AWAITING HIS RETURN

Insights From First And Second Thessalonians
On The Rapture And Second Coming

MARC WHEWAY PHD

Ark House Press
arkhousepress.com

© 2024 MARC WHEWAY PHD

All rights reserved. Apart from any fair dealing for the purpose of study, research, criticism, or review, as permitted under the Copyright Act, no part may be reproduced by any process without written permission.

Scriptures taken from the Holy Bible, New International Version®, NIV®. Copyright © 1973, 1978, 1984, 2011 by Biblica, Inc.™ Used by permission of Zondervan. All rights reserved worldwide. www.zondervan.com The "NIV" and "New International Version" are trademarks registered in the United States Patent and Trademark Office by Biblica, Inc.™

Cataloguing in Publication Data:
Title: Awaiting His Return
ISBN: 978-1-7635572-5-3 (pbk)
Subjects: REL006870   RELIGION / Biblical Studies / New Testament / Revelation; REL067060 RELIGION / Christian Theology / Eschatology; REL085000 RELIGION / Eschatology;

Design by initiateagency.com

I want to express my deepest gratitude to all those who have contributed to the creation of this book, a project that has been both challenging and profoundly rewarding. I am especially grateful to my church community, Kingdom Seekers Wesleyan Methodist Church, for their unwavering support throughout this journey. I would also like to acknowledge the role of technological assistance in making this work. While the concept, theological perspectives, and principal narrative are solely mine, I utilised an AI tool, ChatGPT, in various ways, such as generating preliminary drafts, assisting in data compilation, and editing. However, it is important to emphasise that the technology served only as a tool, not a co-author, and I made all final decisions regarding content and interpretation. The use of AI has enhanced my research and writing style, but the essence of this book is undeniably human and, more importantly, biblical.

This acknowledgment seeks to be transparent about the role of AI, clearly demarcating the boundaries of its contribution while assuring readers that the essence and intellectual ownership of the work remain the authors.

INDEX

Introduction to 1st and 2nd Thessalonians vii

First Thessalonians

Introduction to 1st Thessalonians.. 3
   Wait for the Son from Heaven (1:2-10) 11
   God's Wrath has Come at Last (2:1-16) 27
   Before our Lord Jesus Christ at His Coming (2:17-3:5) 38
   Blameless in Holiness ... at the Coming of the Lord
      Jesus Christ (3:6-13) 53
   The Lord is an Avenger (4:1-12) 62
   The Coming of the Lord (4:13-18) 75

The Evolving Landscape of Rapture Theories................................. 85
   Pre-Tribulation Rapture Theory 88
   Mid-Tribulation Rapture Theory 108
   Post-Tribulation, Pre-Wrath Rapture Theory..................... 116
   The "No Rapture" Argument:.. 130

Conclusion: Compelling Evidence for the Pre-Tribulation
Rapture Theory 142
    The Day of the Lord Will Come Like a Thief in the
        Night (5:1-11) 147
    Be Kept Blameless at the Coming of Our Lord Jesus
        Christ (5:12-28) 162

Second Thessalonians

Introduction 177
    Steadfast Faith as We Await His Return (1:1-12) 179
    Understanding the Signs (2:1-12) 189
    Introduction to Millennialism 201
    Introduction to Pre-Tribulation (Dispensational)
        Pre-Millennialism: 204
    Pre-Tribulation (Dispensational) Pre-Millennialism 213
    Post-Tribulation, Historical, and
        Pre-Wrath Pre-Millennialism 221
    Post-Millennialism 227
    Amillennialism 237

Conclusion: Compelling Evidence for Pre-Millennial
Dispensationalism 245
    Firm / Hold Fast (2:13-17) 248
    Faithful and Steadfast in the Light of His Coming (3:1-5) . 256
    Imitate us as we wait for the return of Jesus Christ (3:6-15) 266
    Purpose and Peace in the Last Days (3:16-18) 276

INTRODUCTION TO 1ˢᵗ AND 2ᴺᴰ THESSALONIANS

1st and 2nd Thessalonians are among Paul's earliest writings, directed to an emerging Christian congregation in Thessalonica, situated in the Roman province of Macedonia. This fledgling church grappled with societal ostracisation and persecution stemming from Roman authorities and conflicting religious and cultural elements within the larger Hellenistic community. Despite these adversities, the congregation remained resilient. However, the hostile environment led to a burgeoning interest in eschatological matters, specifically concerning the dead's resurrection, the church's rapture and the Second Coming of Christ. Their inquiry is because some church members were misled by false teachings suggesting that the tribulation was already underway and that there was no resurrection for the dead.

In both letters, Paul engages with crucial issues related to the end times: the resurrection of the deceased, the rapture of the church, the antichrist revealed, and the Second Coming of Jesus Christ. In his first letter, Paul addresses the emotional turmoil within the community concerning the fate of their loved ones who had passed away. The Thessalonian believers were anxious that these individuals might be left out of the coming resurrection or the millennial kingdom. To appease their concerns, Paul confirms that those who have died in faith will also be resurrected (1 Thess. 4:13-18). In his second letter, Paul rectifies misconceptions about the timing and nature of the "Day of the Lord." Contrary to later theological categories like Postmillennialism and Amillennialism, Paul is chiefly concerned with correcting the urgent misunderstandings the Thessalonians held. He clarifies that a "man of lawlessness" must first be first revealed, setting the stage for subsequent end-time events before the Day of the Lord (2 Thess. 2:3-12).

In sum, the theme of eschatology serves as the most potent link between the 1st and 2nd letters to the Thessalonians. While the first letter lays the groundwork with initial teachings on the Parousia—the return of Christ—and the idea of resurrection, the second letter revisits these subjects to address misunderstandings and dispel false teachings that had arisen. The prominent theme of holiness is also intertwined with the anticipation of Christ's return. In both letters, Paul offers a framework for living meaningfully in 'the present' while keeping an eye on 'the future.' This present-focused guidance includes a strong call for perseverance amid persecution, a topic that further underscores the need for holiness. The theme of faithfulness—a recurring motif across Paul's epistles—serves as a unifying thread, connecting the various subjects and challenges discussed in these letters.

FIRST THESSALONIANS

INTRODUCTION TO 1ST THESSALONIANS

1 Thessalonians is a letter from the Apostle Paul to the Christian community in Thessalonica, a city in ancient Macedonia (now part of modern-day Greece). Written around 50–51 A.D., it is likely one of the earliest Christian documents. The letter aims to encourage and strengthen the believers in Thessalonica who were enduring persecution for their faith. It also clarifies some misconceptions about Christian teachings, particularly the rapture of the church and the second coming of Jesus Christ.

In the Book of Acts, Paul and Silas embark on a missionary journey that is as impactful as it is tumultuous. Beginning with Acts 16, they set out for the region of Macedonia after receiving a vision, eventually reaching the city of Philippi. Here, they encounter a variety of responses to their ministry, from the conversion of Lydia, a businesswoman, to the expulsion of an evil spirit from a slave girl, which leads to their arrest. Imprisoned and beaten, they nonetheless maintain their faith, leading to a miraculous release from jail that also results in the conversion of the jailer and his household. They then head to Thessalonica upon leaving Philippi, as recorded in Acts 17. In this bustling city, their ministry takes on a pattern: Paul visits the synagogue for three Sabbaths, arguing from the Scriptures that Jesus is the Messiah. While some Jews and a considerable number of Gentiles believe, the opposition grows fierce.

Accused of turning "the world upside down" and defying Caesar's decrees, Paul and Silas face hostility and unrest once more. Eventually, they are forced to leave the city at night due to escalating threats. This ministry in Thessalonica is foundational for the fledgling Christian community there. It serves as the backdrop for Paul's first letter to the Thessalonians, where he revisits themes and lessons that emerged during this challenging but fruitful time.

In the first letter to the Thessalonians, Paul stresses the centrality of Jesus' death and resurrection as the foundation of Christian hope, aligning closely with his initial proclamation of the gospel in Acts 17. In Thessalonica, as recorded in Acts 17:2-3, Paul had reasoned with the Jews from the Scriptures, "explaining and proving that the Messiah had to suffer and rise from the dead," asserting that "this Jesus I am proclaiming to you is the Messiah." Back in the epistle, Paul revisits this central theme, reminding the Thessalonians to "wait for His Son from heaven, whom He raised from the dead—Jesus, who rescues us from the coming wrath" (1 Thess. 1:10). Here, the resurrection is not merely a historical event but a powerful manifestation of divine power that provides a basis for salvation and future hope. This is intimately tied to the eschatological anticipation that permeates the letter. When discussing the return of Jesus, Paul reassures the Thessalonians that "the Lord Himself will come down from heaven, with a loud command, with the voice of the archangel and with the trumpet call of God, and the dead in Christ will rise first" (1 Thess. 4:16). The resurrection of Jesus thus serves as a guarantee of the future resurrection and gathering of believers at His return for the church. Through this lens, Jesus' death and resurrection become the foundation of the gospel message

INTRODUCTION TO 1ST THESSALONIANS

initially preached in Acts 17 and the cornerstone of Christian hope for the rapture of the church and the Second Coming, as elaborated in 1 Thessalonians.

The big idea of 1 Thessalonians is to offer guidance and encouragement to a young church. Paul commends the Thessalonians for their faith, hope, and love and encourages them to continue living righteous lives in anticipation of Jesus Christ's return. As mentioned above, the letter also corrects misunderstandings concerning the "Day of the Lord," assuring believers that those who have died will also be resurrected at Christ's return, referring to the rapture (cf. 1 Cor. 15:51-52).

In the first letter to the Thessalonians, the anticipation of Christ's second coming is a recurring theme. The letter instructs believers to "wait for His Son from heaven, whom He raised from the dead—Jesus, who rescues us from the coming wrath" (1 Thess. 1:10). Paul also emphasises the importance of being "blameless and holy in the presence of our God and Father when our Lord Jesus comes with all His holy ones" (1 Thess. 3:13).

Paul strongly emphasises the pursuit of holiness as integral to the Christian life, particularly in the context of anticipating Christ's return. He prays that the Thessalonians may be "blameless and holy in the presence of our God and Father when our Lord Jesus comes with all His holy ones" (1 Thess. 3:13). The emphasis on holiness is not a stand-alone concept but is inextricably tied to eschatological themes. The pursuit of a holy life, according to Paul, has eternal implications. This is highlighted when he reassures believers that they have not been "destined for wrath, but to obtain salvation through our Lord Jesus Christ" (1 Thess. 5:9), drawing a line between living a holy life and escaping the divine wrath that is to come. Both the pursuit of holiness and the assurance of salvation through Christ point to an ultimate future event—the Second

Coming of Jesus—where the true significance of living a holy life will be fully realised. Therefore, holiness in 1 Thessalonians is not merely a spiritual requirement but serves as preparation for the eschatological reality that awaits believers.

Paul often employs the verb "urge" as a strong impetus for the faithful to follow distinct moral and communal principles. For instance, he declares, "We urge you, brothers and sisters, to reprimand the inactive, console the dispirited, support the vulnerable, and be tolerant with everyone" (1 Thess. 5:14). In a similar vein, he advocates that they "live in ways that are pleasing to God" (1 Thess. 4:1) and calls on the congregation to "show respect to those who labour diligently in your midst" (1 Thess. 5:12). These exhortations are designed to cultivate a community of mutual care, moral rectitude, and while they were already acting that way toward all the brothers in Macedonia. Still, Paul emphasises the importance of intensifying these efforts (1 Thess. 4:10), all with an eye towards the anticipated return of Christ.

Interwoven with these exhortations are calls to "imitate" exemplary behaviour. Early in the letter, Paul commends the Thessalonians for becoming "imitators of us and of the Lord" despite "severe suffering" (1 Thess. 1:6). Later, he refers to the Thessalonians as imitators of "God's churches in Judea" (1 Thess. 2:14). The notion of imitation serves to create a cohesive Christian community that emulates not only Paul but also Christ Himself, especially in the context of hardship and adversity.

By urging the believers to live in certain ways and by highlighting the importance of imitating godly examples, Paul is steering the Thessalonian church toward a life prepared for the rapture and the Second Coming of Jesus. Both the urgings and the calls to imitation underscore that the Christian life is not simply about individual

INTRODUCTION TO 1ST THESSALONIANS

righteousness but about fostering a community that collectively anticipates and prepares for Christ's return, first for the church and then to judge.

The letter also contains warnings, cautioning that "the day of the Lord will come like a thief in the night" (1 Thess. 5:2) and that people should be prepared for "sudden destruction, as labour pains on a pregnant woman" (1 Thess. 5:3). As mentioned above, in the midst of these warnings, Paul provides solace, reminding the "blameless" church that "God did not appoint us to suffer wrath but to receive salvation through our Lord Jesus Christ" (1 Thess. 5:9, cf. 1:10).

Furthermore, Paul points out the importance of the Thessalonian believers as the crowning glory in his ministry, stating, "For what is our hope, our joy, or the crown in which we will glory in the presence of our Lord Jesus when He comes? Is it not you?" (1 Thess. 2:19). This shows that Paul's anticipation of Christ's return is deeply intertwined present suffering, and with his love and care for the spiritual well-being of his converts.

The notion of enduring hardship and experiencing persecution is a recurring theme in Paul's first letter to the Thessalonians. Paul contextualises this struggle within the broader eschatological narrative of facing challenges while awaiting Christ's second coming. Paul's own experiences underscore this perspective: after surviving a stoning in Lystra instigated by envious Jews, he made many converts in Derbe and urged them to persevere in their faith, declaring, "Through many tribulations, we must enter the kingdom of God" (Acts 14:22). Early in his letter, Paul applauds the Thessalonians for their unwavering faith despite difficult circumstances: "You became imitators of us and of the Lord, for you welcomed the message in the midst of severe suffering with the joy given by the Holy Spirit" (1 Thess. 1:6). This capacity to find joy in suffering points to a profound hope in the forthcoming return of Jesus.

Echoing the accounts recorded in the Book of Acts, Paul discusses the harsh conditions he endured in order to minister to the Thessalonians, noting that "we dare to tell you about this gospel in the face of strong opposition" (1 Thess. 2:2 paraphrased). Despite the hardship, Paul emphasises the worthiness of the cause, reminding the Thessalonians, "For you, brothers and sisters, became imitators of God's churches in Judea, which are in Christ Jesus: You suffered from your own people the same things those churches suffered from the Jews" (1 Thess. 2:14).

Thus, suffering and persecution in 1 Thessalonians are not isolated topics but are intrinsically connected to the broader theme of eschatological hope. Paul makes it clear that the trials and tribulations faced are part of the Christian journey but should be navigated with an eternal perspective, eagerly awaiting the return of Jesus Christ and the reward that comes with faithful perseverance.

Many contemporary churches have shifted their focus away from the biblical teachings on enduring suffering, choosing to embrace messages like "Your Best Life Now" or "Destined to Reign." These prosperity-centric ministries depart from the scriptural emphasis on suffering and prioritise immediate material gain over spiritual truths. Instead of looking forward to the things to come, they are fixated on the here and now.

In stark contrast, Paul's first letter to the Thessalonians lays bare the ethical foundations of his ministry, directly refuting any suggestion that he preached for personal or material advantage. In 1 Thessalonians 2:5, he states unequivocally, "You know we never used flattery, nor did we put on a mask to cover up greed—God is our witness." He further clarifies in 1 Thessalonians 2:6: "We were not looking for praise from people, not from you or anyone else, even though as apostles of Christ we could have asserted our authority." These remarks highlight that Paul's chief aim was the spiritual well-being of the Thessalonian congregation rather than his own enrichment.

Paul further highlights his self-sacrificial approach in his ministry: "Surely you remember, brothers and sisters, our toil and hardship; we worked night and day in order not to be a burden to anyone while we preached the gospel of God to you" (1 Thess. 2:9). Here, the apostle signals that he abstained from receiving material benefits from the church, choosing instead to suffer hardship and labour so as not to be a burden.

These principles are deeply interwoven with the themes of suffering, perseverance, and the expectation of Christ's return. Paul is not merely setting a standard for ethical behaviour in ministry; he is laying out a theological model that ties in with eschatological hope. The idea is that enduring hardship and avoiding the trap of pursuing material gain in this life aligns with the true Christian journey—one characterised by suffering but also by hope in the rewards that come with the return of Jesus Christ. This starkly contrasts the "prosperity gospel," which emphasises material wealth and success as indicators of God's favour.

The prosperity gospel claims that faith can directly lead to material blessings in this life, often sidestepping the scriptural emphasis on suffering and the trials that come with being a follower of Christ. Paul's model, as seen in 1 Thessalonians, serves as a counter-narrative to such teachings. His ministry was not about accumulating wealth or comfort; rather, it was about preparing believers for the rapture of the church and the Second Coming. The reward that Paul looks forward to is not material but spiritual, awaiting the day when he can stand "blameless and holy in the presence of our God and Father when our Lord Jesus comes with all His holy ones" (1 Thess. 3:13).

As mentioned earlier, Paul even characterises the Thessalonians as his future "crown" in the presence of Jesus: "For what is our hope, our joy, or the crown in which we will glory in the presence of our Lord Jesus when He comes? Is it not you?" (1 Thess. 2:19). Here, the reward is relational and spiritual, grounded in the community of believers he has helped nurture, rather than in material gain.

In summary, the teachings in 1 Thessalonians provide:

- A cohesive message against preaching for greed and material gain,
- Emphasising instead the virtues of suffering,
- Perseverance, and,
- Spiritual readiness for Christ's return.

In conclusion, in Paul's first letter to the Thessalonians, the apostle weaves themes of perseverance through suffering, the centrality of Christ's death and resurrection, and the imminence of the Second Coming into a coherent and comforting message for a young church grappling with internal and external challenges. The apostle combines stern exhortation with consolation to guide the believers towards a holistically Christian life grounded in the expectation of Christ's return. Paul seeks to instil correct doctrinal beliefs about the rapture and the Second Coming and foster an ethical and spiritual lifestyle conducive to greeting this pivotal event with both readiness and joy. The letter serves as a timeless guide for modern believers, cautioning against the allure of prosperity-centric teachings that shift focus away from the eschatological hope central to the Christian faith. Ultimately, Paul's message to the Thessalonians is one of enduring hope amid suffering, amid societal pressure, and constant readiness for the ultimate return of Jesus Christ, themes that resonate across the millennia to challenge and comfort believers today.

WAIT FOR THE SON FROM HEAVEN

'From Idols to God: Awaiting the Resurrected
Son Who Saves from Coming Wrath'
(1 Thess. 1:2-10)

To fully understand the context of 1st Thessalonians, one must delve into Acts 17:1-9, which describes the pioneering visit of Paul and Silas to Thessalonica. During three consecutive Sabbaths, they eagerly preached about the suffering, death, and resurrection of Jesus Christ, capturing the hearts and minds of some Jews and numerous devout Greeks. Their impact was so profound that it led the local Jewish community to level against them with the evocative accusation of "turning the world upside down" and advocating for a new king in the form of Jesus.

Enraged by this seismic shift in religious loyalties, the local Jews orchestrated the arrest of several new converts, dragging them before the city officials. They charged them with subversion against Caesar, causing enough alarm among the authorities to pressure Paul and Silas to make a secret departure for Berea. Even there, the Thessalonian opponents were relentless, tracking them down and stirring up hostilities. This compelled Paul to leave Berea, though Silas and Timothy remained.

Following these tumultuous events, Paul penned 1st Thessalonians, likely around 51 A.D., during his second missionary journey. This letter starts with a greeting from Paul, Silas, and Timothy to the fledgling Christian community in Thessalonica.

Throughout 1st Thessalonians, Paul's thanksgiving for the Thessalonian believers is hard to miss. Initially, he thanks God for all of them, a sentiment he elaborates on by acknowledging that their acceptance of the gospel was not seen as mere human words but as the very word of God. This sentiment carries over into his second letter to the Thessalonians, where he praises their growing faith and love.

The backdrop for this deep gratitude is the Thessalonians' transformation from idol worshippers to devout followers of God and their resilience in the face of suffering. Paul is elated by their thriving faith, rooting his expressions of thanksgiving in this profound change and constancy. It's worth noting that this sense of thanksgiving is not exclusive to the Thessalonians; it is a recurring theme in Paul's epistolary tradition.

In the broader landscape of Paul's correspondence, this practice of starting his letters with an expression of thanksgiving is inescapable. Whether it's Romans, Corinthians, Ephesians, Philippians, Colossians, or Philemon, Paul makes it a point to initiate his discourse with gratitude. These introductory thanksgiving notes establish rapport and set an uplifting tone for the remainder of the text.

Paul's thankfulness in his letters to the Thessalonian church is deeply rooted in the authentic faith, love, and steadfastness that the congregation displays. He is especially touched by their unquestioning acceptance of the gospel as the true word of God, a transformative force at work within them. The fact that their faith is both personal and communal, increasing in intensity and reach, significantly moves Paul.

This sense of thanksgiving becomes even more meaningful when viewed against the challenges facing the Thessalonian believers. Formed

INTRODUCTION TO 1ST THESSALONIANS

in the crucible of religious and social upheaval, the Christian community in Thessalonica found itself embroiled in external hostilities, including religious persecution and accusations of political activism. As a fledgling church in a predominantly non-Christian society, they were vulnerable to societal pressures and possibly internal doubts and divisions. In this complicated environment, Paul's reiterated thanksgiving acts as both an affirmation of their emerging faith and a fortifying agent against the multitude of challenges they are contending with.

In summary, Paul's epistles to the Thessalonians are laced with heartfelt gratitude for their steadfast faith and love, set against a backdrop of societal pressures and hostilities. It serves as a form of spiritual validation and encouragement, helping the fledgling community solidify their faith even amid adversity. His expressions of thanks align with a broader practice seen throughout his letters, creating a sense of continuity and highlighting the universal virtues of faith, love, and resilience in the face of challenges.

Paul's recurring expressions of thanks for his converts are deeply significant and transcend the immediate context. Beyond mere words of gratitude, they have eschatological implications—concerning the ultimate destiny of individuals and the world. In 1 Thessalonians 2:19, Paul elucidates this eternal perspective: "For what is our hope, our joy, or the crown in which we will glory in the presence of our Lord Jesus when He comes? Is it not you?" Here, Paul identifies the Thessalonian believers as his "eternal joy and crown," positioning them within the grand narrative of God's redemptive plan that culminates in the second coming of Jesus Christ.

This eschatological theme is not unique to his letters to the Thessalonians; it permeates other Pauline writings. For instance, in Philippians 4:1, Paul calls the Philippian believers his "joy and crown," emphasising the eternal significance of their faith journey. Likewise, in 2 Timothy 4:8, Paul refers to the "crown of righteousness" that the Lord will award him on "that day," pointing forward to a future hope grounded in Christ's return. Additionally, in 1 Corinthians 3:12-14, Paul talks about the "work" each person has done being tested by fire at the end of times. The quality of this work has eternal implications, and those who have laboured faithfully are promised rewards. This passage can be seen as a conceptual parallel to Paul's identification of the Thessalonians as his "crown," both referencing the eternal rewards waiting for the faithful.

Similarly, in Colossians 1:5, Paul speaks of the "hope stored up for you in heaven," linking their present faithfulness with future glory. The sense that believers' lives have eternal consequences is pervasive throughout his writings. Even in his letter to the Romans, which opens with a grand theological exposition, Paul interweaves this eternal perspective. He commends the Romans for their faith, which is "being reported all over the world" (Rom. 1:8). While not directly speaking of crowns or end times, the idea that the faith of the Roman believers is a cause for global recognition suggests a sense of eternal consequence on a cosmic scale.

Paul's sense of gratitude is thus twofold: He is thankful for the present faith and steadfastness of these early Christian communities and is also filled with joy and hope for the future, seeing them as his "crown" when he stands before the Lord. This unique blend of immediate and eternal gratitude encourages believers in their current struggles and sets their sights on the ultimate eschatological horizon (cf. 1 Thess. 1:10).

By repeatedly pointing to this eschatological aspect, Paul accomplishes several things. First, he affirms the value and significance of the believers' faith and suffering, not just as transient experiences but as

INTRODUCTION TO 1ST THESSALONIANS

critical elements in unfolding God's ultimate plan. Second, he places their individual and communal narratives within the larger cosmic story, culminating in Christ's return and the establishment of His millennial kingdom. Third, by identifying the believers as his "joy and crown," Paul subtly emphasises his role—and, by extension, the role of apostolic teaching and leadership—in preparing the community for this eschatological fulfilment.

Paul's ministry is notable for its dual focus on the immediate task and the eschatological horizon. While he eagerly anticipates Jesus Christ's return, this longing does not detract from his immediate responsibilities; instead, it fuels them. Understanding this tension requires a closer examination of Paul's terminology regarding "work" and "labour," as well as the way he commends the Thessalonian believers for their commitment to these endeavours.

In 1 Thessalonians 1:3, Paul gives thanks for the Thessalonians' "work of faith, a labour of love, and steadfastness of hope in our Lord Jesus Christ." The "work of faith" refers to the actionable aspects of their belief, which likely encompassed both personal transformation and active proselytising. The "labour of love" might include acts of charity and mutual support within the community, consistent with Jesus' command to love one another (Jn. 13:34-35). Paul's own work and labour included evangelistic missions, pastoral care, and often manual labour to support himself financially, as he discusses in 2 Thessalonians 3:7-10, thereby setting an example of self-sufficiency and commitment to the gospel message.

Again, Paul's "work" and "labour" concept is not limited to earthly endeavours but is deeply rooted in an eschatological framework. For example, in Philippians 2:16, he talks about "holding fast to the word of life, so that in the day of Christ I may be proud that I did not run in vain or labour in vain." Here, Paul's work and labour validation come from immediate results and their eternal implications.

Similarly, in 1 Corinthians 15:58, Paul exhorts the Corinthians to be "always abounding in the work of the Lord, knowing that in the Lord your labour is not in vain." The 'work of the Lord' here includes evangelism and personal sanctification, anchored by the resurrection hope. In Colossians 1:10, he prays that the Colossians may "walk in a manner worthy of the Lord, fully pleasing to Him: bearing fruit in every good work and increasing in the knowledge of God."

Paul is diligent in connecting this work and labour with the ultimate return of Jesus. In 2 Thessalonians 1:11-12, he prays that God may "fulfil every resolve for good and every work of faith by His power, so that the name of our Lord Jesus may be glorified in you, and you in Him." Once again, the undertone is eschatological; the good works and acts of faith have an end-times significance that complements their immediate impact.

By weaving the immediate ("work of faith, a labour of love") with the eternal ("crown of boasting before our Lord Jesus at His coming"), Paul illustrates that Christian life should be a seamless integration of present service and future hope. The eschatological dimension validates the immediate labour and enriches it, providing both the worker and the observer with a fuller understanding of its eternal value. Thus, Paul's commendation of the Thessalonians affirms their faith and is a powerful motivator to persevere, with the understanding that their work and labour contribute to an everlasting kingdom.

Integrating the message of Jesus' parables, especially those concerning His second coming, with Paul's teachings reveals a cohesive theological narrative. The parable of the minas, as recorded in Luke 19:11-27, serves as a poignant illustration. When Jesus taught this parable,

His disciples mistakenly believed that He would establish His kingdom immediately (Lu. 19:11). Yet the story makes it clear that Jesus would first have to leave, receive the kingdom from His Father, and return at a later time (vv. 12, 15). In His absence, His followers are entrusted with responsibilities—akin to Paul's "work of faith and labour of love"—and are called to 'occupy until He comes' (Lu. 19:13).

In a sense, this 'occupying' reflects engagement in 'kingdom business.' This phrase captures both the urgency and the importance of the earthly and heavenly tasks that believers are assigned. Those who excel in this 'business,' like the first two servants in the parable (Lu. 19:16-19), are rewarded with authority in the coming kingdom, mirroring Paul's eschatological "crown of boasting."

However, the story also presents a stark warning about religious complacency. Just as Paul warned the Thessalonians about idleness in 2 Thessalonians 3:6-10, Jesus criticised the servant who failed to engage in kingdom business (Lu. 17:20-21). This servant's failure was rooted in his lack of anticipation for the return of Jesus (Lu. 17:22). He symbolises a congregation focused on temporal success rather than eternal significance, reminiscent of the Laodicean church described in Revelation 3:17-20. In both cases, the self-satisfaction of earthly life led to spiritual short-sightedness and exclusion from the future kingdom.

In this context, when someone remarks, 'I do not want to hear about the end times; I am just going to occupy until He comes,' it is important to scrutinise what this 'occupying' entails. Based on the full scope of biblical teaching, disinterest in Jesus' return can translate into a dangerous spiritual stance. Just 'doing church' is insufficient; one needs to be actively 'engaged in kingdom business,' which should be underscored by an eschatological focus, as Paul so vividly models.

As Luke 21:34-36 and Matthew 25:14-30 reiterate, neglecting or delaying preparation for Jesus' return can have eternal consequences. Therefore, aligning oneself with Paul's teachings and Jesus' parables reinforces that true discipleship involves a dynamic interplay between present responsibilities and future hope. As Paul reminds the Thessalonians and Jesus' parables affirm, these are not mutually exclusive but deeply interconnected realms that define the Christian experience.

Building on this concept of engagement in 'kingdom business' while awaiting the return of Jesus, it's crucial to understand that God's choice plays a role in directing this work. In Acts 17:26, Paul explains that God has determined the times set for men and the boundaries of their habitation, suggesting that individuals are divinely placed in specific contexts to hear, receive, and spread the gospel message. This is mirrored in Paul's commendation of the Thessalonian church in 1 Thessalonians 1:4: "Loved by God, He has chosen you." These men from Thessalonica were not randomly caught in the currents of history; they were intentionally handpicked by God and situated in their city at their particular time to be witnesses to the gospel. They "received the word in much affliction, with the joy of the Holy Spirit" (1 Thess. 1:6), showcasing a transformative faith that enabled them to "turn to God from idols" (1 Thess. 1:9).

Such divine choosing and human response are not isolated to the Thessalonians. Throughout Biblical history, God calls individuals for specific tasks—think of Abraham, Moses, Esther, or Paul himself. The broader narrative of scripture even encapsulates this idea with phrases like "many are called, but few are chosen" (Matt. 22:14). Essentially. In contrast, the call may go out broadly, but it is those who respond—who actively "engage in kingdom business"—that become living examples to both their contemporaries and future generations of believers.

INTRODUCTION TO 1ST THESSALONIANS

Just as the Thessalonians became "an example to all the believers in Macedonia and Achaia" (1 Thess. 1:7) and beyond (1 Thess. 1:8), their response to God's choosing echoes down through history, encouraging others to work earnestly while waiting for Jesus' return, all the while holding fast to "this hope...as an anchor for the soul, firm and secure" (Heb. 6:19). This aligns perfectly with the underlying eschatological focus that both Paul and Jesus emphasised: a life devoted to God's current call-in anticipation of future glory.

The term "brothers" used by Paul in his letters to the Thessalonians carries a weighty significance, as it underscores the familial relationship among believers in the body of Christ. This wasn't just a casual form of address but a profoundly theological one that conveyed a shared spiritual lineage. In Galatians 3:26, Paul elaborates on this idea, stating, "For you are all sons of God through faith in Christ Jesus." In Romans 8:15, he even speaks of the "Spirit of adoption" that enables believers to cry out, "Abba, Father," signifying an intimate relationship with God that extends to our relationships with each other. By referring to the Thessalonians as "brothers," Paul affirms their shared identity as God's adopted children, a commonality that transcends cultural, ethnic, and social divisions (cf. Col. 3:11).

In a more practical sense, addressing them as "brothers" creates a sense of unity and mutual accountability, crucial for a community under external pressures and persecution, as was the case with the Thessalonian church. The term encourages spiritual kinship, reminding them that they are part of a more prominent family that shares the same heavenly Father, the same foundational faith, and the same ultimate hope in the return of Jesus Christ (1 Thess. 1:10, 4:13-18). It fosters a mutual concern and care for each other's spiritual well-being, echoing Paul's other admonitions to "bear one another's burdens" (Gal.

6:2) and "encourage one another and build one another up" (1 Thess. 4:18, 5:11). In a sense, by calling them "brothers," Paul emphasises that their unity in Christ should be a living testimony to the gospel's transformative power.

In aligning with this new identity as "brothers," the Thessalonian believers did not merely encounter a message; they experienced the gospel's transformative power. Paul affirms this in 1 Thessalonians 1:5, stating, "Our gospel came to you not simply with words but also with power, with the Holy Spirit and deep conviction." This was not a superficial or transient change but a total transformation brought about by the Holy Spirit. It embodied what Paul later declares in Romans 1:16: "For I am not ashamed of the gospel, because it is the power of God that brings salvation to everyone who believes." This supernatural power laid the foundation for the new spiritual identity and family of which they were now a part.

Moreover, the characters of Paul, Silas, and their companions also served as living testimonies to the gospel's truth. In 1 Thessalonians 2:10, Paul reminds them, "You are witnesses, and so is God, of how holy, righteous and blameless we were among you who believed." The credibility and integrity of these messengers enhanced the impact of their message. Paul and Silas were not mere orators or philosophers; they were men transformed by the gospel they preached, men willing to suffer for the sake of their message (Acts 16:25; 2 Cor. 4:8-12).

In doing so, they provided a tangible example for the Thessalonians to emulate. It was an example of how to believe, live, act, and relate to their new family of "brothers" and "sisters" in Christ. In this sense, the gospel was not just a proclamation but a powerful life-changing reality modelled by men who had been transformed by it. This lifestyle of deep conviction and exemplary conduct reinforced the importance of

INTRODUCTION TO 1ST THESSALONIANS

awaiting Christ's return with vigilant preparation and active love for the community of believers.

The phrase "our gospel," as used by Paul in 1 Thessalonians 1:5, carries with it a weighty distinction from other 'gospel' messages that circulated then and continue to do so today. Paul is emphasising a gospel rooted in the person and work of Jesus Christ, one that is accompanied by transformative power through the Holy Spirit. This stands in stark contrast to diluted or distorted versions of the gospel, such as hyper-grace messages that minimise the need for repentance or prosperity gospels that equate God's favour with material wealth. These alternative messages lack the transformational potency that the true gospel possesses. As Paul declares in Galatians 1:6-9, anyone who preaches a gospel contrary to the one he delivered is to be accursed. He underscores this point in 2 Corinthians 11:4, warning against those who preach "another Jesus" or a "different gospel." Such messages are void of the life-changing power that leads to genuine faith, deep conviction, and a life lived in eager anticipation of Christ's return. Only the gospel of Jesus Christ has the ability to bring about the radical change of heart and life that Paul witnessed among the Thessalonians and countless others.

Continuing the theme of the gospel's transformative and eschatological power, it's crucial to highlight the specific kind of "power" Paul references in 1 Thessalonians 1:5. While Paul does not define this in the Thessalonian letter, he elaborates in Romans 15:18-19 that his apostolic mission among the Gentiles was marked by "signs and wonders," implying that this divine power manifested in miraculous ways. This aligns with his descriptions in 1 Corinthians 12:8-10, where spiritual gifts like healing and miracles are catalogued as visible manifestations of divine power.

In this way, Paul's gospel differed fundamentally from various 'gospel' messages we encounter today, like the prosperity gospel or the message of hyper-grace, which often lack the transformative, miraculous power Paul speaks of. Paul's gospel came not just in word but in the power of the Holy Spirit, validating his message and deepening its transformative impact. In comparison, contemporary faith healers may claim to operate in the realm of "signs and wonders." Still, the critical question remains: Does their message hold the same transformative and sanctifying power as Paul's gospel? Are their 'wonders' leading to a community of believers who are, as the Thessalonians were, examples of faith and endurance, living in eager anticipation of Christ's return?

Thus, for Paul, the gospel was not just a message to be heard; it was a force to be felt. It led to immediate transformation and set believers on the path of progressive sanctification, all while keeping their eyes fixed on the eschatological hope of Christ's return.

In contrast to the transformative gospel that Paul preached, a gospel devoid of the Holy Spirit's power results in a form of dead religion characterised by empty rituals and works-based self-righteousness. Without the Spirit's regenerating and sanctifying work, there is no real change in the 'believer's' life, no conviction of sin, and no passion for Christ or His imminent return. Such a powerless gospel fails to provide eschatological hope and leads to spiritual complacency or self-deception. Scripture itself warns against such an outcome. In 2 Timothy 3:5, Paul warns of those who have "a form of godliness but deny its power." In Matthew 7:21-23, Jesus cautions that not everyone who calls Him 'Lord' will enter the Kingdom of Heaven, but only those who do the will of His Father. It is a sobering reminder that a gospel without the power of the Holy Spirit is not just ineffective but eternally detrimental. Therefore,

INTRODUCTION TO 1ST THESSALONIANS

examining the gospel we adhere to is crucial, ensuring it aligns with the transformative, hope-filled message delivered by apostles like Paul.

While the power of the gospel indeed transforms lives, it is essential to clarify that it does not guarantee a life free from suffering, distress, or tribulation. Contrary to some modern teachings that equate the gospel's power with earthly prosperity or safety, Paul and his converts in Thessalonica understood that trials and hardships were not inconsistencies in the Christian life but signs pointing toward Christ's imminent return. As mentioned in 2 Thessalonians 1:5-10 and elaborated in 1 Thessalonians 3:2-4, distress or tribulation served as a precursor to the second coming, or parousia, of Christ. Far from being a reason to lose hope or faith, these hardships were seen as indicators that the promise of final redemption was close at hand. This divinely inspired joy in the face of persecution was not an act of delusion or denial. Still, it was deeply rooted in the theological framework Paul had imparted to his converts. The gospel's transformative power is not about escaping trials but equipping believers to face them with unwavering hope and conviction in Christ's ultimate victory.

The experience of persecution not only strengthens and purifies individual faith but also fortifies the collective resilience of the church, acting as an indisputable testament to the power of the gospel. This was especially true for the Thessalonian believers, whose reputation for steadfastness under pressure had spread far and wide, as Paul notes in 1 Thessalonians 1:8: "The Lord's message rang out from you not only in Macedonia and Achaia—your faith in God has become known everywhere" (paraphrased). The spread of their reputation highlights the contagious effect of a faith that stands unshaken amid trials, creating a ripple effect that encourages other communities of believers. As the Apostle Peter articulates in 1 Peter 1:6-7, the ordeal of suffering serves to refine faith, likening it to gold that withstands the test of fire, resulting in "praise, glory, and honour" at the revelation of Jesus Christ. Paul echoes this in Philippians 1:12-14, stating that his own imprisonment led not to discouragement but to the advancement of the gospel. Indeed, Jesus Himself blessed those who endure persecution for righteousness, declaring that theirs is the kingdom of heaven (Matt. 5:10). In facing persecution with unyielding faith, believers grow individually and contribute to the fortification and spread of the gospel. They make evident the gospel's transformative power even in life's harshest trials.

The gospel's transformative power is vividly manifested in the way it turns people's hearts completely away from idols and towards the living God. In 1 Thessalonians 1:9-10, Paul remarks that the Thessalonian converts "turned to God from idols to serve the living and true God, and to wait for His Son from heaven." This dramatic shift was a matter of changing religious affiliations and a wholesale redirection of life's purpose and devotion. The book of Acts provides another compelling example in the city of Ephesus, where new converts dramatically burned their magic books, representing a total estimated value of 50,000 pieces of silver, as an unequivocal act of turning away from their former lives (Acts 19:19). Similarly, in Acts 14:15, Paul and Barnabas urged the people of Lystra to "turn from these worthless things to the living God, who made the heavens and the earth and the sea and everything in them." The turning away from idols is not merely an external act but a profound internal transformation, showcasing the irresistible force of the gospel's power. This turning is total, radical, and immediate, leaving no room for a middle ground. It is the compelling evidence of a life fully captured by the grace and truth of Jesus Christ, effectively demonstrating the gospel's ability to transform lives fully.

INTRODUCTION TO 1ST THESSALONIANS

In the Christian walk, it is crucial to recognise that anything contrary to the gospel has no rightful place in our lives. As mentioned above, the Apostle Paul warned the Galatians about accepting "another gospel" that was not in line with the true gospel of Jesus Christ (Gal. 1:6-9). In the same vein, New Age practices and syncretic blends of religious beliefs under the umbrella of ecumenicalism dilute and contradict the core tenets of the Christian faith. Whether it's New Age spirituality that promotes self over the Saviour or an ecumenical approach that seeks to meld the doctrines of various religions into a convoluted whole, such practices compromise the integrity and exclusivity of the gospel message. 2 Corinthians 6:14-17 explicitly tells us not to be "unequally yoked" with unbelievers and to separate ourselves from practices and beliefs that are not aligned with the Word of God. The gospel is not a mere add-on to a life of mixed beliefs; it demands complete allegiance and transformative power that is incompatible with a diluted or syncretic faith. Hence, as believers committed to the transformative and exclusivist claims of the gospel, it is imperative to reject any practice or belief that stands in opposition to the "faith that was once for all entrusted to God's holy people" (Jude 1:3).

Building on the need for doctrinal purity and exclusivity in Christian belief, 1 Thessalonians 1:2-10 offers a distinctively Christological focus that culminates in the much-anticipated return of Jesus Christ. This passage highlights the gospel's transformative power and underscores the centrality of waiting for Christ's return as a marker of genuine faith. Those who are truly waiting for Jesus, the one who "rescues us from the coming wrath" (1 Thess. 1:10), will necessarily find themselves separating from worldly concerns and false practices. In doing so, they demonstrate an authentic conversion experience characterised by turning away from idols "to serve the living and true God" (1 Thess. 1:9). This eschatological hope is not merely a future event to anticipate but serves as a present force for sanctification. Those who stand fast in this hope are those who will be spared the coming wrath (1 Thess. 1:10, 5:9). By focusing on the return of Christ; believers are inspired to remain vigilant and free from the entanglements of worldliness and false teachings, solidifying their calling and election in a world that desperately needs the true gospel.

In conclusion, the message of 1 Thessalonians 1:2-10 serves as a reminder of the gospel's transformative, convicting, and sanctifying power. It calls believers to a new identity as brothers and sisters in Christ and a life of steadfast faith, holy conduct, and eschatological hope. Paul's teaching serves as a poignant reminder against the allure of diluted teachings, be it hyper-grace, prosperity gospels, or a blend of New Age and syncretic beliefs. As Paul articulated, the gospel is rooted in the power of the Holy Spirit and comes with immediate and progressive transformation. It does not promise worldly safety or prosperity but does assure us of ultimate deliverance from the coming wrath.

Moreover, genuine faith is refined and spread through persecution, emphasising that the gospel is not just a set of beliefs but a life-changing power. A life genuinely touched by this gospel power will be marked by a radical turning from idols, worldly practices, and false teachings, living in anticipatory hope of Christ's return. Thus, the passage reaffirms the unwavering truth that the gospel of Jesus Christ fully convicts, fully transforms, and fully prepares us for the day of His glorious return.

GOD'S WRATH HAS COME AT LAST

'Pleasing God, Not Man'
(1 Thess. 2:1-16)

In the first chapter of Paul's First Letter to the Thessalonians, the apostle commends the church for their exemplary faith in the face of suffering. This fledgling community had readily accepted the gospel despite intense social, religious, and political persecution, and they had done so with joy inspired by the Holy Spirit. This resilience, Paul notes, had turned them into a model for other believers. Yet, a robust eschatological hope empowers their unyielding faith—a sincere belief in the Second Coming of Jesus Christ. In the second chapter, Paul takes a closer look at the themes of suffering and eschatological hope. He further explains his own experiences and motivations in sharing the gospel. Paul highlights the importance of having an eternal perspective, which helps overcome present challenges and shapes the conduct of Christian ministry and fellowship.

In chapter 2's opening sentence, Paul writes, "For you yourselves know, brothers (and sisters), that our coming to you was not in vain." This statement refers back to his initial visit to Thessalonica and the ministry he and Silas conducted there. When looking at this verse in the context of Acts 17, a fuller picture is seen of what Paul means by "not in vain."

In Acts 17:1-10, Luke describes Paul's journey to Thessalonica, where he reasoned with the Jews and God-fearing Greeks in the synagogue for three Sabbaths. Although some people were persuaded to join Paul and Silas, others became jealous and instigated a mob. The turmoil was such that Paul and Silas had to be sent away at night for their safety.

Despite the harsh circumstances and opposition, Paul's visit was "not in vain" for several reasons. First, a community of believers was established, a fact he praises in 1 Thessalonians 1. Second, the Thessalonian Christians had become exemplary in their faith and love, even amid persecution. Third, their eschatological hope had been kindled—they awaited Jesus' return as the deliverer of the wrath to come.

Paul's words in 1 Thessalonians 2:1 serve as a transition from the commendation in chapter 1 to his defence and elaboration of his apostolic ministry in chapter 2. By acknowledging that his visit was not "in vain," Paul highlights his ministry's fruitfulness despite hardships, reinforcing the importance of perseverance and hope for the Thessalonian Christian community facing persecution and suffering.

Paul and his fellow missionaries were far from being leisurely travellers; their journey to Thessalonica was imbued with a divine sense of urgency and purpose. Fresh from a harrowing experience in Philippi, where they were flogged and imprisoned for the gospel's sake (Acts 16:22-24), they arrived in Thessalonica with battle scars that bore witness to their commitment. These were not men seeking to exploit their audience for personal gain or prestige; they were willing to pay a high personal cost to deliver a message they believed was of eternal importance.

Drawing from a reservoir of divine courage, Paul and his companions boldly stepped into the synagogue in Thessalonica to proclaim the same gospel message that had incited persecution against them in

Philippi. "For our appeal does not spring from error or impurity or any attempt to deceive, but just as we have been approved by God to be entrusted with the gospel, so we speak, not to please man, but to please God who tests our hearts" (1 Thess. 2:3-4). Unwavering in their mission, they continued to preach even when opposition flared up in the new city, echoing the words of the apostle in Romans 1:16, "For I am not ashamed of the gospel, for it is the power of God for salvation to everyone who believes."

Paul urges the Thessalonians to remember these efforts as a testament to their genuine commitment to God and His gospel. He essentially says, "You are witnesses, and God also, how holy and righteous and blameless was our conduct toward you believers" (1 Thess. 2:10). The resilience shown by the missionaries was not self-manufactured but was an evident sign of God's power and grace working through them. As Paul wrote in 2 Corinthians 12:10, "For the sake of Christ, I am content with weaknesses, insults, hardships, persecutions, and calamities. For when I am weak, then I am strong."

Paul and his companions' unyielding faith in the face of severe trials stood as irrefutable testimony to their sincerity and unwavering integrity. Their lives were clearly anchored in the teachings of Christ, who had already warned His disciples that they would encounter persecution but also encouraged them by saying, "In this world, you will have trouble. But take heart! I have overcome the world" (Jn. 16:33). This steadfastness harkens back to Paul's earlier exhortation in Acts 14:22, where he strengthened the souls of the disciples, encouraging them to continue in the faith and saying, "Through many tribulations, we must enter the kingdom of God."

Paul and his companions were the embodiment of a faith that transcended mere lip service; it was a faith that had been tried and purified in the crucible of affliction, resonating deeply with James' challenge, "Show me your faith apart from your works, and I will show you my faith by my works" (Ja. 2:18). In essence, their resolute boldness amid significant opposition was not just an aspect of their character; it was a divine affirmation, manifesting the work of God within them. Their courage and perseverance were not just human traits but potent markers of divine activity, proving that God was mightily at work in and through His servants.

In 1 Thessalonians 2:3-6, Paul elucidates the principles that govern his ministry, stating, "For our appeal does not spring from error or impurity or any attempt to deceive, but just as we have been approved by God to be entrusted with the gospel, so we speak, not to please man, but to please God who tests our hearts. For we never came with words of flattery, as you know, nor with a pretext for greed—God is witness. Nor did we seek glory from people, whether from you or others, though we could have made demands as apostles of Christ."

Paul's ministry, he insists, is fundamentally different from those who seek personal gain or validation, whether they be religious leaders of his own era or contemporary figures. While he and his companions were unyielding in the face of external adversities like persecution—a recurring theme noted in Acts 16:22-24 and 14:22—they were equally vigilant against internal dangers, specifically, the pitfalls of deception, greed, and ego.

The contrast between external and internal threats is notable. Externally, the early Christians faced brutal persecution, both socially and politically, as well as the ever-present danger of physical harm or death. These external threats were visible, tangible, and easily recognisable. Internally, however, the dangers were more insidious but equally perilous: false teachings, greed disguised as spirituality, and the vainglorious pursuit of human approval. Paul confronts these internal dangers head-on by emphasising the integrity, sincerity, and divine approval behind his ministry.

The relevance of Paul's warning extends into our modern context, particularly seen in some segments of the charismatic movement. While some charismatic leaders may be sincere in their beliefs and actions, a good number echo the self-interested religious figures Paul warns against. Whether it is prosperity gospel preachers promising miracles in exchange for financial gifts or charismatic leaders whose methods appear designed more for spectacle than for meaningful spiritual engagement, the internal dangers of deception and self-interest persist alongside the external threats of scepticism and outright hostility toward faith.

In sum, Paul's teachings serve as an enduring safeguard against the two-fold dangers that ministries face. They caution us to be vigilant not only against the external threats of persecution and societal disdain but also against the equally detrimental internal dangers of deception, self-interest, and the corrupting pursuit of personal gain at the expense of the gospel's truth. The apostle underscores that the ultimate metric of any ministry's success should be its faithfulness to the gospel and its aim to glorify God above all else.

In 1 Thessalonians 2:7-8, Paul delineates the essence of his apostolic ministry, saying, "But we were gentle among you like a nursing mother taking care of her own children. So, being affectionately desirous of you, we were ready to share with you not only the gospel of God but also our own selves because you had become very dear to us." These verses show the stark contrast between Paul's approach and those who exploit or harm the faithful for personal gain.

Paul's nurturing metaphor of being like a "nursing mother" echoes Christ's own words about leadership, where Jesus instructs His disciples,

"The greatest among you will be your servant" (Matt. 23:11). Paul's care for the Thessalonians was not merely about conveying a message; it was about forming a bond akin to a parent-child relationship.

In a world where charisma can often eclipse character, Paul's principles offer a litmus test for spiritual leadership. While the church must be vigilant in confronting external threats, the internal threats—especially those stemming from within the pulpit—need equally scrupulous discernment and courage to address. Paul's life and teachings serve as a reminder that the ultimate objective of Christian ministry should be the unadulterated proclamation and practice of the gospel, guided by love, integrity, and a selfless desire to see the Kingdom of God grow.

In 1 Thessalonians 2:9-12, Paul continues to elaborate on the character of his ministry: "For you remember, brothers, our labour and toil: we worked night and day, that we might not be a burden to any of you, while we proclaimed to you the gospel of God. You are witnesses, and God also, how holy, righteous, and blameless our conduct toward you believers was. For you know how, like a father with his children, we exhorted each one of you, encouraged you, and charged you to walk in a manner worthy of God, who calls you into his kingdom and glory."

In these verses, Paul underscores his commitment to self-sufficiency, labouring "night and day" to ensure he would not financially burden the community. This aligns with his broader teaching on work and responsibility found in 2 Thessalonians 3:10, "If anyone is not willing to work, let him not eat." His point is clear: the ministry was never about personal gain but rather the spiritual enlightenment of the Thessalonian church.

Again, Paul's example starkly contrasts leaders who manipulate or exploit their congregations. He could have invoked his apostolic authority to demand support, but instead, he modelled the teachings of Christ, who said, "Freely you have received; freely give" (Matt. 10:8). This approach directly opposes those who would exploit the flock, as warned by Jesus in John 10:12-13: "The hired hand is not the shepherd and does not own the sheep. So when he sees the wolf coming, he abandons the sheep and runs away."

Paul's ethical conduct, paternal care, and ceaseless labour set the standard for what Christian ministry should embody. He was not simply disseminating information; he was guiding, "exhorting," "encouraging," and "charging" the believers to live lives "worthy of God." This nurturing attitude reflects the ideal expressed in Ephesians 4:11-12 that spiritual leaders are given "to equip his people for works of service, so that the body of Christ may be built up."

The dual themes of external and internal threats provide a sobering but necessary lens through which we can evaluate contemporary Christian leadership. Paul's life and teachings in these verses offer an enduring standard that cuts through the complexities of the modern Christian experience. His emphasis on sincerity, hard work, and relational, sacrificial ministry provides a beacon to guide the church towards faithfulness, irrespective of its era or challenges.

In 1 Thessalonians 2:13-16, Paul expresses gratitude for how the Thessalonians received the Word of God: "And we also thank God constantly for this, that when you received the word of God, which you heard from us, you accepted it not as the word of men but as what it really is, the word of God, which is at work in you believers. For you, brothers, became imitators of the churches of God in Christ Jesus that are in Judea. For you suffered the same things from your own countrymen as they did from the Jews, who killed both the Lord Jesus and the prophets, and drove us out, and displease God and oppose all mankind."

Here, Paul rejoices over the Thessalonians for accepting the gospel and enduring persecution, similar to what he and the Judean churches had faced. He acknowledges that the true gospel carries with it a cost—the cost of discipleship, in alignment with Jesus' own words: "If they persecuted Me, they will persecute you also" (Jn. 15:20).

The striking element here is the type of gospel Paul preached—a gospel that not only promised eternal life but also forewarned of earthly trials. This contrasts sharply with other versions of the gospel encountered today, again, particularly within segments of the charismatic movement. While Paul and the early Christians faced persecution for their faith, some modern-day preachers promised a gospel of prosperity, divine protection, and physical health. Such teachings misinterpret, misuse, and abuse scriptural promises and, as a result, create a distorted gospel that neither Jesus nor Paul would recognise.

Externally, the church has always faced threats, from societal scorn to outright persecution. But as Paul's letters and the broader biblical narrative indicate, the more dangerous threats are internal—false teachings that promise an easier, more comfortable Christian walk. These false teachings stand in stark contrast to Paul's words in 2 Timothy 3:12: "Indeed, all who desire to live a godly life in Christ Jesus will be persecuted."

Paul's gratitude for the Thessalonians' acceptance and application of the authentic gospel serves as an indelible mark of its divine origin. The gospel Paul proclaimed was not designed to appeal to worldly desires or offer a quick path to personal prosperity. Instead, it demanded a radical commitment, even in the face of adversity. This high-stakes, authentic gospel reflects the sentiments of 2 Corinthians 4:14: "For we do not preach ourselves, but Jesus Christ as Lord, and ourselves as your servants for Jesus' sake."

INTRODUCTION TO 1ST THESSALONIANS

In an age where messages of divine favour devoid of sacrifice or service increase, Paul's words offer a much-needed corrective. The gospel has never been a means to worldly success or personal enrichment. The gospel preached by Paul, with its promise of trials and tribulations, validates its divine source as a crucial touchstone for measuring contemporary proclamations.

In 1 Thessalonians 2:15-16, Paul elaborates on the notion of "God's wrath," specifically targeting those who "inhibit us from speaking to the Gentiles that they might be saved." One school of thought posits that Paul could be alluding to the catastrophic fall of the Jerusalem Temple in 70 A.D. as a tangible example of this divine wrath. The devastation wrought by this event, which resulted in the loss of thousands of lives and the dislocation of even more, marked a profound shift in the centrality of Jerusalem in Jewish life. Some theologians argue that this calamity was God's judgment on the Jewish leaders for their rejection of the gospel and their efforts to hinder its dissemination.

Paul further explores the topic of God's wrath in 1 Thessalonians 5:3, indicating that sudden destruction will come upon those who proclaim "peace and safety." However, he offers a glimmer of hope for believers in 1 Thessalonians 5:9 and 4:16-17. In these verses, Paul implies that Christians are not slated for this divine wrath, supporting the notion of a pre-tribulation rapture. This view contends that the faithful will be "caught up" (1 Thess. 4:17) before the tribulation, a period characterised by intense suffering and divine judgment, as vividly depicted in the Book of Revelation.

Additionally, Paul reassures the faithful that they will not be surprised by this "thief in the night" (1 Thess. 5:4), an idea that resonates with the warning to the church in Sardis in Revelation 3. This suggests a kind of spiritual alertness among genuine believers, contrasting sharply with those who thwart the true gospel message from being disseminated.

The act of obstructing the gospel is not merely a matter of historical record; it continues in contemporary times. Present-day preachers who propagate a skewed version of the gospel are effectively leading people away from the truth. These modern circumstances could also be categorised under the overarching theme of God's wrath, as discussed by Paul. Whether looking at the ancient destruction of the Jerusalem Temple or the prospective tribulation, the recurring message is that any rejection or obstruction of God's Word can result in severe consequences. History reveals that obstructing the gospel has led to harsh outcomes in the past and will ultimately manifest in the future wrath of the tribulation.

In conclusion, Paul's approach to ministry, as revealed in the second chapter of 1 Thessalonians, remains a timeless model for Christian leadership. His ministry is characterised by sincerity, self-sacrifice, and an unyielding dedication to delivering an uncompromised gospel. Verses 1 to 16 in the chapter offer invaluable insights into the essence of Christian leadership, drawing a stark contrast with those who would distort or manipulate Christ's message for personal benefit.

Paul's words also caution us against both external and internal threats to the Christian faith. External threats, such as societal disdain and outright persecution, have been present since the inception of the church. Yet, there are internal threats that are potentially more harmful. These include false teachings that promise a Christian life devoid of suffering, resembling the distorted gospel peddled by some modern charismatic leaders. Such messages deviate from the rigorous teachings of Christ and the apostles, opting for teachings catering to worldly desires.

Notably, Paul discusses the concept of "God's wrath" in the context of those who obstruct the gospel message, be it the Jewish leaders who

INTRODUCTION TO 1ST THESSALONIANS

faced devastating consequences in 70 A.D. with the destruction of the Jerusalem Temple or modern preachers who misrepresent the gospel today. He further expands on this concept in the fifth chapter, indicating that while sudden destruction may come, the church is not destined for wrath but will be removed before the tribulation (1 Thess. 5:3, 5:9, cf. 4:16-17). These teachings offer a framework for vigilance against external threats and internal distortions from the pulpit.

Paul's teachings serve as a grounding force in an era where the line between worldly success and spiritual integrity is often blurred. His ministry stands as a beacon of what Christian leadership should aspire to: a life rooted in love, integrity, and selfless commitment to the Christian community's preservation and spiritual growth. His words continue to echo through time, reminding his readers that the true power of the gospel is not in the promises of earthly riches but in the transformative work of Christ in the lives of believers, even if and when that comes at the cost of comfort or worldly approval.

In a world where authenticity is often sacrificed for artifice, Paul's first letter to the Thessalonians serves as more than a historical note. It offers timeless guidelines for discerning and practising a faith that, while challenging, is immeasurably rewarding.

BEFORE OUR LORD JESUS CHRIST AT HIS COMING

'Satan Hindered Us'
(1 Thess. 2:17-3:5)

In 1 Thessalonians 2:17-3:5, Paul reveals his emotional and spiritual connection with the Thessalonian church, underlining a stark contrast between his ministry and that of leaders who seek their own glory or peddle a "gospel of prosperity." Paul's absence from the community has been a burden to him, yet his concern is entirely for the well-being of the Thessalonians. His sending of Timothy to strengthen and encourage them in the face of affliction highlights the sacrificial nature of his pastoral care. Unlike those who proclaim a gospel centred on immediate earthly gains, Paul acknowledges the reality of suffering for the gospel's sake. He does not promise an easy life but prepares the Thessalonians for the inevitable trials that come with living a life in Christ. His focus is not on the material comfort or personal glory that false teachers promote but on the spiritual fortitude that sustains true believers through life's adversities. Within this suffering, there is an eschatological tension, a 'looking forward' to the return of Christ. Paul instils a sense of eternal perspective, encouraging the Thessalonians—and, by extension, his readers—to endure, knowing that present sufferings are not worth comparing with the glory that will be revealed when Christ returns.

The depth of Paul's emotional connection with the Thessalonian church is palpably expressed in 1 Thessalonians 2:17, where he says,

INTRODUCTION TO 1ST THESSALONIANS

"We were torn away from you." The phrase, often used in contexts of deep familial separation, such as orphaned children or bereaved parents, underscores the agony Paul felt in his physical absence from the community. This poignant emotion needs to be understood in the context of Acts 17, where Paul and Silas initially established the church in Thessalonica. They faced intense persecution and had to leave abruptly for their own safety. Despite the promising start of this fledgling community, opposition from local Jewish leaders forced an abrupt separation. Paul's words echo the deep-rooted care he has for his spiritual children, similar to sentiments expressed in other epistles, like when he tells the Corinthians, "For though you might have ten thousand guardians in Christ, you do not have many fathers. Indeed, in Christ Jesus I became your father through the gospel" (1 Cor. 4:15). The phrase "torn away" captures the anguish of a spiritual father separated from his children, eager to see how they are faring, and desiring to nurture them in faith despite adversity. It adds an intensely personal and emotional layer to the challenges of apostolic ministry and underscores the sincerity of Paul's commitment to the Thessalonians.

The emotional weight of Paul's separation from the Thessalonians is somewhat alleviated by his assertion that the separation is "for a short time" (1 Thess. 2:17). This phrase implies an anticipated reunion and underscores Paul's intent to return. However, Paul also notes in verse 18 that he had "made every effort to come to [them]" but that "Satan blocked [his] way." This adds a layer of spiritual warfare to the account, suggesting that evil cosmic forces acted to keep Paul and the Thessalonians apart.

While 1 Thessalonians does not specify the exact mechanisms by which Satan obstructed Paul's return to Thessalonica, the book of Acts and other letters from Paul furnish deeper insight. Particularly illuminating is Acts 20:24-35, where Paul underscores the importance of proclaiming "the whole counsel of God" and warns against self-serving, false teachers who could infiltrate the church. These impostors would not labour with their own hands, as Paul did. However, they would greedily exploit the congregation for personal gain, introducing a distorted 'gospel' that omits the authentic message of suffering and grace that Paul had taught.

In 1 Thessalonians 2:16, Paul says Satan hindered him from revisiting the Thessalonian church, a community he aimed to bolster in faith. Again, in 1 Thessalonians 3:5, he expresses his anxiety that the evil one might tempt the believers during his absence. These passages suggest that Satan's interference was not just an attempt to obstruct Paul but to create a vacuum wherein false teachers could spread their self-centred, corrupt interpretations of the gospel. By keeping Paul away, Satan was opening the door for these misleading influences, leading some members of the Thessalonian church potentially astray.

In Acts 14, we gain further understanding of Satan's tactics as Paul and Barnabas encounter various forms of opposition, ranging from hostile crowds to explicit plots against them. These incidents serve as additional examples of Satan's attempts to impede Paul's ministry. Similarly, in 2 Timothy, Paul describes how Demas abandoned him for worldly interests, which, although not directly attributed to Satan, could be viewed as another form of satanic hindrance. This is especially true considering that Demas later became a priest of idols, according to early church writings.

Paul's letter to the Corinthians also provides insight. In 1 Corinthians 16:9, he says a "wide door for effective work" had opened for him but also mentioned "many adversaries." Though these adversaries are not

INTRODUCTION TO 1ST THESSALONIANS

explicitly identified as satanic forces, the context suggests a form of spiritual opposition.

Paul himself was keenly aware of these spiritual hindrances. He discusses the need for spiritual discernment in 2 Corinthians 2:11 and advises believers in Ephesians 6:13-18 to put on spiritual armour. These exhortations indicate Paul's understanding that the challenges in his ministry were not merely physical or circumstantial but also spiritual.

Though the Bible does not explain how Satan obstructed Paul's journey back to Thessalonica, a composite understanding can be formed when considering other scriptural narratives detailing Paul's multifaceted challenges during his ministry. These obstacles were both situational and spiritual in nature, designed to derail Paul's mission and to create opportunities for leading the faithful off track and away from the narrow and difficult path.

The notion that Satan could actively obstruct the apostolic mission highlights the intense spiritual warfare that is an inherent aspect of spreading the gospel. However, in the face of these spiritual hindrances, Paul is far from resigned. Instead, he draws strength from the eschatological promise that such trials are fleeting compared to the eternal glory awaiting believers upon Christ's return. This sense of hope is not just theoretical for Paul; it manifests in his earnest desire to be reunited with the Thessalonians. His intent for earthly reunion serves as a microcosm of a larger, more profound hope—that of eternal communion in God's kingdom. This dynamic interplay between spiritual warfare and eschatological hope illuminates Paul's resilience and enduring commitment to his ministry.

In the context of spiritual warfare, the New Testament, including insights from Acts 28:18, offers a compelling examination of the ceaseless cosmic battle between the forces of good and evil. On one side stands God, accompanied by His angelic legions, and on the other, Satan with his demonic followers. The scriptures provide a nuanced and layered understanding of this eternal struggle, giving depth to our perception of the spiritual conflict that perpetually unfolds.

Thus, the New Testament provides a comprehensive and nuanced understanding of spiritual warfare that goes beyond the celestial clash of good and evil to include the human endeavour of coming to faith, abiding in Christ, and actively participating in the discipleship and retention of believers.

Ephesians 6:12 clarifies that our struggle is not against humans but against otherworldly spiritual forces of wickedness. This perspective is amplified by John 10:10, where Jesus delineates the stark difference between His mission to bring abundant life and the devil's aim, which is solely "to steal and kill and destroy."

Building on this foundation, 2 Corinthians 10:3-5 dives into the mental and ideological dimensions of spiritual warfare. It asserts that although we live in a physical world, the weapons of our warfare are divinely powerful for tearing down strongholds. Here, it is crucial to understand that the strongholds, thoughts, and imaginations being demolished are often our own, especially when influenced by satanic seeds of deceit. These false thoughts and imaginations can elevate themselves against the actual knowledge of God. If left unchecked, they can manifest into sinful behaviour, leading victims further away from God's truth.

In accordance with Paul's teaching to capture every thought and bring it under submission to Jesus Christ, James instructs believers to "submit to God and resist the devil" (Ja. 4:7), while 1 Peter 5:8 portrays Satan as a lion prowling around, seeking someone to devour, emphasising the need for watchfulness. Other verses, such as 2 Corinthians 2:11, caution God's elect against being ignorant of Satan's tactics, underscoring the importance of being aware of spiritual warfare.

While these scriptural passages offer a nuanced and complex view of spiritual warfare, they also project a fundamentally hopeful message. Contrary to the dualistic perspective of Manicheanism, which posits an eternal struggle between equally powerful forces of good and evil, the Bible clearly affirms the supreme authority and power of God over all creation, including Satan and his fallen angels. These verses are not merely warnings but empowering testaments to God's ultimate sovereignty.

In this Biblical view, the forces of good and evil are not co-equal combatants locked in an endless tug-of-war. Instead, God is the Creator and Ruler of all things, superior in every way to Satan and his minions. The scriptures indicate that God permits Satan a limited period of influence before the inevitable fulfilment of prophetic scriptures, which culminate in Christ's return and the casting of Satan into the bottomless pit. In this grand narrative, the forces of good led by God are not only engaged in a battle against evil but also predestined for ultimate and complete victory.

In charismatic circles, spiritual warfare takes on a more dramatic form, including practices such as "binding" and "rebuking" Satan and his demonic forces. They often rely on texts like Matthew 16:19, where Jesus grants Peter the "keys of the kingdom," which they interpret as conferring authority to bind or loose spiritual entities. These practices extend beyond a straightforward interpretation of the biblical text and incorporate elements from non-Christian philosophies like Manichaeanism, which, again, proposes a dualistic cosmos in a perpetual struggle between good and evil. During the first three centuries, the early Christian church emphasised living holy lives and enduring persecution was a form of spiritual warfare.

In discussions about spiritual authority, the verse Luke 10:19 is frequently mentioned within charismatic circles, where Jesus assures His followers, "I have given you authority to trample on snakes and scorpions and to overcome all the power of the enemy; nothing will harm you." At first glance, this verse may initially seem to offer a blanket authority over demonic powers, but its meaning takes on added depth when juxtaposed with the lived experiences of Christians throughout history. In the Old Testament, the Israelites bitten by serpents in the wilderness were not saved by avoiding the threat but by looking upon the bronze serpent raised by Moses—a symbol of Christ's future redemptive power. This suggests that spiritual authority does not preclude them or us from facing challenges or dangers.

The lives of the apostles serve as profound lessons in the reality and the complexities of spiritual warfare and the Christian journey. With the exception of John, who lived in exile, all the apostles met their end through martyrdom, embodying the essence of spiritual discernment discussed in Hebrews 5:14. Their stories resonate deeply with the experiences described in Hebrews 11:35-40, which details the trials of believers who faced torture, mockery, flogging, and imprisonment, but remained unswerving in their faith. Just like the individuals highlighted in Hebrews 11, the apostles demonstrated remarkable discernment in distinguishing between the transient allure of worldly comforts and the eternal weight of spiritual commitment. This discernment equipped them to stand firm in the face of intense suffering, making them enduring examples in the ongoing spiritual warfare that challenges believers to this day. Both the apostles and the heroes of faith in Hebrews 11 illustrate that spiritual warfare is not merely a struggle against external forces but also an internal battle requiring constant practice to discern good from evil.

Building on the example set by the apostles and the heroes of faith in Hebrews 11, it is essential to consider the complexities of spiritual authority as outlined in Luke 10:19. In this verse, Jesus proclaims that He has endowed believers with the authority "to trample on snakes and scorpions and to overcome all the power of the enemy." While it may be tempting to interpret this as a promise of a life devoid of suffering, the experiences of those who have walked the path of faith suggest otherwise. The trials faced by these believers reveal that spiritual authority and earthly suffering are not contradictory but are, in fact, complementary facets of the Christian journey. This more nuanced understanding affirms that Christians may still encounter hardships even with divine authority to overcome spiritual adversaries. These challenges serve as crucibles for faith, helping to refine spiritual discernment and fortify the soul in its ongoing engagement with spiritual warfare.

Similarly, the apostle Paul, who was steeped in spiritual matters, had to contend with a "thorn in the flesh, a messenger of Satan," as detailed in 2 Corinthians 12:7. Adding further distinction from the charismatic claims is the fact that another commonly cited scripture, Mark 16:17-18, is absent from some of the more literal Bible translations. The closest biblical narrative to this Mark 16 passage is the account of Paul in Malta, where he handled a snake and was bitten before ultimately being unharmed—a sequence that mirrors the experience of the Israelites and the bronze serpent.

In summary, while verses like Luke 10:19 do affirm a degree of spiritual authority vested in believers, this authority is exercised in a world still rife with spiritual warfare. Such authority does not render one impervious to the trials, obstacles, and even the possibility of martyrdom that are a part of the human experience.

Contrary to that of the charismatics, mainstream evangelicalism takes a more balanced approach. While evangelicalism acknowledges the reality of spiritual battles, it also emphasises the redemptive work of Christ and the importance of the "full armour of God," as described in Ephesians 6. Unlike in charismatic traditions, the practice of "binding Satan" is not a mainstream evangelical concept.

The Armor of God, as detailed by the apostle Paul in Ephesians 6, serves as a metaphorical guide for living a Christian life resilient to spiritual warfare. Each element of the armour— the belt of truth, the breastplate of righteousness, shoes of the gospel of peace, the shield of faith, the helmet of salvation, and the sword of the Spirit—is elaborated upon in the preceding chapters of Ephesians. For example, the breastplate of righteousness is directly related to the call to live righteously, as expounded earlier in the epistle. While charismatic Christians often speak of "putting on the armour" each day, the more profound implication of Paul's teaching is that one should embody these virtues consistently. In other words, rather than ceremonially putting on the armour daily, the aim is to live so that one never has to take it off.

Without contradiction, Christians do hold spiritual authority, as the Bible makes abundantly clear. The account of Paul's encounter with a spirit-possessed slave girl in Acts 16:16-18 serves as a poignant example. Here, Paul exercises his spiritual authority by directly confronting the evil spirit and commanding it to leave the girl, which it promptly does. Another scriptural example can be found in Acts 13:12, where Paul, filled with the Holy Spirit, confronts a sorcerer and renders him blind, leading the proconsul to believe in the Lord. Furthermore, Luke 10:17 describes the seventy-two disciples returning from their mission

INTRODUCTION TO 1ST THESSALONIANS

as elated that even demons are subject to them in Jesus' name. This spiritual authority is not limited to the apostolic era but extends to modern believers. Ephesians 6:12 establishes the theological context for spiritual warfare, emphasising that God empowers believers to engage against "the powers of this dark world and against the spiritual forces of evil in the heavenly realms."

It is essential to note that while this spiritual authority provides the means to confront and overcome evil forces, it does not offer immunity from life's challenges, obstacles, or even martyrdom, as history shows through the experiences of apostles and believers alike. This delegated authority operates within the greater framework of God's divine plan, pointing towards a Creator actively battling evil and predestined for ultimate victory. This understanding is fundamental to the Christian worldview of life in a fallen world, stressing that spiritual warfare is both real and ongoing and that the believer's authority in Christ is a testament to God's kingdom's impending, complete triumph.

In 1 Thessalonians 2:19, Paul describes the Thessalonian believers as his "hope, joy, and crown of boasting", pointing to his and their complete triumph before Jesus at His coming. This eschatological perspective resonates deeply with the hardships and obstructions, notably satanic hindrances, that believers face, as described in 1 Thessalonians 2:17-3:5. Therefore, Paul's anguish over being separated from the Thessalonians ("We were torn away from you") wasn't merely sentimental; it was rooted in a deep spiritual concern. As mentioned earlier, but worth repeating, Paul understood that Satan often works to undermine the faith of believers, sometimes through his ministers who preach a false gospel that promises prosperity without suffering, thereby leading people astray (cf. 2 Cor. 11:12-15). This starkly contrasts with Paul's own ministry, which did not seek glory or gain but aimed to prepare believers for the reality of suffering for the gospel.

In 1 Thessalonians 3:3-5, Paul expresses concern that the Thessalonians should not be "moved" by afflictions, recognising that persecution is one of the tools Satan uses to destabilise believers. This makes the integrity of the church's faith even more crucial, and it is why Paul sent Timothy to strengthen and encourage them (1 Thess. 3:1-2). In all these struggles, however, Paul never loses sight of the ultimate hope: the return of Christ. Paul's deepest fear is losing some of the flock to the deceptive ploys of Satan and his ministers, but his greatest joy and hope lie in standing before Jesus on the Day of His return alongside those who have remained faithful. This balances the immediate struggles with a future, eschatological perspective, a balance that is central both to Paul's ministry and to the New Testament's overall teachings on spiritual warfare.

Paul's writings, particularly in passages like 1 Thessalonians 3:3-5, also challenge the Calvinistic doctrine of "once saved, always saved," a perspective influenced by Augustine. Paul clearly expresses concern that believers could be "moved" or led astray by sufferings or false teachings, a sentiment that aligns more closely with Arminian views on conditional security. His proactive steps in sending Timothy to strengthen and encourage the Thessalonians indicate that he saw their faith as something that could be shaken or lost. Paul's ongoing concern for the spiritual well-being of his converts shows that he considered the perseverance of the saints as contingent upon lasting faith and commitment, not as an inevitable outcome guaranteed at the moment of initial salvation. This Arminian perspective emphasises human free will and the necessity of continued faithfulness for ultimate salvation.

INTRODUCTION TO 1ST THESSALONIANS

In 1 Thessalonians 3:1 and again in verse 5, Paul articulates an acute sense of urgency, stating that he "could no longer bear" being apart from the Thessalonians without knowing the state of their faith. This anxiety further questions the Calvinistic doctrine of "once saved, always saved," as it demonstrates Paul's genuine concern for the spiritual welfare of his converts. His fear that the "tempter had tempted them" and rendered his labour "in vain" indicates a recognition that the community's faith was vulnerable to challenges that could lead them away from salvation. Paul's decision to send Timothy—despite personal loneliness and difficulty—is a testament to how pressing he considered the matter of their spiritual stability and growth. The potential for the Thessalonians to be "moved" by trials or the "tempter" was a real and present danger in Paul's mind. Hence, and again, his theology aligns more closely with Arminianism, which emphasises the conditional nature of salvation and the continual need for faithfulness and spiritual vigilance.

In his letters to the Thessalonians and other early Christian communities, Paul outlines various ways Satan could tempt and "move" believers away from their faith. As mentioned earlier, one key avenue is through false teachings or deceptive philosophies that distort the gospel, which Paul warns against in several of his epistles, such as in Galatians 1:6-9. Another means could be through moral compromise, where believers start to adopt the practices and values of the surrounding culture, thereby diluting their Christian witness—a concern Paul addresses in 1 Corinthians 5. Additionally, persecution and social ostracisation could make the cost of discipleship seem too high, causing some to abandon their faith, an issue Paul deals with directly in the context of Thessalonians. As mentioned earlier, an example of someone succumbing to such temptations is Demas, whom Paul mentions in 2 Timothy 4:10 as having "loved this present world" and deserted him.

Paul's fears for the Thessalonians are rooted in a realistic understanding of the many pressures and pitfalls that could lead them away from steadfastness in their faith.

As mentioned earlier, the passage in Hebrews 11:35b-39 attests to the faithfulness of those who refused to recant their belief in Christ, even in the face of extreme suffering or death. This enduring faith was deeply rooted in the eternal hope offered by Christ, a yearning so powerful that it could not be exchanged for mere earthly release from torment. This aligns closely with Paul's sentiments in 1 Thessalonians 2:19 and 3:5, where he emphasises the future hope of Christ's appearing as the ultimate triumph and fears that the Thessalonians may waver under the temptations or persecutions they face. Apostasy, the complete renunciation of faith, was seen as losing one's eternal reward in Christ.

In the early church, the recanting stakes were considered extremely high. For instance, some Christians renounced their faith during the Roman persecutions to avoid death or torture. These individuals were generally considered to be spiritually lost by the Christian community. A historical example could be the story of the early Christian bishop Marcellus of Ancyra, who reportedly sacrificed to pagan gods to avoid martyrdom and was subsequently considered an apostate by many in the church. A path back to spiritual restoration often involved a complex process of repentance and, at times, the intercession of a saint facing martyrdom. The belief was that these imminent martyrs, being closer to God at that time, could hear directly from Him and extend forgiveness to the apostate.

In sum, the juxtaposition of eternal hope and immediate suffering offers a profound exploration of what it means to truly live by faith. In this light, Paul's fears for the Thessalonians—and his ultimate rejoicing

INTRODUCTION TO 1ST THESSALONIANS

at their steadfastness—gain even greater depth, set against the backdrop of early Christian experiences and an eternal, eschatological hope.

In conclusion, the scriptures, spanning from 1 Thessalonians 2:17-3:5 to Acts 20:24-35 and Acts 28:18, offer a deeply nuanced look at the multi-dimensional hardships Paul and the early Christians faced. These were not merely physical, emotional, or psychological tribulations; instead, they were embedded in the overarching context of spiritual warfare, a ceaseless cosmic struggle between God's forces of good and Satan's forces of evil. The New Testament provides an intricate and layered understanding of this eternal battle, which will continually unfold in heavenly realms and human experiences until Christ returns.

Paul's persistent endeavours to return to Thessalonica, agonising absence, and decisive action to send Timothy to fortify the Thessalonians' faith speak volumes about his commitment to safeguarding their spiritual well-being against the enemy's machinations. Acts 20:24-35 further elucidates this by highlighting Paul's emphasis on proclaiming "the whole counsel of God" while cautioning against false teachers who distort the gospel for their own gain.

Coupled with insights from Acts 28:18, it becomes evident that the New Testament presents a comprehensive understanding of spiritual warfare that goes beyond mere celestial confrontations. It encompasses the human journey of coming to faith, remaining rooted in Christ, engaging in discipleship and nurturing believers.

Therefore, these texts' emotional, spiritual, and eschatological aspects come together to form a compelling call to vigilance for believers: to remain steadfast in faith and hold an eternal perspective that guides them through life's challenges. This vigilance is not a matter of fleeting concern but of eternal significance, affecting both individual lives and the collective faith of the Christian community.

Paul's warnings and actions thereby stand as a timeless model that serves multiple purposes: they guide spiritual leadership, offer a framework for the Christian community, and set an example for individual perseverance in the face of adversity. This integrated approach to spiritual warfare calls all believers to look beyond merely heavenly concerns and to grapple with their earthly responsibilities, including discipleship and pastoral care, as part of an ongoing, collective endeavour with eternal implications.

BLAMELESS IN HOLINESS ... AT THE COMING OF THE LORD JESUS CHRIST

'We Live "IF" You are Standing Fast in the Lord'
(1 Thess. 3:6-13)

In the early part of 1 Thessalonians chapter 3, specifically verses 1 through 5, Paul talks about his worries and his love for the church of Thessalonica. He is concerned about their spiritual health. Moving on to verses 6 through 13 in the same chapter, Paul opens up more, offering guidance to the Thessalonians about increasing faith and God's love, establishing the church in preparation for Christ's return. Paul does not just recollect events; he reveals divine truths, showcasing the Thessalonians' unwavering faith and passionate love—a picture painted clearer by Timothy's updates when he was in Corinth.

The initial verse of this passage, 1 Thessalonians 3:6-13, transitions from the preceding by mentioning Timothy, who has returned to Paul, presumably in Corinth, with a report on the Thessalonians. This presumption about Corinth as the location stems from the chronological clues in Paul's journey. It is written that Paul, while in Athens, dispatched Timothy to Thessaloniki (1 Thess. 3:1-2), and after his stop in Athens, he proceeded to Corinth (Acts 18:1).

From 1 Thessalonians 3:6, the mood changes. It goes from a feeling of worry and longing to a feeling of joyful revelation. It is within these parts of scripture that we see the robust and lively faith of the

Thessalonians, a faith that is fruitful and steadfast, filling Paul with a joy that is beyond words—a joy that only comes from the gospel itself (1 Thess. 3:9). The enduring faith of the Thessalonians and their deep desire to reunite are met with Paul's ongoing hope and strong desire to see them again (1 Thess. 2:18, 3:7, 10, 11).

Timothy's safe return to Paul was a moment marked with immense relief and joy for Paul. Initially, Paul had sent Timothy to the Thessalonians, a decision made out of deep concern and sacrificial love (1 Thess. 3:1-2). This meant that Paul had to stay alone, showcasing his selfless nature and desire to ensure the well-being of the Thessalonians over his own comfort.

Paul must have been concerned about Timothy, considering him a son in the faith (1 Cor. 4:17; 1 Tim. 1:2; 2 Tim. 1:2; Phil. 2:22), so seeing him return safely was a great relief. However, Timothy's return was more than a reunion; he brought good news about the Thessalonians' faith and love. "But now that Timothy has come to us from you and has brought us the good news of your faith and love and reported that you always remember us kindly and long to see us, as we long to see you" (1 Thess. 3:6). This news was a joy to Paul, soothing his worries and strengthening the bond between him, Timothy, and the Thessalonians.

As a result of Timothy's report and "good news", this segment of Paul's epistle to the Thessalonians marks another transition in tone and content. The earlier articulated apprehensions of Paul regarding the church (1 Thess. 3:5) metamorphose into expressions of joy (1 Thess. 3:9). This joyful revelation is a response to learning that the church, which was established amidst significant personal tribulations (1 Thess. 3:4, 7), against all odds, continues to flourish, defying all adversities (1 Thess. 2:14, 3:3, 5).

INTRODUCTION TO 1ST THESSALONIANS

Interestingly, Paul uses the Greek translation of "proclaiming good news" (1 Thess. 3:6) to describe the report Timothy brings back. Initially, this verb was used to denote any announcement of good news (1 Thess. 3:1-2). Though it might have this meaning in this context, Paul's word choice likely has a deeper resonance. It seems to be a deliberate play on words, echoing the term frequently used by early Christians to convey the core message of Christianity. This term is crucial in Christian communications, as seen in passages like 1 Corinthians 15:1 and Galatians 1:8, 11, and 16, where it symbolises the proclamation of the Christian message. This illustrates Paul's nuanced use of language to imbue his message with layers of meaning, connecting Timothy's news from the Thessalonians to the broader Christian narrative of spreading the gospel in this section of the scripture, unveiling a heightened motivation for Paul's desire to revisit them. This alteration in intentionality is brought to the forefront upon receiving the good news of their persistent faith and burgeoning love (1 Thess. 3:1). The motivating force now behind Paul's desire is no longer solely grounded in concern but is overwhelmingly infused with joy (1 Thess. 3:9).

Again, Paul's oscillation between fear and joy reflects his deep-rooted care and concern for the Thessalonian believers. His joy is amplified, knowing that the believers in Thessalonica are standing firm in their faith, overcoming the challenges and persecutions that are their lot (1 Thess. 2:14). It is evident that the joy Paul experiences is not superficial; instead, it is an overflow of his spiritual connection and commitment to the Thessalonians, embodying a sense of relief and spiritual peace derived from the steadfastness of the Thessalonians in their faith. This transformation from apprehension to elation underscores the dynamic and profound relationship between Paul and the Thessalonian church, highlighting the resilient and enduring nature of the faith community he had nurtured and established (Acts 17:1-8).

The Thessalonian church's enduring perseverance and spiritual vigour serve as a beacon of hope and a testament to the gospel's transformative power amid trials and tribulations.

Paul's apprehensions about the church ignited a fervent desire in him to return to the Thessalonians multiple times (1 Thess. 2:18), especially after experiencing the emotional turmoil of being forcibly separated from them, a feeling likened to a parent being wrenched away from their infant child, and vice versa (1 Thess. 2:17). Again, this intense longing illustrates Paul's deep, familial bonds with the Thessalonian believers, underscoring the parental concern and love he held for them in their spiritual journey (1 Thess. 2:7-8).

In the eschatological context of the letter, Paul's desire to be with the Thessalonian church gains a deeper significance. He is not just looking forward to reuniting with them due to personal affection or concern for their well-being, although those elements are present. Instead, his desire is intensified by his anticipation of the return of Christ, marked by increased tribulation for both him and the Thessalonians (1 Thess. 2:14, 3:3-4, 7). Paul understood his sufferings as part of a larger, prophesied period of trial and tribulation that would precede the ultimate reunion at Christ's Second Coming by way of the rapture (1 Thess. 1:10, 2:19, 3:13, 4:15-17, 5:9) and then followed by the tribulation (1 Thess. 5:2-3).

With an unwavering focus on Christ and His impending return, Paul perceives his present sufferings and sacrifices as minor when juxtaposed with the forthcoming divine promises. By maintaining this perspective, he fosters encouragement within the exceptionally steadfast church to persist in their resilience and allegiance to the Lord (1 Thess.

INTRODUCTION TO 1ST THESSALONIANS

3:7, 4:10). This enduring spiritual stance is pivotal, ensuring that upon Christ's return, the congregation is deemed blameless in their holiness in the presence of God, the Son, and the saints (1 Thess. 3:13).

In the interim before the glorious appearing of Christ, Paul conveys, with profound resonance, "For now, we live," a statement steeped in conditionality, denoting, "If you (the church) are anchored firmly in the Lord" (1 Thess. 3:8). Again, the backdrop of this statement is the resilient endurance of the church amidst relentless persecution (1 Thess. 2:14, 3:4) and the persisting, albeit resisted, enticements of Satan (1 Thess. 3:5). The term "life," as invoked by Paul, represents a transcendent joy born out of the spiritual robustness of the church, his converts, who remain unswerving in their devotion, a stark divergence from the doctrines propounded by the charismatic movement. Often cloaked in the garb of a prosperity "gospel," these doctrines equate "abundant life" with material wealth and physical well-being. In sharp contrast, Paul's joy is extricated from divine experiences, independent of worldly affluence or satisfaction; it is a spiritual joy stemming from the unwavering faithfulness of the church amidst adversities, symbolising his eternal joy and crown at the second coming of Jesus (1 Thess. 2:19). Paul's teachings emphasise spiritual enrichment and enduring joy in Christ over transient worldly gains, portraying "abundant life" as an embodiment of spiritual resilience and eternal hope amid life's ephemeral and tumultuous journey, aligning with scriptures advocating for spiritual wealth, divine contentment, and refined faith over material accumulation (Matt. 6:19-21; Phil. 4:11-13; Heb. 12:7-11).

Continuing, it becomes pivotal to address another prevalent theological perspective, namely Calvinism, and its doctrine of "once saved, always saved." This doctrine posits that once an individual is saved, they remain saved, irrespective of their subsequent actions or beliefs, essentially proposing an unconditional security in salvation. However, Paul's epistles present a nuanced understanding of salvation, marked by conditional perseverance and enduring faithfulness. The conditional "If" (1 Thess. 3:8), central to Paul's discourse, accentuates this very idea, supported by his voiced apprehensions about the church potentially being "moved" amidst tribulations (1 Thess. 3:3) or succumbing to temptation (1 Thess. 3:5).

Paul's fears elucidate the constant spiritual battle and vigilance required to maintain one's faith, indicating that falling away is a real and present danger, and the believer's journey is one of continual growth, resilience, and steadfastness in faith. This is corroborated by various other scriptures, underscoring the necessity for enduring faith and perseverance in righteousness until the end (cf. Matt. 10:22, 24:13; Heb. 10:35-39; Rev. 2:10). For instance, 1 John 2:24 advises believers to let what they have heard from the beginning abide in them, implying that if one continues in the Son and in the Father, the promise of eternal life remains with them, signifying the contingency of eternal life on continuous abidance in divine teachings. These scriptural intricacies reflect the multifaceted nature of salvation, underlining the importance of sustained spiritual integrity, continual growth in Christ, and enduring adherence to divine precepts, thereby offering a more balanced and biblically aligned perspective on the dynamics of salvation and eternal life in contrast to the absolute, unconditional assurances posited by the doctrine of "once saved, always saved."

In the "prosperity gospel" context, Paul's letters offer a stark contrast. As aforenoted, Paul writes to a congregation facing various physical and spiritual trials from both visible and invisible sources. Despite these challenges, the church continues to thrive and hold on to the hope of being reunited with Paul (1 Thessalonians 3:11, 2:18, 3:6, 9,

INTRODUCTION TO 1ST THESSALONIANS

10). Paul fervently prays for their continued growth in love and holiness, which is a recurring theme in his letters, including 1 Thessalonians 4:12, where he encourages them to "do more and more."

Paul's invocation for "increase" (1 Thess. 3:12) is not a call for material accumulation but a heartfelt prayer for a burgeoning love among believers, fostering an environment wherein hearts are fortified in sanctity in anticipation of Christ's triumphant return, accompanied by all His saints. This deepening love is envisioned as encompassing sacrificial giving and selflessness amidst hardships, fundamentally differing from the prosperity gospel's focus on material acquisition and worldly success. While Paul paints a vision of believers strengthening each other in love, awaiting a heavenly kingdom to be established with the return of Jesus, prosperity teachings, such as those adhering to the Seven Mountain Mandate, divert focus towards establishing an earthly kingdom, prioritising temporal gains over spiritual growth. In contrast, the gospel message emphasises compassion, selflessness, love, sacrifice, and holiness, resulting in a blameless standing before God, the Son, and the saints on Judgment Day.

The essence of standing blameless at the return of Christ, a central theme in New Testament teachings, epitomises a state of spiritual sanctification and moral uprightness achieved through a life steeped in faith, love, and grace. In his numerous letters, Paul underscores this by urging believers to shine as lights in the world, holding fast to the word of life, and exemplifying God's transformative power in a sin-tainted world. This is particularly evident in his encouragement to the Philippians to be "blameless and harmless, children of God without fault…" and his assertion in Colossians 1:22 about the reconciling power of Christ to present believers as holy and blameless. Peter also reverberates this call for diligence in spiritual purity in 2 Peter 3:14. Ephesians 5:27 portrays the church as the embodiment of sanctified purity, free from blemish, reflecting the redeeming work of Christ. The intricate interweaving of these scriptural insights with Romans 14:12 and 1 Corinthians 3:13-15 further illustrates the profound importance of individual accountability and the enduring need to align one's life with God's eternal standards of love and holiness. This holistic transformation, anchored in an authentic relationship with God and manifested through righteous living and selfless love, prepares the believer to enter into eternal communion with the Creator on the day.

In sum, reflecting on 1 Thessalonians 3:6-13, the spiritual dynamics between Paul and the Thessalonians demonstrate a transformative journey of faith and love. The Thessalonians' steadfast faith and love, conveyed by Timothy, shifted Paul's concerns to joy, revealing the enduring and profound spiritual bond between them. Paul's use of "proclaiming good news" in describing Timothy's report alludes to the Christian narrative of spreading the gospel, adding layers of meaning to his communications. Paul's intense longing to reunite with the Thessalonians was not just based on affection but also his anticipation of the return of Christ, marking a period of increased tribulation. This longing exemplified Paul's understanding of his and the Thessalonians' sufferings as part of a larger prophesied period preceding Christ's Second Coming. Paul's nuanced teachings focus on spiritual enrichment and enduring joy in Christ over transient worldly gains, presenting a balanced view of salvation marked by conditional perseverance and enduring faithfulness. This contrasted sharply with the doctrines of "once saved, always saved" and the prosperity gospel, which equated abundant life with material wealth and presented salvation as unconditionally secure. Instead, Paul's letters to the Thessalonians underscored the importance of continuous growth in Christ and enduring adherence to divine precepts, emphasising the need for increased love and holiness among believers in anticipation of Christ's return. The genuine Christian life, as Paul portrays, centres on compassion, selflessness, love, and holiness, ensuring blamelessness in holiness at the coming of the Lord Jesus Christ. The teachings and revelations within these scriptures provide a roadmap for spiritual resilience and unwavering faith, encouraging believers to remain steadfast in the Lord, to live in alignment with divine precepts, and to be motivated by a profound spiritual joy independent of worldly affluence or satisfaction, in anticipation of Christ's triumphant return.

THE LORD IS AN AVENGER

'Live Holy Lives'
(1 Thess. 4:1-12)

The teachings of Paul in 1 Thessalonians 3 and 4 articulate deep spiritual truths, portraying an affectionate relationship between Paul and the Thessalonian church, rooted in mutual love and shared faith. Paul's deep concern for the Thessalonians transforms into immense joy upon receiving Timothy's reassuring report of their steadfast faith and genuine love. This is not mere earthly joy but one intertwined with the gospel's transformative power, illuminating the resilience of the Thessalonians amidst tribulations and their longing to reunite with Paul. It is in this divine joy that Paul's yearning to revisit the Thessalonians gains momentum, infused with the anticipative hope of witnessing their spiritual growth before the return of Christ. The central theme within these passages accentuates living a life of increasing holiness and love, thus being found blameless at Christ's coming.

As mentioned in the previous sections, Paul's teachings starkly contradict the prevailing prosperity teachings and the doctrinal perspective of "once saved, always saved," emphasising instead a call to conditional perseverance, eternal hope, and spiritual growth, highlighted by the conditional "if" in 1 Thessalonians 3:8, representing the necessity of steadfastness in faith and continual abidance in divine teachings. His message is one of enduring spiritual resilience, transcending worldly wealth and physical well-being, emphasising the pursuit of spiritual enrichment through increasing faith. Paul's invocation for the increase is a prayer for overflowing love and holiness, a call to spiritual fortification in anticipation of Christ's return, again bluntly contrasting to teachings prioritising temporal gains and diverting focus towards establishing an earthly kingdom. The essence of Paul's teachings culminates in preparing oneself to stand blameless in holiness at the return of the Lord Jesus Christ, living in unwavering faith, unceasing love, and growing holiness.

In 1 Thessalonians 4:1, Paul's "urging" underscores an emotional plea to his brothers and sisters in Christ to lead lives pleasing to God, a theme deeply embedded in the eschatological context, emphasising the imminent return of Jesus Christ. Paul's eschatological message is echoed in his warnings against being led astray by divergent gospels, notably those promoting a prosperity gospel void of suffering and service, as mentioned in 2:5-6. He poignantly reminds the Thessalonians of the inevitability of afflictions in a believer's journey (3:4, 7), denouncing doctrines that equate God's favour solely with material prosperity and physical well-being. Paul's concern about believers being tempted away (3:5) underscores the necessity of spiritual vigilance and resilience in maintaining true faith. This continuous emphasis on holiness and unswerving faith is integral to Paul's teachings, as he underscores the importance of steadfastness in faith, consistently warning against regression and admonishing believers to live a life steeped in sanctity and increasing love, ever-ready for the awaited return of the Lord, on a day, and at an hour they do not know (Matt. 24:36, 42, 44, 50; 5:13). In essence, Paul's eschatological urging resonates with a call to live in unwavering holiness, withstanding temptations and false teachings, thus preparing oneself to be found blameless in holiness at the advent of Jesus Christ.

Continuing Paul's emphasis on spiritual growth and righteous conduct in 1 Thessalonians, he repeatedly "urges" the Thessalonians to do "more and more" (4:1, 10), highlighting the importance of progressive sanctification in their Christian walk. Although Paul acknowledges the evident maturity and spiritual accomplishments of the Thessalonians, as seen in 4:9, again, he implores them not to be complacent but to continually strive to excel more in living a life pleasing to God. This thematic repetition serves as a clarion call to every believer to persist in cultivating a deeper love for God and one another and refining one's godly character, even when substantial progress has already been made. It is reminiscent of Philippians 3:12-14 where Paul articulates his relentless pursuit of the upward call of God, emphasising the ongoing nature of the Christian journey. Even as he commends their love for one another, he encourages relentless progress, insinuating that the pursuit of holiness and love is limitless and should permeate every aspect of one's life. It is a consistent biblical principle, echoed in 2 Peter 3:18, which encourages believers to grow in the grace and knowledge of our Lord and Saviour, Jesus Christ. Paul's repetitive urging underscores a relentless pursuit of a Christ-centred life, reflecting an understanding that spiritual maturity is an ever-advancing journey, emphasising continual growth, ceaseless love, and enduring perseverance in anticipation of Christ's return.

The danger of stagnation and lack of maturity in the Christian faith is emphatically highlighted in Hebrews 5:11-6:8. This passage warns against the peril of remaining spiritually immature, likening those who have not progressed beyond elementary teachings to infants, unable to digest solid spiritual food. Hebrews warns of the grave risk of falling

INTRODUCTION TO 1ST THESSALONIANS

away, portraying the impossibility of renewing to repentance those who have once been enlightened but have turned away, likening it to crucifying the Son of God all over again. Such a stark depiction serves as a sombre reminder that the Christian journey demands continual growth and maturation in faith. Similarly, 2 Peter 2:20-22 warns of the implications of knowing the way of righteousness but then turning back to the corruption of the world, depicting it as a dog returning to its vomit, emphasising the severe repercussions of reverting to one's old ways after having experienced the knowledge of the truth. The apostle Paul also echoes this sentiment in 1 Corinthians 9:27, expressing his discipline to keep his body in subjection, lest after preaching to others, he himself should become disqualified. The scriptural consensus is unequivocal; a failure to progress and mature in faith can lead to spiritual peril, and thus, believers are encouraged to press on towards maturity, grounded in sound doctrine and steadfast in the faith, continually growing in the grace and knowledge of Jesus Christ. The overarching narrative of these passages is a clear call to believers to be vigilant, to persevere in faith, to mature in spiritual understanding, and not to allow themselves to drift away from the truth, for the consequences of such neglect are eternally significant.

Reflecting on 1 Thessalonians 4:2, Paul places paramount importance on abiding by the sanctity of God's word and the emphasis on shunning sexual immorality. In his epistle to the Thessalonians, Paul urges believers to uphold a life of holiness and sanctification, maintaining control over their bodies in an honourable and holy manner. This teaching is echoed and amplified in 1 Corinthians 6:18-20, where believers are exhorted to flee sexual immorality, treating their bodies as temples of the Holy Spirit, destined to honour God. Additionally, Hebrews 13:4 reinforces the sanctity of marriage and the divine judgment awaiting those who defile it through sexual immorality. The implications of such immoral actions are further elucidated in Galatians 5:19-21, categorising sexual immorality as an act of the flesh and cautioning that those who practice such will not inherit the Kingdom of God. There is a serious warning in Revelation 2:20 regarding sexual sin, which may lead to being thrown into the Great Tribulation unless repentance is sought first (2:22). Various other verses also caution about the consequences of living an immoral life, painting a fearful picture of eternal separation from God in a fiery lake of burning sulphur (Rev. 21:8 and 22:14). These scriptures' seamless continuity and unanimity underscore the enduring battle against sin, highlighting the urgency of living in persistent righteousness, ongoing repentance, and unyielding adherence to divine commandments for inheriting eternal life.

Connected with sexuality purity, Paul reminds the believers of the importance of brotherly love, "not to wrong a brother" (4:6), urging them to love one another more and more, to lead a quiet life, to mind their own business, and to work with their hands so that their daily conduct may win the respect of outsiders (4:9-11). Further, he exhorts the Thessalonians to maintain their hope in the return of Jesus, comforting one another with the assurance of the resurrection and the reunion with their loved ones who have died in Christ (4:13-18). Further again, Paul instils the urgency of being alert and sober, wearing the breastplate of faith and love and the hope of salvation as a helmet (5:6-8). These instructions are not just good and goldy guidelines for living but are deeply rooted in the eschatological hope of Christ's return. They represent a holistic approach to Christian living, integrating love, moral purity, mutual support, diligent work, and hopeful anticipation, underscoring the multifaceted dimensions of a life pleasing to God as they, and we, await the return of our Lord Jesus Christ.

INTRODUCTION TO 1ST THESSALONIANS

Among Paul's instructions, to the Thessalonians, the reference: "Make it your ambition to lead a quiet life: You should mind your own business and work with your hands, just as we told you" (4:11), is worth some amplification. Here, Paul is not simply advocating for manual labour but is urging believers to lead a life characterised by peaceable conduct and diligence, thereby gaining the respect of outsiders. This warning to work is contrasted with Paul's words in 1 Thessalonians 4:14 and 2 Thessalonians 3:6-15, where he explicitly condemns idleness. In 2 Thessalonians, Paul commands the church to keep away from every believer who is idle and disruptive and does not live according to the teachings received from the apostles. He reiterates that those unwilling to work should not eat and recalls how he and his companions worked day and night to set an example. The idle are admonished to settle down and earn the food they eat. Paul's consistent message across these passages is clear: believers are to avoid idleness to be diligent and productive in their endeavours, thus reflecting life in accordance with the gospel. The comparison between those who work diligently and those who are idle illustrates the broader theme of Christian responsibility and righteous living in anticipation of the Lord's return. The emphasis is not merely on the avoidance of idleness but on active engagement in righteous and productive living as a testimony to the gospel's transformative power.

The reason Paul instructs believers to "make it your ambition to lead a quiet life: You should mind your own business and work with your hands, just as we told you, so that your daily life may win the respect of outsiders and so that you will not be dependent on anybody," is fuelled by misconceptions about the imminent return of Christ. Some believers thought His return was so immediate that engaging in daily work was futile. Paul addresses these misconceptions extensively in both epistles.

In 1 Thessalonians, he clarifies the nature of Christ's return and emphasises the need for preparedness and continual commitment to responsibilities. In 2 Thessalonians, Paul confronts the disturbance caused by a counterfeit letter, purportedly from him, suggesting that the Day of the Lord had already arrived (2 Thess. 2:1-3). He admonishes the church against idleness and disorderly conduct, urging them to persevere in doing good and to work diligently (2 Thess. 3:6-12), reminding them of his own example of working tirelessly so as not to be a burden to anyone (2 Thess. 3:7-9).

Continuing from the above, the call to holiness in the life of a believer is unequivocally intertwined with active engagement in natural work, good works, and spiritual development, a theme resonant in Paul's letters. Paul emphasises the necessity of living blamelessly, a mandate echoed three times in 1 Thessalonians (2:10, 3:13, 5:23), accentuating the need for believers to present themselves faultless in preparation for the day of the Lord's return. This encompasses a holistic approach to righteous living, embracing integrity in everyday activities, dedicated involvement in charitable deeds, and continuous spiritual growth. The unequivocal teaching is that Christ is returning for a church without spot or blemish (Col. 1:22; 2 Pet. 3:14; Jude 24), a sanctified assembly prepared in righteousness, leaving those unredeemed in their transgressions. Paul's epistles harmonise with other scriptural affirmations, as in Titus 2:14, where believers are instructed to be zealous for good works, and Ephesians 2:10, which posits believers are created for good works in Christ. This confluence of spiritual teachings serves as a vivid reminder to the believers of their divine calling to live blameless lives, saturated in good works and spiritual maturity, in ardent anticipation of the imminent return of Jesus Christ.

INTRODUCTION TO 1ST THESSALONIANS

Expanding on the aforementioned themes, Paul's recurrent emphasis on holiness permeates the text of 1 Thessalonians, notably highlighted in 1 Thessalonians 4:6 and reiterated in 3:13, 4:4, and 4:7. This vividly accentuates the supreme importance of purity and adherence to Christian doctrine. The phrase "The Lord is an avenger" serves as a potent reminder of the grave consequences that ensue when God's commandments are transgressed. It underscores the profound implications for those who embrace unholiness and who transgress against their fellow believers in Christ.

This admonition is far more than just precautionary counsel; it is a resounding warning about divine retribution, resonating with the grave assertion made in Hebrews 10:31, "It is a fearful thing to fall into the hands of the living God." These warnings coalesce with the teachings found in 2 Thessalonians 1:5-10, where Paul speaks about God's righteous judgment and the revelation of the Lord Jesus in flaming fire, inflicting vengeance on those who do not know God and do not obey the gospel of our Lord Jesus.

These elements integrate to magnify the essential need for holiness, urging believers to maintain purity per Christian doctrine to avoid facing the severe and fearful repercussions mentioned in Hebrews and Thessalonians. The stern warnings serve as an impetus for the followers of Christ to persist in righteousness, aligning their lives with the divine teachings and mandates of holiness in anticipation of the Lord's return.

Once again, Paul's warnings to the Thessalonian church spotlight a need for vigilance and ongoing sanctification within the early Christian communities, addressing existing moral and ethical challenges facing the nascent church. Paul's warning juxtaposes Calvinistic teachings, which primarily adhere to predestination and irresistible grace. The argumentative contention lies in the apparent tension between the emphatic call to righteousness and the doctrinal assertions of predetermined salvation. Paul's letters' stern warnings and exhortations reflect an underlying belief in human responsibility to adhere to a holy and righteous path, contrasting with a deterministic view of salvation and grace.

The essence of these warnings implies an understanding of the free will and human responsibility in maintaining holiness, tying in with the biblical assertions in 1 Peter 1:15-16 which commands, "But just as He who called you is holy, so be holy in all you do; for it is written: 'Be holy because I am holy.'" This continuity of thought magnifies the essence of sanctity and moral uprightness in Christian living, framing it as an indispensable component of one's faith journey. It is designed to align believers with God's righteous standards, preparing them for His return.

In harmonising the avenging nature of the Lord with the recurrent theme of Christ's return found at the conclusion of every chapter in 1 Thessalonians, we glean a compelling portrait of divine justice and redemptive culmination. Paul's deliberate positioning of the Second Coming of Christ is a sombre reminder that the return of the Messiah will be a time of reckoning, a moment when the righteous will be distinguished from the unrighteous. Each will receive according to their deeds, as reflected in 2 Corinthians 5:10. The Lord as an "avenger" reinforces the notion of divine justice and retribution, highlighting the inevitable consequences of living contrary to God's holiness and standards, as delineated in Romans 2:5-6.

Paul's letters reverberate with urgent anticipation and profound moral reflection regarding Christ's return, serving as a clear call for believers to uphold righteousness and holiness persistently. This urgent expectation resonates well with the messages of vigilance and preparation articulated in Matthew 24:42-44 and echoed intensely in Luke

INTRODUCTION TO 1ST THESSALONIANS

21:34-36, where believers are cautioned against the hearts being weighed down by excessiveness and the anxieties of life. They are encouraged to pray for the strength to escape the impending calamities and stand before the Son of Man.

These scriptural passages collectively underscore the imperative for believers to remain watchful, continually aligning their lives with the teachings of Christ. They interweave warnings and anticipations, creating a divine tapestry of revelation that communicates the imminent reality of Christ's return. This event symbolises the culmination of God's redemptive plan and the pinnacle of divine justice and mercy, fostering a milieu of continual self-examination and perpetual moral and spiritual realignment.

The synthesis of these scriptures promotes a devout lifestyle marked by holiness, love, and earnest expectation of the Parousia—the glorious appearance of our Saviour, Jesus Christ. It compels believers to vigilant reflection on holiness and steadfast adherence to Christ's teachings and path, maintaining a stance of readiness and alignment with divine principles in anticipation of fulfilling the ultimate divine promise.

With the advent of verse 8 in 1 Thessalonians 4, the severity of the divine warning is accentuated as it explicitly underscores that the warning stems directly from God Himself. This unequivocal declaration acts as a clarion call, reiterating the grievous consequences of disregarding God's commands, a theme recurrent in both the Old and New Testaments. The Old Testament is replete with instances where Israel, in its obstinacy, ignored divine warnings and subsequently encountered severe repercussions, as vividly depicted in the calamities and exiles illustrated in the Books of Jeremiah and Ezekiel.

The narrative of Israel's continual cycle of disobedience, punishment, repentance, and restoration reverberates through the annals of biblical history, serving as sober reminders of the implications of straying from God's path. The New Testament also echoes these sentiments, emphasising the gravity of neglecting such divine admonitions. Hebrews 2:1-3 expounds on this by emphasising the peril in neglecting such a great salvation offered by Christ, highlighting that every transgression and disobedience received a just recompense of reward under the Mosaic law. The deliberate amplification of God being the originator of this warning in verse 8 is not only a reminder of His holiness and justice but also serves as a stark reminder of the inevitable ramifications of disregarding His divine will and commands, thus urging believers to heed the warnings and align their lives according to God's holy standards, to avert the peril of divine judgment.

In the reflections on 1 Thessalonians 4:1-12, it is paramount to draw a stark contrast between the authentic Christian life advocated by Paul and the behaviours exhibited by those who peddle the gospel for greedy gain mentioned in 2:5-6. Paul's exhortations are underlined by an urge to foster self-sufficiency and a quiet, diligent life, eschewing unwarranted dependence and focusing on maintaining a lifestyle that is a testament to Christian values, thus earning the respect of non-believers. This is diametrically opposed to the exhibitionism and self-glorification that often characterise the pursuits of those who distort the gospel for personal gain as they boast about their achievements and wealth. Paul's counsel in 4:11 to aspire to lead a quiet life and mind one's own business is a call to humility and modesty that counteracts the ostentation and self-promotion prevalent among many. It is a call to live in a manner that avoids drawing attention to oneself but instead reflects the glory of God through a life of integrity, diligence, and genuine faith. This holistic and humble approach to Christian living, emphasising both spiritual and practical dimensions, is integral in maintaining a

INTRODUCTION TO 1ST THESSALONIANS

robust and authentic witness in the world, setting a distinct example that magnifies Christ and serves as a beacon of His transformative love and power.

The distortions and divergent gospels deviate from the essence of Christ's teachings. In conclusion, Paul's fervent urgings and solemn warnings within these verses illuminate a path of unwavering holiness, steadfast love, and continual spiritual growth, all deeply entrenched in the eschatological anticipation of Christ's imminent return. Paul's insistent plea serves not merely as a moral guideline but as a resounding call for a profound transformation of heart and conduct, leading to lives that are pleasing to God and are reflective of His holiness and love.

The urgency intertwined in Paul's letters to the Thessalonians underscores a holistic approach to Christian living. It intertwines purity, mutual love, diligent work, and hope-filled anticipation of Christ's return, embodying the multifaceted dimensions of a life pleasing to God. Paul's emphasis on progressive sanctification and his call to "more and more" mirror the unending journey towards spiritual maturity and Christlikeness, against which complacency and stagnation are persistently warned.

Paul's eschatological urging and his emphasis on righteous and productive living are aligned against a backdrop of divine justice and impending reckoning, depicting the avenging nature of the Lord and underscoring the gravitas of living in contravention of God's standards. The severe warnings against spiritual negligence, portrayed both in the Old and New Testaments, resonate as perpetual reminders to believers to align with divine precepts, avoiding the repercussions of straying from God's ordained path.

In sum, Paul's passionate letters to the Thessalonians, layered with fervent pleas, moral exhortations, eschatological reminders, and divine warnings, resonate as a timeless echo in the corridors of Christian theology. They call believers of all generations to a life marked by unswerving holiness, boundless love, continual growth, and unwavering hope in ardent preparation for the glorious advent of our Lord, Jesus Christ.

THE COMING OF THE LORD

'The Sound of the Trumpet'
(1 Thess. 4:13-18)

In the initial verses of 1 Thessalonians 4, Paul depicts "The Lord as an Avenger," emphasising Christ's imminent return through the Rapture. Those superficially participating in the faith, merely playing "church," will face the stark reality of His judgment, being left behind to endure the seven-year tribulation. Yet, even in this grave act, the grace of God remains evident. This tribulation acts as a judgment and a final signal for souls to genuinely embrace Christ during these unparalleled times of adversity. Chapter 4 stands as a dual reminder: it serves as an urgent call for the church to remain steadfast and alert while simultaneously offering hope to bolster the spirit of the faithful. The latter part of chapter 4 and into chapter 5 reiterates this comforting assurance: Jesus is on the brink of returning, even sooner than we anticipate.

Building on our exploration of 1 Thessalonians 4, verse 13 addresses a pressing concern within the early church regarding those who had "fallen asleep," or in other words, those believers who had passed away. Given the anticipation of Christ's imminent return, many were distressed about the fate of their deceased loved ones. Would they miss out on this glorious event? In his epistle to the Thessalonians, the apostle Paul seeks to provide comfort and clarity on this matter. He assures them that those who have died in Christ will not be disadvantaged.

On the contrary, they will be the first to rise at the sound of the trumpet, preceding even those who are alive at the time of Jesus's return (1 Thess. 4:16b). This revelation served to allay fears and offer hope and a renewed sense of purpose. The message was clear: Death could not sever the bond between the believer and the promise of Christ's return. The teaching provided consolation to those mourning the loss of fellow believers, emphasising the eternal continuity of faith and the unshakable hope in the face of death.

Another misconception regarding the term "fallen asleep" is that some misinterpreted it to suggest "soul sleep," a concept where the soul remains dormant after death until the resurrection. However, Paul's teachings offer a clear counterpoint to this notion. In his other letters, Paul asserts that for a Christian, to be "absent from the body" is to be "present with the Lord" (2 Cor. 5:8; cf. Phil. 1:23; 1 Thess. 5:10). Thus, the "sleep" Paul refers to in 1 Thessalonians 4:13 is not of the soul, but instead of the body, resting until its eventual resurrection and glorious transformation, at which point it reunites with the soul (1 Cor. 15:35–57; 2 Cor. 5:1–9).

It is important to note that the "soul sleep" doctrine is not a biblical teaching but originates from various religious traditions and sects. Some proponents of this doctrine base their belief on literal interpretations of scriptural references to death as sleep. The doctrine gained prominence during the Reformation, introduced by certain Anabaptist groups, and was later adopted by denominations like the Seventh-day Adventists and the Jehovah's Witnesses.

Elaborating further, Paul provides comfort and clarity to the early church in the face of grief and loss. Unlike those outside the faith, who grapple with hopelessness when confronted with death, Christians possess a distinct hope, characterised not by wishful thinking but

INTRODUCTION TO 1ST THESSALONIANS

by confident expectation. This hope rests firmly on the promises of Christ's resurrection and the assurance of eternal life. Paul's intention was clear: he desired the Thessalonians to neither remain ignorant nor grieve as those devoid of hope, specifically referring to unbelievers. While Christians are not immune to the pain of loss, their grief is fundamentally different. Even Jesus, in His humanity, grieved at the death of His friend Lazarus, as captured in the shortest verse of the Bible, "Jesus wept" (Jn. 11:35). However, the assurance of future bodily resurrection lessens the mourning of believers. Their sorrow is eased by the promise that their departed loved ones will rise again, standing shoulder to shoulder with them, before and alongside Christ (1 Thess. 4:16).

In the midst of the anguish that accompanies the loss of a loved one, the distinct difference between those engulfed in prolonged grief and those who find solace relatively quickly is the gospel. Paul emphasises the significance and power of the gospel repeatedly in his letters to the Thessalonians. In 1 Thessalonians, he refers to the gospel six times (1:5, 2:2, 4, 8, 9, 3:2) and twice more in 2 Thessalonians (1:8, 2:4). Through these references, he differentiates the authentic gospel of Jesus Christ from counterfeit versions that pander to worldly desires, devoid of the transformative power that often accompanies suffering for one's faith. In 2 Thessalonians 2, Paul warns of God sending a strong delusion so that those not genuinely seeking truth might be ensnared by falsehood. While this delusion ultimately alludes to the antichrist, Paul suggests that many deceptive teachings already exist, with various pulpits worldwide being sources of these false doctrines. Such teachings mislead countless souls, priming them for the deceptive allure of the future antichrist.

In 1 Thessalonians 4:14, Paul highlights the foundational belief that if we believe that Jesus died and rose again, even so, God will bring with Him those who sleep in Jesus. Believing, however, extends far beyond mere intellectual assent or acknowledgment. In this context, the original Greek word for "believe" is "pisteuō," which implies passive faith, active trust, dependence, and a commitment to what is believed. When the text reads, "For if we believe that Jesus died and rose again," it calls believers to accept this truth cerebrally and let it influence their behaviour and life choices. This actionable aspect of faith is echoed in verses like James 2:17, which says, "Even so faith, if it has no works, is dead, being by itself." In essence, true belief necessitates obedience. It is not merely about acknowledging the truth but about letting that truth manifest in our actions, choices, and lifestyles. As John 14:15 underscores, "If you love Me, you will keep My commandments." The intertwining of faith and action in the scriptures shows that believing, in its deepest sense, is a transformative and responsive journey where the heart and hands work in tandem.

Intertwining the actionable faith, as described in the previous scriptures, with the notion of believers "falling asleep" and the hope of the resurrection, Paul continually emphasises this theme across his letters. This idea of believers who have "fallen asleep" echoes the same theme we find in 1 Corinthians 15:6, where Paul recounts how, after Jesus' resurrection, He appeared to over five hundred brethren, many of whom were still alive at the time of Paul's writing. However, some had "fallen asleep." Delving into 1 Corinthians 15:1-10, we find a succinct yet profound encapsulation of the gospel: Christ died for our sins according to the scriptures, was buried, rose again on the third day in accordance with the scriptures, and made post-resurrection appearances to various individuals, including Peter, the apostles, and even to Paul himself. These foundational events—Christ's death, resurrection, and ascension—are the bedrock of Christian hope. For our hope finds its

INTRODUCTION TO 1ST THESSALONIANS

roots in His victory over death (Rom. 6:9). As declared in Acts 1:11, just as Jesus ascended to heaven, He will return in like manner. Thus, the gospel is not merely a historical account but a living testament of hope for all believers, anchored in the reality that Christ conquered death and is set to return (1 Thess. 4:15-17).

The revelations Paul shares in 1 Thessalonians 4:15 — "For this, we say to you by the word of the Lord, that we who are alive and remain until the coming of the Lord will by no means precede those who are asleep" — emerge from a blend of sources and divine experiences. First, Paul was a Pharisee, thoroughly trained in Jewish law. The writings of the Old Testament (cf. Phil 3:5). Many Old Testament passages, such as the writings of the prophets, speak of the day of the Lord and the resurrection (Job 19:25-27; Isa. 26:19; Hos. 4:13; Dan. 12:2). Paul would have been intimately familiar with these texts. Additionally, ancient Jewish writings, like the apocalyptic literature found among the Dead Sea Scrolls, discuss themes of end times, resurrection, and the Messiah, further shaping the broader Jewish understanding. Moreover, after his dramatic conversion on the road to Damascus (Acts 9:1-19), Paul spent a significant period in Arabia (Gal. 1:17-18). While the Bible does not provide exhaustive details about this time, it is traditionally understood that he received direct revelations from the Holy Spirit, further deepening and transforming his understanding of Christ's teachings and the mysteries of God. Furthermore, Paul was "caught up to heaven" (2 Cor. 12:2-4). The firsthand glimpse into the heavenly realms could have provided insight into the mysteries of life, death, and resurrection. This combination of rigorous scriptural training, Jewish cultural and theological understanding, and direct divine revelation culminated in the profound insights Paul shared with the early Christian communities, including the Thessalonians.

Paul's epistles, particularly to the church of Thessaloniki, radiate a deep sense of expectancy concerning the return of Christ. He was steadfast in his belief that the rapture was forthcoming and could manifest at any moment. This is evident in verses such as 1 Thessalonians 1:10, where he highlights Jesus' role in delivering us from impending wrath (cf. 1 Thess. 5:9), signalling an acute hope among the faithful. In 1 Corinthians 7:29, Paul accentuates the brevity of time, declaring, "The time is short." This urgency is echoed in Philippians 4:5 with the reminder that "The Lord is near." For Paul, the imminence of Christ's return was more than just a theological principle; it was a source of solace. As he points out in 1 Thessalonians 4:18, believers should draw comfort from this imminent hope. Yet, this expectancy was not passive; it carried an exhortation. Paul consistently urged believers to live holy lives, ensuring that they would be found blameless on that anticipated day of Christ's return (1 Thess. 2:13). Through this, Paul intertwined the hope of Christ's imminent return with the call to righteousness, emphasising the significance of both readiness and sanctity.

In 1 Thessalonians 4:16-17, Paul delves deeper into the events of Christ's anticipated return, painting a powerful scene that stands for expectant believers. He describes "the Lord Himself" descending "from heaven with a shout, with the voice of the archangel, and with the trumpet of God." This triumphant imagery is reflective of divine authority and power. The dead in Christ, those who have already passed away with faith in Jesus, will rise first. This resurrection, a cornerstone of Christian belief, is also touched upon in 1 Corinthians 15:51-52, where Paul speaks of a mystery: "We shall not all sleep, but we shall all be changed—in a moment, in the twinkling of an eye, at the last trumpet." After the resurrection of the dead, those who are still alive will be caught up or raptured, together with them in the clouds, meeting the Lord in the air. The underlying message here is profound: regardless of whether a believer is deceased or living at the moment of Christ's return, all will be united with Him. This reunion will be eternal, as Paul concludes, "so we will always be with the Lord." Such a grand revelation further stresses the urgency and significance of Paul's earlier call to readiness and holiness.

In 1 Thessalonians 4:16-17, the blast of the trumpet resonates as a symbol deeply entrenched in Jewish customs, echoing throughout New Testament scriptures. Traditionally, the trumpet has been associated with significant spiritual occurrences, marking divine interventions or pivotal transitions. A significant parallel can be found in the Jewish Feast of Trumpets, presently recognised as Rosh Hashanah. This sacred day within the Jewish liturgical calendar is punctuated by the resonant tones of the shofar, a ram's horn, serving as a clarion call to introspection and repentance, heralding the advent of the Jewish New Year. This sound is emblematic of both culmination and commencement. Venturing into the New Testament, trumpet blasts often precede eschatological phenomena, delineating events associated with the end times and the awaited return of Christ. Revelation 4:1 offers a further layer to this imagery when John discerns "a voice like a trumpet," beckoning him with the words, "Come up here," indicating the rapture's commencement and the ensuing divine reckoning. This trumpet sound acts as a dual signal – a summoning for the faithful and a stark admonition for those remaining. Paul's allusion to the trumpet in relation to Christ's second advent forges a link between cherished Jewish traditions and emergent Christian eschatological expectations. Hence, the trumpet becomes a unifying motif, seamlessly bridging Old Testament rituals with New Testament prophetic insights, all converging on the pivotal moment of Christ's triumphant return.

When Jesus returns for His church, the magnitude of this event will resound across the globe, leaving an indelible mark on humanity. Such a monumental occurrence will be impossible to overlook, as Christ's return for His saints will reverberate from heaven with undeniable force. Every corner of the earth will be privy to this awe-inspiring event. The ground itself will testify to this event as graves burst open. This seismic activity has a precedent in scripture, evoking memories of key events:

1. At the crucifixion of Christ, Matthew recorded a significant earthquake: "And behold, the veil of the temple was torn in two from top to bottom, and the earth shook, and the rocks were split" (Matt. 27:51).
2. Following this, when Christ had given up His spirit, there was another awe-striking occurrence: "The tombs broke open, and the bodies of many holy people who had died were raised to life" (Matt. 27:52-53).

The Bible's portrayal of these past earthquakes as signs accompanying divine actions suggest that similarly when the rapture occurs, the world might experience seismic tremors signalling the monumental spiritual shift. Just as the earth quaked at the crucifixion and resurrection, we might expect creation to once again bear witness, in its own way, to the return of Christ and the rapture of His saints. Nevertheless, believers are urged to always be watchful, not necessarily for physical signs, but for fulfilling God's promises. As 1 Thessalonians 4:16-17 says, "For the Lord Himself will descend from heaven with a shout, with the voice of the archangel and with the trumpet of God, and the dead in Christ will rise first. Then we who are alive and remain will be

INTRODUCTION TO 1ST THESSALONIANS

caught up with them in the clouds to meet the Lord in the air, so we shall always be with the Lord."

Furthermore, every child under the age of accountability will vanish in the blink of an eye as the world reels from the aftermath of this unparalleled occurrence; confusion and chaos will ensue. However, in the midst of this global turmoil, there will be those who will craft deceptive narratives to obfuscate the truth, including tales of alien invasions. The universal shock and desperation for understanding will prompt world leaders to offer explanations, paving the way for a singular global leader, the antichrist, to rise. Proposing solutions for "peace and security," he endeavours to assuage the distress of the masses, fulfilling prophecy and setting the stage for the unfolding of future events.

Luke 21:5-36 provides a prophetic discourse wherein Jesus details the signs that will precede His second coming and the end of the age. These signs encompass diverse phenomena such as wars, natural disasters, celestial disturbances, and global persecution of the faithful. Yet, the culmination of these harbingers will be the removal of the church, as depicted in verses 35-36. This sudden extraction of God's people is a seminal event, serving as the clearest signpost that the tribulation period is imminent and then triggered by the signing of the Middle East peace treaty (Isa. 28:15, 18; Dan. 9:24-27). Just as a building's foundation quakes under immense pressure, the world will similarly reel from the weight of this unprecedented event. Amidst the dread and uncertainty leading into the tribulation, only those vigilant with faith, those who "watch themselves" (Lu. 21: 34) and "stay awake" (Lu. 21:36), will truly discern the times and evade the snares set by the world.

While the earth plunges into turmoil and the population of the world 'left behind' grapples with disarray, a stark contrast emerges in the experiences of those who were ready and waiting for Jesus. These believers, alongside the faithful who had previously passed away in Christ, will be united with their Saviour in the air. This transcendent reunion marks a pivotal transition in the believer's journey: from that moment forth, they will dwell in everlasting communion with Jesus, never to be separated from His tangible presence again. Paul's concluding exhortation in chapter 4 emphasises the profound weight of this eternal promise. Recognising the challenges and tribulations that the Thessalonians and all believers currently face, Paul implores his reader to draw strength from this hope. His words, "therefore, encourage one another," serve as a timeless reminder for all followers of Christ to uplift and fortify each other with the hope of His imminent return and the eternal union that awaits.

In essence, 1 Thessalonians 4 delves deeply into the concept of Christian hope, illuminating the magnificent future that awaits believers at Christ's second advent. Responding to the early church's apprehensions, Paul elucidates the destiny of those who have passed on, dispelling fears of them being overlooked at the resurrection and emphasising the certainty of their ascent. Rooted in Old Testament teachings and prophetic revelations, Paul seamlessly bridges ancient scriptures with imminent prophecies, reinforcing the continuum of God's eternal plan. In a world riddled with doubt and turmoil, 1 Thessalonians 4 emerges as a beacon of hope, guidance, and comfort. It champions a steadfast hope anchored in Christ's resurrection, the anticipated gathering of the saints, and the ensuing everlasting communion with the Redeemer. Through time, Paul's message reverberates, calling believers to uphold sanctity, vigilance, and resilience, bolstering each other with the promise of Christ's glorious reappearance. For genuine followers of Christ, the pinnacle of blessings is still on the horizon, whereas those merely masquerading in faith will soon confront their reckoning.

THE EVOLVING LANDSCAPE OF RAPTURE THEORIES

The concept of the rapture, a moment when believers are suddenly and miraculously "caught up" to meet Christ, has been a focal point of Christian eschatology for centuries. The very essence of this belief carries with it hope and anticipation of reuniting with the Saviour. However, while the overarching theme remains consistent, there are divergent views regarding the timing of the rapture relative to the prophesied tribulation period. These variations in understanding have led to the formulation of four primary theories: pre-tribulation, mid-tribulation, post-tribulation, and the perspective that no rapture will occur. Each viewpoint holds its unique interpretation of scripture, historical context, and set of proponents and detractors. The following briefly summarises the four positions, followed by a detailed account.

1. Pre-Tribulation Rapture

The pre-tribulation rapture theory posits that believers will be taken to heaven before the onset of the seven-year tribulation period. Rooted in scriptures like 1 Thessalonians 4:16-17 and Revelation 3:10, this viewpoint suggests that God's intention is to spare His church from the forthcoming global turmoil. Historically, figures like John Nelson Darby in the 19th century have been attributed with popularising this perspective, especially within dispensationalist circles. Advocates argue that it aligns with God's nature of mercy and grace. At the same time, critics feel it might foster a sense of complacency among believers, presuming an escape from end-time tribulations.

2. Mid-Tribulation Rapture

According to the mid-tribulation stance, the rapture will occur halfway through the seven-year tribulation period, saving believers from the latter half's intense wrath, the Great Tribulation (Matt. 24:21). This theory is supported by passages like Revelation 11:1-2, which describes a temple being trodden for 42 months, equivalent to 3.5 years, half the tribulation. The phrase "Come up here" (Rev. 11:12) is cited as evidence of the midpoint rapture. Proponents of this theory believe that it reconciles different biblical timelines. In contrast, opponents argue that the mid-tribulation view does not clearly differentiate between the church and Israel.

3. Post-Tribulation Rapture

According to the post-tribulation theory, believers will endure the entirety of the tribulation and will be raptured at its conclusion, just before Christ's millennial reign. Verses such as Matthew 24:29-31 are often cited in support. Early church fathers introduced this theory, who taught that the church's triumphant entry into heaven must come after intense trial and purification. Proponents argue it aligns with the broader theme of Christian perseverance. In contrast, some critics argue that the full force of the tribulation goes against its purpose, which is to bring about salvation. Furthermore, the post-tribulation view does not clearly differentiate between the church and Israel.

4. No-Rapture Theory

Lastly, there's a perspective that suggests no rapture will occur at all. Proponents of this view often interpret rapture scriptures allegorically or symbolically, viewing them as representations of spiritual truths rather than literal future events. This stance is more common among amillennialists, who see many end-time prophecies as fulfilled or non-literal. The strength of this perspective lies in its simplicity and avoidance of the complexities of rapture timing. However, critics argue that it disregards or overly spiritualises clear scriptural promises.

Subsequent sections of this book will delve deeply into the diverse perspectives of pre-, mid-, post-, and no-rapture. After examining each view, we will conclude by determining which stands out as the most compelling.

PRE-TRIBULATION RAPTURE THEORY

The pre-tribulation rapture doctrine has intrigued and inspired believers for centuries, presenting a hope-filled scenario where the faithful are divinely spared from a period of global cataclysm. This eschatological viewpoint is rooted in numerous New Testament scriptures and suggests that the church will be "caught up" with Christ in the clouds before the earth faces its darkest hour. Scriptures ranging from Luke to Revelation articulate elements of this belief, with the Letters to the Thessalonians and the Book of Corinthians providing particularly vivid insights. Furthermore, historical records reveal that this concept is not just a modern novelty but has its foundations deep within early Christian writings, teachings, and anticipations. A journey through these biblical and historical landscapes not only elucidates the contours of the pre-tribulation rapture theory but also offers comfort to believers in Christ's protective providence and His imminent return.

Bible verses supporting the pre-tribulation rapture:

- Zephaniah 2:1-3 (others include Isaiah 26:20-21; I disagree)
- Luke 21:34-36
- John 14:2-3
- Romans 5:9
- 1 Corinthians 15:51-52
- 1 Thessalonians 1:10, 4:16-17, 5:9
- 2 Thessalonians 2:1, 2-8
- Titus 2:11-13
- Hebrews 9:28

THE EVOLVING LANDSCAPE OF RAPTURE THEORIES

- James 5:7-8
- 2 Peter 3:1-13
- 1 John 2:28
- Jude 20-23
- Revelation 3:10, 4:1 (cf. 11:12)

As seen with the list provided above, the pre-tribulation rapture doctrine finds support in various Bible verses, including Zephaniah 2:1-3, which calls for seeking righteousness and shelter before the day of the Lord's anger. Luke 21:34-36 reminds believers to stay watchful and pray for strength to escape all that is coming. John 14:2-3 assures us of Christ's promise to prepare a place for His followers and return to receive them. Romans 5:9 speaks of deliverance from God's wrath through Christ. In 1 Corinthians 15:51-52, the mystery of the transformation of believers at the last trumpet is unveiled. 1 Thessalonians 1:10, 4:16-17, and 5:9 emphasise the hope of being saved from the coming wrath. 2 Thessalonians 2:1, 2-8 discusses the removal of the restrainer (the Holy Spirit-empowered church) before the revelation of the lawless one. Titus 2:11-13 encourages godly living while awaiting the blessed hope. Hebrews 9:28 anticipates Christ's return to bring salvation to His people. James 5:7-8 urges patience for the Lord's coming. 2 Peter 3 underscores scoffers mocking Christ's return. 1 John 2:28 exhorts abiding in Christ for confidence at His coming. Jude 20-23 also deals with scoffers. Revelation 3:10 promises being kept from the hour of trial, while Revelation 4:1 marks the church's absence on earth, not reappearing until chapter 19, aligning with the pre-tribulation rapture perspective.

Further exploring the concept of a pre-tribulation rapture, the often-overlooked Letter to the Hebrews offers a theological perspective that aligns with other foundational New Testament writings. When placed beside letters like 1st and 2nd Thessalonians and 1 Corinthians, Hebrews uses terms such as "end of the ages" and "last days" as critical markers within God's grand scheme of redemption. At the epicentre of this divine plan is the incarnation of Jesus Christ, His sustaining work through the church, and His much-anticipated return.

Therefore, Hebrews 9:28 becomes central in this discussion: "So Christ was offered once to bear the sins of many. To those who eagerly wait for Him, He will appear a second time, apart from sin, for salvation." The emphasis here on "salvation" rather than judgment crystallises the underpinning rationale for the pre-tribulation rapture thesis. It posits that Christ, in His mercy, will usher His church away before the onset of the tribulation, a period marked by an unparalleled divine retribution.

Paul's letters provide deeper nuances to this perspective. Notably, 1 Thessalonians 1:10 encourages believers to "wait for His Son from heaven, whom He raised from the dead, Jesus who delivers us from the wrath to come." Moreover, 2 Thessalonians 2:3-11 sketches the sequence of eschatological events, reassuring believers. Crucially, this passage suggests the antichrist's unveiling is postponed until a hindering entity, widely believed to be the church, is removed. Such a notion is consistent with prophecies that indicate the antichrist's inauguration of the tribulation via a peace treaty in the Middle East (Isa. 28:15, 18; Dan. 9:24-27).

Further supporting the pre-tribulation rapture theory, Thomas D. Ice from Liberty University examines the interpretation of 2 Thessalonians 2:3 in the context of pretribulationism. Ice discusses the Greek noun "apostasia," traditionally translated as "apostasy," suggesting it might be more accurately rendered as "departure." This interpretation refers to the rapture occurring before the Day of the Lord, supporting the pretribulationist view.

To support this, Ice details how the first seven English translations of the Bible rendered "apostasy" as "departure" or "departing," and only later translations, starting with the King James Version, began using "falling away." He argues that this shift lacks a solid rationale. The article also highlights the use of a definite article with "apostasia" in the Greek text, indicating a specific, known event rather than a general concept. This specificity, Ice argues, aligns better with the idea of a physical departure, like the rapture, rather than a general falling away from faith.

Ice concludes that interpreting "apostasia" as "departure" provides a more coherent understanding of the biblical passage, fitting within the broader context of Paul's teachings and offering a more comforting message to believers concerned about the end times. According to Ice, this interpretation aligns with the sequence of events in pretribulationism, where the rapture precedes the Day of the Lord and the emergence of the antichrist.

Additional insights emerge from 1 Corinthians 15:51-52 and 1 Thessalonians 4:16-17, which portray the rapture and metamorphosis of the faithful. The juxtaposition of 1 Thessalonians 4:13-18, emphasising solace and anticipation in the rapture, against 1 Thessalonians 5:1-11, which underscores the unpredictable arrival of the Day of the Lord, amplifies the pre-tribulation rapture thesis.

Scriptures like Romans 5:9 and 1 Thessalonians 5:9 bolster this perspective by stating unequivocally that believers are predestined not for God's wrath but for salvation, fortifying the argument for the church's pre-tribulation departure.

The Book of Revelation adds additional weight to this argument. The conspicuous absence of the church from the narrative after Chapter

3 is telling. The divine summons in Revelation 4:1, "Come up here," is echoed later in Revelation 11:12 for the two witnesses, symbolising the church's anticipated pre-tribulation rapture.

In Luke 21:34-36, Jesus' counsel for alertness and prayer to be deemed "worthy to escape all these things that will come to pass" strengthens the conviction that the church will receive divine exemption from the looming tribulation era.

A holistic study of Hebrews, 1 and 2 Thessalonians, 1 Corinthians, Romans, Revelation, and Luke crafts a compelling biblical narrative advocating for a pre-tribulation rapture. The recurrent theme is the church's promised deliverance and salvation, underscoring the hope that the devout will escape the imminent era of divine judgment. This narrative offers solace to expectant believers while signifying profound challenges for those left behind.

From the Greek, Revelation 3:10 is a pivotal verse in discussions surrounding the pre-tribulation rapture theory and the timing of the tribulation events. In this verse, Jesus addresses the church of Philadelphia, commending them for their steadfastness in "keeping" or "guarding" His word with patient endurance. The Greek word used for "keep" here is "τηρέω" (tereo), signifying not only preservation but also protection. This choice of words is essential in the debate over the pre-tribulation view. It suggests that the church of Philadelphia (also symbolic of the end times faithful church) will be shielded "from" the impending "hour of trial" set to engulf the entire world, a trial designed to test those dwelling on the earth.

A compelling comparison can be drawn by examining the message to the church in Smyrna, as conveyed in Revelation 2:10. In this letter, Jesus forewarns them of impending suffering, including imprisonment and a specified period of tribulation. While the Greek word "θλίψις" (thlipsis), signifying distress or tribulation, is used here, it is noteworthy that the word "ἐκ" (ek), meaning "out of" or "from," is not explicitly used in the context of Smyrna, as it is the church of Philadelphia (Rev. 3:10). Unlike the church in Philadelphia, the church in Smyrna is not promised an exemption from this tribulation but is instead encouraged to endure it. The church era can be divided into distinct timelines, with Smyrna as the initial faithful church and Philadelphia as the final one.

In the context of these passages, proponents of the pre-tribulation rapture theory argue that the choice of the Greek word "τηρέω" (tereo) in Revelation 3:10, along with the implication of being "kept from" the hour of trial, implies distinct preservation and protection for the latter church of Philadelphia, suggesting that they will be kept "out of" the hour of trial, aligning with the idea of a pre-tribulation rapture. This interpretation hinges on the specific terminology used in these verses to paint a picture of different destinies for various churches within the overarching eschatological framework.

Tracing the Historical Development of the Pre-Tribulation Rapture Doctrine:

The idea of the pre-tribulation rapture, which suggests that believers will be taken up to heaven before a period of tribulation, has been a part of Christian thought for centuries. In the 1st century, subtle hints of this doctrine can be found in Clement of Rome's First Epistle to the Corinthians (23, 24, 34, 35), Polycarp's The Epistle to the Philippians (2, 5, 6), and The Didache (1st or 2nd century, 16.3-8, n.14, n.16, n.17), alluding to the gathering of the faithful before or after tribulation. Further insight on the topic is provided by the 2nd-century writings of Irenaeus' Against Heresies (5.5.1; 29.1; 30.4; 31.2; 32.1) and Tertullian's "A Treatise on the Soul" (50), which discuss the church's potential catching up, either before or after the tribulation. Victorinus'

Commentary on the Apocalypse (15.1) in the 3rd century supports the idea of a pre-tribulation rapture, while Methodius of Olympus expands on this rapture topic. In the 4th century, the thoughts of Ephraim the Syrian and a sermon attributed to him, the "Sermon on the End of the World," anticipates a pre-tribulation gathering of saints. However, from the 5th to the 17th centuries, eschatological silence dominated, later overcome by figures like Increase Mather. It was not until the 18th and 19th centuries that John Nelson Darby played an influential role in popularising the pre-tribulation rapture, which was bolstered by C.I. Scofield's annotations in the Scofield Reference Bible.

The following chart breaks down the individuals and writings mentioned in the preceding introduction that appear to support the concept of the rapture.

Who	When	What	Rapture
Clement of Rome's First Epistle to the Corinthians (23, 24, 34, 35) Polycarp's The Epistle to the Philippians (2, 5, 6) The Didache (1st or 2nd century, 16.3-8, n.14, n.16, n.17)	1st Century	Clement of Rome's First Epistle to the Corinthians (23, 24, 34, 35), Polycarp's The Epistle to the Philippians (2, 5, 6), and The Didache (1st or 2nd century, 16.3-8, n.14, n.16, n.17) contain references and allusions that suggest early Christian anticipation of the gathering of believers, which could be before the tribulation, or at the conclusion.	Pre-, or Post-Tribulation

THE EVOLVING LANDSCAPE OF RAPTURE THEORIES

Who	When	What	Rapture
Irenaeus' Against Heresies (5.5.1; 29.1; 30.4; 31.2; 32.1)	2nd Century	Irenaeus' Against Heresies (5.5.1; 29.1; 30.4; 31.2; 32.1) contains various passages where he discusses future events related to the church being caught up, with some suggestion it maybe before a period of tribulation, or afterwards.	Pre-, or Post-Tribulation
Tertullian's A Treatise on the Soul (50)		Tertullian's A Treatise on the Soul (50) offers insights into a bodily resurrection and translation of the saints, either before the reign of the antichrist, or afterwards.	
Victorinus' Commentary on the Apocalypse (6.14; 15.1)	3rd Century	Victorinus' Commentary on the Apocalypse (6.14; 15.1) contains passages that are often interpreted as supporting the idea of a pre-tribulation rapture, with references to believers being spared from tribulation.	Pre-Tribulation *"And I saw another great and wonderful sign, seven angels having the seven last plagues; for in them is completed the indignation of God. For the wrath of God always strikes the obstinate people with seven plagues, that is, perfectly, as it is said in Leviticus; and these shall be in the last time, <u>when the church shall have gone out of the midst.</u>"* (15:1)
Methodius of Olympus		Methodius of Olympus, in "Symposium, Discourse 7," Methodius discusses the resurrection and translation of the saints, either before or after the reign of the antichrist.	

Who	When	What	Rapture
Ephraim the Syrian	4th Century	Ephraim the Syrian, a prominent Christian theologian and hymnographer, wrote a text titled "On the Last Times." This work discusses eschatological themes and speaks about the gathering of the saints and the elect before the tribulation. While Ephraim did not develop a comprehensive doctrine of the rapture, he did express an expectation that there would be a gathering of the saints before the coming tribulation. His work reflects some of the early Christian thought about eschatology and the end times.	Pre-Tribulation
Pseudo-Ephraem	4/5th Century	An anonymous author, often attributed to Ephraim the Syrian, wrote a sermon titled "Sermon on the End of the World." In this sermon, the writer discusses a future gathering of the elect before the period of tribulation, asserting that believers would be spared from the trials to come. This text is one of the early Christian writings that have been used to support the idea of a pre-tribulation rapture, though like Ephraim the Syrian's work, it does not fully develop this into a comprehensive doctrine.	Pre-Tribulation

THE EVOLVING LANDSCAPE OF RAPTURE THEORIES

Who	When	What	Rapture
None known	Silent years	From the 5th to the 12th centuries, and with relatively few exceptions until the 18th century, the concept of the rapture, as it is understood in some modern Christian denominations, was largely absent from theological discourse. Several factors contribute to this. During the early medieval period, the church was preoccupied with establishing orthodoxy, combating heresy, and surviving politically rather than developing detailed eschatological theories. Even during the Scholastic era, theological inquiry focused more on questions of metaphysics, ethics, and the nature of God than on the end times. Furthermore, early, and medieval Christian eschatology often focused on collective events like the Last Judgment and the general resurrection rather than the individualised notion of believers being "caught up" before, or after the tribulation. As a distinct theological concept with varied views on its timing in relation to other end-time events, the rapture began to retake its modern form in the rise of dispensationalism and premillennialism in the 17th and 18th centuries.	

Who	When	What	Rapture
Increase Mather	17/18th Century	Increase Mather, a prominent Puritan minister, mentioned the concept of a gathering or translation of believers in his writings. While he did not provide an extensive doctrine of the rapture, he acknowledged the idea of believers being taken to be with Christ before the tribulation.	Pre-Tribulation
John Darby and C.I. Scofield	18/19th Century	John Nelson Darby, an Irish theologian and one of the founders of the Plymouth Brethren movement played a significant role in popularising the concept of the pre-tribulation rapture. His views were further popularised through the notes and commentary provided by C.I. Scofield in the Scofield Reference Bible.	Pre-Tribulation

The above-listed ancient Christian text known as the "Didache" or "Teaching of the Twelve Apostles" from the 1st and 2nd centuries contains profound teachings that revolve around key themes, weaving together important aspects of early Christian belief and practice. These themes guide believers in their spiritual journey and help them remain vigilant in their faith. The first theme is the anticipation of the rapture, which the text underscores as a central belief. It encourages steadfast faith, warning against doublemindedness, and emphasises that the return of Christ will occur suddenly, as prophesied in scripture. Another significant theme is the call for required holiness. The Didache instructs believers to lead lives of holiness, steering clear of sinful behaviours such as slander, covetousness, strife, deceit, and other unrighteous acts. It underscores the importance of adhering to God's commandments and living blamelessly before Him.

Furthermore, the text urges Believers to avoid worldliness. It encourages them to resist worldly temptations and to live in a manner that pleases God, cautioning against being swayed by the sinful behaviours and values of the secular world. In addition, the Didache warns against the peril of apostasy and apostates. It cautions against the rise of false prophets and corrupt individuals who will lead people astray, emphasising the need for believers to safeguard their spiritual well-being and be discerning in identifying false teachers and deceivers.

The Didache also contains practical guidance concerning Christian assembly on the Lord's Day, the responsibilities of different members within the Christian community (including deacons, young men, virgins, and presbyters), and underscores the importance of forgiveness and reconciliation among believers. Incorporated within the Didache are sections from Irenaeus' "Against Heresies," which introduce crucial theological concepts: Irenaeus emphasises the concept of recapitulation, asserting that Christ, being both the Word of God and the Son of Man, rectified humanity's disobedience through His perfect obedience, offering salvation to all. He staunchly upholds the significance of Apostolic Succession, contending that teachings passed down directly from the apostles are trustworthy sources of Christian doctrine, guarding against the idea of an unbroken, guaranteed salvation. Irenaeus highlights the indispensable role of the Holy Spirit within the church, guiding its interpretation of scriptures and reinforcing the importance of active faith throughout one's spiritual journey. He addresses themes such as the resurrection of the righteous and the judgment of the wicked, emphasising the influence of individual free will in determining these destinies and rejecting the notion of predestination.

These sections collectively underscore Irenaeus' theological stance on Christology, the authority of the church, the role of the Holy Spirit, eschatology, and the rejection of the Calvinist doctrine of "once saved, always saved," which posits that salvation is irrevocably secured upon initial belief, regardless of subsequent actions or choices.

The subsequent sections address and counter the criticisms levelled against the rapture theory, including claims that the term 'rapture' does not appear in the Bible and the accusation that proponents of pre-tribulation are advocating for 'escapism.' Additionally, support for the pre-tribulation rapture is presented through the examination of the Jewish Feasts and the Galilean Wedding tradition.

The word "Rapture" is not in the Bible:

As depicted in the reference chart provided, the doctrine of the rapture has a well-established presence in the annals of church history. Nevertheless, the absence of the term "rapture" within the Bible has led some to reject this concept. While the term "Rapture" is not found in the Bible, nor is the term "Trinity," but the concept of the triune nature of God is derived from various passages that speak of the Father, Son, and Holy Spirit. Early church theologians developed the term and doctrine of the Trinity to articulate the belief in God as three persons in one essence.

The term "rapture," stemming from the Latin "raptura," signifying "seizure" or "snatching away," encapsulates the belief that believers will be caught up or taken away from the earth to meet the Lord in the air (Gk. Harpazo). Though the specific word itself does not find direct usage in biblical texts, like the term "Trinity," the underlying concept

THE EVOLVING LANDSCAPE OF RAPTURE THEORIES

of a gathering or catching up of believers can be discovered in passages like 1 Thessalonians 4:17 and 1 Corinthians 15:51-52. These verses describe a future event when living believers will be "caught up" alongside resurrected believers to meet the Lord.

No one could discover the teaching of the rapture for themselves unless taught:

The Bible contains numerous prophetic and eschatological verses that have intrigued scholars throughout history. These verses discuss end-time events and their mysteries. However, it was only with the revelation received by the apostle Paul in 1 Corinthians 15:51-52 that the concept of rapture became clear. "Listen, I tell you a mystery: We will not all sleep, but we will all be changed—in a flash, in the twinkling of an eye, at the last trumpet. For the trumpet will sound, the dead will be raised imperishable. We will be changed." Paul's revelation served as a beacon, illuminating the transformative event for believers in the end times. This scriptural insight, encapsulated in the term "mystery," highlighted that until Paul's revelation, the full comprehension of the rapture remained concealed. With this foundation, theologians embarked on a dedicated journey of scriptural study, theological contemplation, and the interpretation of biblical prophecy, further shaping and refining the concept of the rapture.

Furthermore, the Holy Spirit guides and illuminates believers' understanding of scripture and empowers believers to discern and interpret biblical truths. Therefore, individuals could discern and understand the rapture concept through the guidance of the Holy Spirit, even without explicit teaching on the subject.

Escapism:

The argument that pre-tribulation believers seek to avoid trouble through the rapture concept overlooks significant historical and present-day realities. The disciples, except John, all faced martyrdom while eagerly awaiting the return of Jesus. Throughout history, countless millions of believers have suffered and given their lives for their faith. Even today, persecution of Christians is on the rise, with increasing hostility towards believers. Jesus Himself referred to the troubles preceding the tribulation as "birth pains," indicating that believers would experience difficulties and trials in this world. The Bible contains numerous verses that affirm the reality of suffering for believers (Jn. 16:33, Acts 14:22, Rom. 5:3-5, 1 Pet. 4:12-13, reinforcing the understanding that tribulation is not something to be escaped but rather a part of the Christian journey.

Jewish feasts:

The idea that the Jewish feasts outlined in Leviticus 23 and other parts of the Old Testament might have an eschatological or "end-times" significance in Christian theology is a topic of discussion and speculation among some theologians and believers. It's important to note that this is an interpretive framework and not universally accepted within Christian circles. However, within this framework, the feasts are often seen as a kind of prophetic calendar, with each feast symbolising a different aspect of God's redemptive plan.

Here's a breakdown of how this eschatological pattern is often interpreted:

1. Passover (Pesach): Seen as pointing to the sacrifice of Jesus, the "Lamb of God," for the redemption of humanity. Jesus' crucifixion coincided with Passover.
2. Feast of Unleavened Bread: Some interpret this as representing the burial of Jesus, where his body would not see corruption (i.e., the absence of leaven, which is a symbol for corruption or sin in some biblical contexts).
3. Firstfruits (Yom HaBikkurim): Seen as pointing to the resurrection of Jesus as the "firstfruits" from the dead, occurring during this feast.
4. Feast of Weeks or Pentecost (Shavuot): Understood to typify the outpouring of the Holy Spirit and the birth of the Church, which took place during the Jewish celebration of Shavuot according to the New Testament.

The Spring Feasts (Passover, Unleavened Bread, Firstfruits, and Weeks) often correspond to the first coming of Jesus and the establishment of the Church. The Fall Feasts are seen as future events in Christian eschatology:

1. Feast of Trumpets or New Year (Rosh Hashanah): This is often linked to the Rapture of the church in Christian eschatology. The blowing of trumpets (shofar) is associated with the trumpet calls mentioned in passages like 1 Thessalonians 4:16-17 and 1 Corinthians 15:51-52 that speak of the catching up of believers to meet Christ in the air. Revelation 4:1 also references a trumpet, signalling the removal of the church.
    1.1 There are strong arguments to consider this festival as a symbolic or even literal precursor to the rapture. Traditional

Jewish wedding customs add weight to this perspective, as a trumpet sound or shout often heralds the bridegroom's unexpected arrival. This aligns closely with the New Testament metaphor of Christ coming like a "thief in the night," suggesting the unpredictability of the rapture or His coming for His bride, the church. Just as the spring festivals in the Jewish calendar were prophetically fulfilled through key events in Jesus' life, the same might hold true for the fall festivals, including the Feast of Trumpets. While it is not definitively established that this feast is identical to the trumpet sound heralding the rapture, dismissing the connection outright ignores compelling biblical and traditional parallels. These correlations provide a strong basis for the argument that the Feast of Trumpets could serve as a symbolic or actual event leading up to the rapture, as described in Christian eschatology.

2. Day of Atonement (Yom Kippur): This day is frequently associated with the physical return of Jesus to Earth. The Day of Atonement involves fasting and repentance. This interpretive framework points to the time of Israel's national repentance when they "look upon him whom they have pierced" (Zechariah 12:10) and recognise Jesus as the Messiah.

3. Feast of Tabernacles or Booths (Sukkot): This feast is often seen as symbolising the millennial reign of Christ on Earth, a time of peace and prosperity, as described in various Old and New Testament prophecies.

4. The Eighth Day or Last Great Day (Shemini Atzeret) is sometimes interpreted to represent the eternal state when God will dwell with humanity forever, as described in Revelation 21-22.

Galilean Wedding:

The Galilean Wedding pattern is a theological framework of the rapture theory. According to this pattern, parallels between the various stages of a traditional Jewish wedding ceremony and the events associated with the rapture incorporate symbolic imagery such as a chariot.

Here is a simplified outline of the Galilean Wedding pattern, including the reference to the chariot and how it is sometimes connected to the rapture:

a) Betrothal: The first stage of a Jewish wedding is the betrothal, which involves a formal agreement between the bride and groom. In this stage, the bride is set apart for the groom, and a dowry is often given. Parallel to the rapture: Some see the betrothal stage as a parallel to the present age in which believers are spiritually betrothed to Christ. The dowry can be seen as representing the price paid by Jesus through His death and resurrection.

b) Groom's Departure: After the betrothal, the groom departs to prepare a place for his bride. This could involve building or adding to his father's house. Some depictions incorporate the imagery of a chariot carrying the groom. Parallel to the rapture: The groom's departure, often associated with Jesus ascending to heaven after His resurrection, can be seen as symbolised by a chariot carrying the groom. This connects to the belief that Jesus is preparing a place for His followers, as mentioned in John 14:2-3.

c) Bride's Preparation: While the groom is away, the bride prepares herself for the wedding day. This includes being ready and watching for the groom's return. Parallel to the rapture:

This stage is often linked to the idea that believers should be prepared, vigilant, and eagerly anticipating the return of Christ, as described in various New Testament passages.

d) Groom's Return and Gathering: At an unexpected hour, the groom returns with a shout and a trumpet blast. He gathers the bride and her attendants to take them to the wedding feast at the groom's father's house. Parallel to the rapture: This stage, symbolised by the groom returning with a shout and a trumpet blast, can be associated with the event of Christ's return, where believers are gathered to meet Him. The imagery of a chariot can be incorporated to represent the gathering and transportation of the bride and attendants.

e) Chariot: When the groom returns, the bride is placed in a chariot and carried away. The imagery of a chariot is connected to the teachings of the rapture as described in the Bible. 1 Thessalonians 4:16-17: "For the Lord himself will come down from heaven, with a loud command, with the voice of the archangel and with the trumpet call of God, and the dead in Christ will rise first. After that, we who are still alive and are left will be caught up together with them in the clouds to meet the Lord in the air. And so we will be with the Lord forever." 1 Corinthians 15:51-52: "Listen, I tell you a mystery: We will not all sleep, but we will all be changed— in a flash, in the twinkling of an eye, at the last trumpet. For the trumpet will sound, the dead will be raised imperishable, and we will be changed."

f) Marriage Ceremony: The bride and groom and their guests celebrate the marriage ceremony together. Parallel to the rapture: The wedding feast is often connected to the parable of ten virgins (Matthew 25:1-13 and Revelation 19:6-10).

THE EVOLVING LANDSCAPE OF RAPTURE THEORIES

Conclusion:

The doctrine of the rapture, signifying the sudden divine removal of believers before a looming tribulation, has long sparked multifaceted interpretations within Christian scholarship. While the specific term "rapture" is not directly inscribed in the Bible, its foundational essence resonates within passages such as 1 Thessalonians 4:15-17 and 1 Corinthians 15:51-52. As this concept matured, it found exponents ranging from these foundational theologians to modern-day scholars. Notably, critics who interpret the rapture as fostering escapism may overlook the Christian ethos centred on enduring trials, drawing from histories of martyrdom to prescriptive biblical teachings on resilience. Symbolic frameworks, such as the Jewish Feast of Trumpets or the Galilean Wedding pattern have also enriched the rapture's intricate tapestry. Nevertheless, while these interpretive lenses provide depth, they must be discerned alongside, and not in lieu of, the direct revelations of scripture.

MID-TRIBULATION RAPTURE THEORY

The concept of the rapture—where believers are caught up to meet Christ in the air—has been a subject of much debate and interpretation among Christians. One view that has gathered attention is the mid-tribulation rapture theory. This perspective posits that believers will be raptured at the midpoint of the seven-year tribulation period. While a relatively modern construct, this view is said to harmonise several biblical texts and offers a balanced approach to end-times scenarios.

The mid-tribulation rapture theory posits that the church will experience a rapture at the midpoint of the tribulation, sparing it from the most intense phase known as the Great Tribulation. This significant period of tribulation is set in motion by signing a peace treaty, an event expected to bear the endorsement of the antichrist. Identifying the antichrist is often expedited by monitoring the signing of the Middle East peace treaty. This treaty is likely to follow a conflict that threatens Israel's very existence, potentially leading to a global conflict akin to the fulfilment of biblical prophecies such as Psalms 83, Isaiah 17, or even Ezekiel 38-39 (cf. Dan. 11:40-45; Rev. 16:12-16).

Once the peace treaty is ratified, a sense of "peace and security" will pervade the world (1 Thess. 5:3). During this deceptive period of false peace, the antichrist will actively engage in rebuilding the tribulation temple, a crucial step in his plan to declare himself as God. This event will usher in a period of "sudden destruction" known as the Great Tribulation (Matt. 24:21), from which no one will be able to escape. The construction of the third temple, predicted to occur up to 3.5 years into the tribulation, coincides with the antichrist mandating his mark, often symbolised as "666" (Rev. 13:11-18).

As mentioned in the previous section, proponents of the pre-tribulation rapture theory believe that the church will be raptured before the signing of the peace treaty. This timing contrasts the mid-tribulation rapture theory, which suggests that the church will be raptured after the peace treaty but possibly before the antichrist's occupation of the temple. These differing perspectives on the timing of the rapture significantly influence how each theory defines the role of the church during the tribulation period.

A notable challenge for the mid-tribulation rapture theory lies in the apparent absence of specific references to the church from Revelation chapter 4 until chapter 19. Mid-Tribulation supporters interpret the saints mentioned during this period as representing the church. However, the pre-tribulation rapture position offers an alternative interpretation. It suggests that these saints primarily refer to Israel and individuals who come to faith through their ministry or other means during the tribulation. This discrepancy in interpretation highlights a significant point of contention between the two theories regarding the identity and role of these saints during the tribulation period.

Scriptural Evidence

When examining biblical passages such as Matthew 24:21-22, Daniel 9:27, and Revelation 11:11-12, supporters claim that a coherent narrative emerges in support of the mid-tribulation rapture theory. In Matthew 24:21-22, Jesus speaks of a "great tribulation" that is cut short "for the sake of the elect," aligning with the theory's notion that the rapture occurs at the midpoint of the tribulation. Daniel 9:27 outlines a seven-year covenant with a significant event at the midpoint, corresponding to this theory's timing of the rapture. Revelation 11:11-12 describes the resurrection and ascension of the Two Witnesses, mirroring a rapture-like event during the tribulation. When combined with 2 Thessalonians 2:1-3, these passages are said to support the idea that a great apostasy within the church precedes the midpoint, coinciding with the rise of the antichrist and that the rapture of the church takes place as a crucial event during this phase of the tribulation.

Proponents of the mid-tribulation rapture theory rely heavily on 2 Thessalonians 2:1-3 to support their belief. Again, according to them, this passage sheds light on the concept of a great apostasy within the church that comes before the rapture and after the signing of the peace treaty. This apostasy is closely linked to the antichrist's revelation at the tribulation's midpoint (2 Thess. 2:4), followed by the removal of the church (2 Thess. 2:6).

From the mid-tribulation rapture perspective, here is how this passage contributes to the theory:

"Now concerning the coming of our Lord Jesus Christ and our being gathered together to Him, we ask you, brothers, not to be quickly shaken in mind or alarmed, either by a spirit or a spoken word, or a letter seeming to be from us to the effect that the day of the Lord has come. Let no one deceive you in any way. For that day will not come, unless the rebellion comes first, and the man of lawlessness is revealed, the son of destruction" (2 Thess. 2:1-3)

This passage underscores the importance of clarity concerning Jesus's return and the believers' gathering. It cautions against being easily swayed by false claims or deceptive messages suggesting that the day of the Lord has already arrived. Instead, it emphasises that the day of the Lord will not occur until a "rebellion" or "falling away" takes place first.

As mentioned, some individuals believe that the verses mentioned above support the mid-tribulation rapture theory. According to this interpretation, the "great rebellion" or "great falling away" refers to the departure from sound biblical doctrine within various church denominations and movements during the first half of the tribulation. The great falling away is seen as a departure from sound doctrine rather than individual Christians simply abandoning their faith. As the tribulation unfolds and reaches its midpoint, this departure from sound doctrine within the church intensifies, culminating in the revelation of the antichrist (2 Thess. 2:4). This revelation marks a pivotal moment in end-times events, as the apostasy within the church aligns with the rise of the antichrist, all in preparation for the ultimate judgment and destruction prophesied in passages like 2 Thessalonians 2:9-12.

In summary, according to the mid-tribulation rapture theory, 2 Thessalonians 2:1-3 provides biblical support. It underscores the idea that a great apostasy within the church occurs before the midpoint of the tribulation, coinciding with the revelation of the antichrist. Therefore, it is argued that this interpretation strengthens the overall framework of the theory, which places the church's rapture at the tribulation period's midpoint. This perspective is said to align with other biblical passages such as Matthew 24:21-22, Daniel 9:27, and Revelation 11:11-12, all of which are claimed to contribute to the coherent narrative of the mid-tribulation rapture theory.

Historical Perspectives

Though the early Christian church did not universally agree on a specific timing for the rapture, early church writings have been interpreted to suggest a period of tribulation before the church is caught up. Church fathers like Irenaeus, in his work "Against Heresies," have been incorrectly cited as offering insights that align with the notion of tribulation preceding a midpoint rapture, albeit not in the highly systematised form we see today.

Jewish Feast Template: Rosh Hashanah

The mid-tribulation argument gains its foundation from Revelation 11:15, which suggests that the last trumpet of the tribulation resounds at its midpoint. This concept intriguingly draws a parallel to the significance of the first trumpet heard at Mount Sinai. The first trumpet, as recorded in Exodus 19:16, marked a momentous occasion: "On the morning of the third day, there were thunders and lightnings and a thick cloud on the mountain and a very loud trumpet blast so that all the people in the camp trembled." Throughout the tribulation period, the Book of Revelation unveils a series of trumpet blasts, each carrying its own intense impact:

- Revelation 8:7: "The first angel blew his trumpet, and there followed hail and fire, mixed with blood, and these were thrown upon the earth."
- Revelation 8:8: "The second angel blew his trumpet, and something like a great mountain, burning with fire, was thrown into the sea."
- Revelation 8:10: "The third angel blew his trumpet, and a great star fell from heaven, blazing like a torch."
- Revelation 8:12: "The fourth angel blew his trumpet, and a third of the sun was struck, and a third of the moon, and a third of the stars, so that a third of their light might be darkened."

- Revelation 9:1: "The fifth angel blew his trumpet, and I saw a star fallen from heaven to earth, and he was given the key to the shaft of the bottomless pit."
- Revelation 9:13: "Then the sixth angel blew his trumpet, and I heard a voice from the four horns of the golden altar before God."

However, the apex of this sequence culminates in Revelation 11:15: "Then the seventh angel blew his trumpet, and there were loud voices in heaven, saying, 'The kingdom of the world has become the kingdom of our Lord and of his Christ, and he shall reign forever and ever.'" This interpretation finds its anchor in the New Testament as well. The last trumpet, as articulated in 1 Corinthians 15:51-52, carries profound significance: "Behold! I tell you a mystery. We shall not all sleep, but we shall all be changed in a moment, in the twinkling of an eye, at the last trumpet. For the trumpet will sound, and the dead will be raised imperishable, and we shall be changed." Furthermore, 1 Thessalonians 4:16 underscores the transformative nature of this last trumpet: "For the Lord himself will descend from heaven with a cry of command, with the voice of an archangel, and with the sound of the trumpet of God. And the dead in Christ will rise first."

In summary, according to this interpretation, the last trumpet symbolises the moment of the rapture, signifying the culmination of the tribulation period and the ascent of the church. Combined with the intriguing connections to Jewish feasts like Rosh Hashanah and Shavuot, these elements paint a multifaceted picture of eschatological events.

Modern Proponents

The Mid-Tribulation theory gained traction in the 20th century, thanks to scholars like Gleason Archer and Harold Ockenga. Moreover, Marvin Rosenthal and Robert Van Kampen have proposed a "Pre-Wrath" view, which, although slightly different, often gets discussed alongside the mid-tribulation theory.

Types and Shadows

The story of Shadrach, Meshach, and Abednego, who were preserved within the fiery furnace rather than being spared from it, could serve as a scriptural "type" of the mid-tribulation view. Like them, believers would go through part of the tribulation while being divinely protected.

In evaluating the evidence presented for the mid-tribulation rapture theory, it becomes evident that while this viewpoint offers a unique and internally consistent interpretation of certain biblical passages, it presents a weak argument when subjected to closer scrutiny.

As previously mentioned, a significant challenge facing the mid-tribulation theory lies in the absence of specific references to the church in the Book of Revelation from chapter 4 until chapter 19. While mid-tribulation supporters interpret the saints mentioned during this period as representative of the church, alternative interpretations, such as those favouring a pre-tribulation rapture, argue that these saints predominantly refer to Israel and individuals who come to faith during the tribulation. This lack of clarity regarding the identity and role of these saints during the tribulation period serves as a notable point of contention.

Although proponents of the mid-tribulation theory provide a comprehensive scriptural argument, citing passages like Matthew 24:21-22, Daniel 9:27, Revelation 11:11-12, and 2 Thessalonians 2:1-12, the coherence of this argument remains to be determined. Interpretations of these verses can vary widely, and they do not conclusively establish a mid-tribulation rapture. Additionally, while offering some historical context, historical perspectives do not provide support for this theory, as early Christian views on the timing of the rapture were diverse and not uniformly mid-tribulation.

Furthermore, while the concept of the last trumpet and its significance is intriguing, connecting it to the mid-tribulation theory requires a degree of interpretation and extrapolation. The biblical passages cited in support of this idea can be understood in different ways, making it a less than robust foundation for the theory.

To sum it up, the mid-tribulation rapture theory has a flawed narrative and relies on specific biblical passages, taken out of context. The evidence presented to support this theory is weak and does not provide a convincing argument. The interpretation of these passages is still a topic of debate, and alternative viewpoints, such as the pre-tribulation rapture theory, provide more plausible explanations according to the scriptures.

POST-TRIBULATION, PRE-WRATH RAPTURE THEORY

The post-tribulation rapture theory posits that the seven-year tribulation period, often referred to as Daniel's 70th Week, begins with the signing of a Middle East peace treaty—a perspective shared by proponents of rapture theology. In this framework, the initial 3.5 years constitute the tribulation phase, followed by a transition into the Great Tribulation, spanning an additional 3.5 years. Evidence for marking this latter half can be found in passages like Matthew 24:15-21, Daniel 7:25, 8:13-14, 9:27b, and Revelation 11:2-3, 12:6, 14, and 13:5-7 (alluding to 1260 days, or forty-two months, which is 3.5 years).

According to the post-tribulation rapture theory, the seals described in Revelation 6 are opened just before the rapture event occurs, symbolising the conclusion of the full 7-year period (cf. Dan 9:26-27). Matthew 24:29 is seen as the culmination of the Great Tribulation. From a post-tribulation perspective, Christ's return and the saints' rapture are considered a single event supported by passages like Matthew 24:30-31, Mark 13:26-27, and Revelation 6:12-13. Following the rapture, Jesus is believed to have executed judgment upon the earth during a period commonly referred to as the Wrath of God. This divine wrath is associated with sounding the seven trumpets (Rev. 8:7-11:19) and the pouring out of the seven bowls (Rev. 16).

After the culmination of God's wrath (cf. Rev. 16:1), Jesus, accompanied by the raptured church and the saints, returns to earth, specifically to Megiddo (Rev. 19), the location linked to the Armageddon event mentioned in Revelation 16:16. Their primary purpose is to pass judgment upon the nations and inaugurate the millennial reign.

However, an interval precedes the commencement of this millennial reign, designed to address final matters. This interval follows the 1260 days of the Great Tribulation and spans 75 days, totalling 1335 days (Dan. 12:12) from the tribulation's midpoint until the millennial kingdom's initiation.

Again, the pre-wrath rapture theory contends that the rapture takes place before the "great day of . . . wrath" (Rev. 6:17). According to this view, believers will endure most of the tribulation but will be spared from God's wrath, which descends just before the end of the tribulation (Matt. 24:21). While the church is expected to endure persecution from Satan (Rev. 2:10: 12:17), the antichrist (Rev. 13:7, 10), and humanity (Rev. 2:9; 3:9), it will be spared from God's wrath.

To summarise, in the post-tribulation, pre-wrath rapture theory, the trumpet and bowl judgments (Rev. 7–16) are seen as God's wrath from which the church is exempted (1 Thess. 5:9). However, the initial six seal judgments (Rev. 6) are not considered God's wrath; instead, they are viewed as "the wrath of Satan" or "the wrath of the antichrist." This interpretation arises from the absence of direct mention of God's wrath until after breaking the sixth seal (Rev. 6:17). According to the pre-wrath rapture theory, the church will be present during the first six seals.

Drawing parallels between Revelation 6 and Matthew 24, proponents of the pre-wrath rapture theory identify the first seal judgments with Jesus' description of the end times in Matthew 24:4-7. Jesus then describes these events as "the beginning of birth pains" (verse 8). In verses 29 and 30, "the sign of the Son of Man" appears in the sky, and according to the pre-wrath rapture theory, this marks the moment of the church's rapture.

However, there are significant weaknesses in the pre-wrath rapture position. One issue is the presumption that the "elect" mentioned in

Matthew 24:22, 31 is the church when these saints are more likely to be individuals saved during the seven-year tribulation (cf. Rev. 6:9-11; 7:9-14; 20:4). Additionally, the teaching that the first seal judgments are not God's wrath is disputed, as scripture portrays the Lamb as the opener of the seals (Rev. 5:5; 6:1), implying they are all God's judgments. Jesus alone is the one worthy to open the seals and administer the judgments (Rev. 5:4-5).

Another significant challenge for the post-tribulation, pre-wrath rapture theory lies in reconciling the belief that the church remains on earth throughout the tribulation while interpreting the removal of the "He" in 2 Thessalonians 2 as the Holy Spirit. If the Holy Spirit is indeed removed, it raises questions about how the church, without the indwelling Spirit, continues its existence during a time of unprecedented turmoil.

Furthermore, if the Spirit's drawing and convicting work cease, the sealing of the 144,000 Jewish evangelists and the conversion of multitudes through their ministry become enigmatic, as scripture asserts that none can come to faith in Jesus except through the drawing of the Spirit (Jn. 6:44). If someone claims to be a believer but does not possess the Holy Spirit, then they cannot have Jesus (Rom. 8:9-11). Additionally, the absence of the Holy Spirit's active presence during the tribulation raises concerns about what divine force counteracts the influence of the antichrist. In this theological puzzle, the role and continuity of the Holy Spirit's work during the tribulation remain subjects of intense debate among proponents of various eschatological views.

In light of the challenge posed by the absence of the Spirit of God, the post-tribulation, pre-wrath view encounters another obstacle within the book of Revelation. This challenge revolves around the notable absence of the word "church" in the text from Revelation 3:10

until its solitary occurrence in chapter 22:16. If the belief were that the church was destined to endure the tribulation, one would naturally anticipate its continuous presence and relevance within the narrative of Revelation, especially in the midst of the turbulent events described in the later chapters. The remarkable silence concerning the church during these tribulation accounts inevitably raises questions about its role or existence during this crucial period, thereby presenting a substantial challenge for proponents of the post-tribulation, pre-wrath perspective.

Furthermore, the promise given to the church of Philadelphia in Revelation 3:10, where they are assured of being kept "from" (Gk. Ek "kept out of") the hour of trial, implies a form of protection or preservation distinct from undergoing the tribulation itself. This distinction becomes apparent when compared to the church in Smyrna, which is encouraged to endure tribulation without the same assurance of being kept "from" it. These disparities in wording within the text intensify the theological tension between the pre-tribulation and post-tribulation viewpoints, casting doubt on the notion that the latter church must endure the entire tribulation period, as suggested by the concluding perspective.

Again, the absence of the word "church" during the tribulation period is a formidable challenge for the post-tribulation, pre-wrath rapture theory, especially after the events of Revelation chapter three. While the earlier chapters explicitly mention the church, represented by the seven churches, the narrative seems to shift away from the church as it progresses into the tribulation events. This departure from the established pattern found throughout the New Testament, where the church is depicted as the primary vehicle for spreading the gospel and as the salt and light of the world (Matt. 5:13-16), raises substantial questions. Instead of the church fulfilling its customary role, we witness the emergence of Jewish evangelists leading the tribulation population to faith, as depicted in Revelation 7 and 14:1-5. Additionally, the spotlight falls on the Two Witnesses, who are also of Jewish descent, as they take centre stage in proclaiming the gospel during this period, as seen in Revelation 11. These observations naturally invite a critical inquiry: If the belief is that the church is meant to endure the tribulation, why is there no explicit mention of it continuing its mission as the light and salt of the world, as prescribed in Matthew 5:13-16?

Yet another significant challenge for the pre-wrath, post-tribulation rapture theory is timing. Considering the seven-year tribulation period, consisting of 42 months (Rev. 11:2, 13:5) and 1260 days (Rev. 11:3, 12:6, 14, 12:6, 14), repeating twice, the entire seven-year span is accounted for (Dan. 9:26-27). This raises a crucial question: What time is left to outpour God's wrath through the seven trumpets and bowls? According to this theory, if the entire seven-year tribulation period has already transpired, it leaves little to no room for the extensive series of trumpet and bowl judgments (Rev. 8-11, 16) that are traditionally associated with God's wrath.

As highlighted above, and in addition, the post-tribulation, pre-wrath rapture theory faces a significant challenge when examining John 14:2 in the context of the believers' experience in the Father's house, often understood as heaven. According to this theory, believers would be raptured just before or at the end of the tribulation and immediately return to earth with Jesus for His millennial reign. This raises a fundamental question: When, under this perspective, would the church have the opportunity to spend any meaningful time in the Father's house, which is traditionally associated with heaven? The concept of a yo-yo theory emerges, where believers are swiftly taken up and then brought back down to earth, bypassing the notion of dwelling with the Father in heaven. This interpretation seems incongruent with the promise of John 14:2, where Jesus speaks of preparing a place for His followers in His Father's house. It is important to consider that the pre-tribulation rapture theory aligns more naturally with the idea of believers dwelling in the Father's house in heaven before returning with Christ during His second coming to establish His earthly kingdom. This incongruity with John 14:2 presents a challenge to the post-tribulation, pre-wrath rapture theory and further supports the pre-tribulation perspective's theological coherence.

From the post-tribulation, pre-wrath perspective, proponents might argue that the timing of the trumpet and bowl judgments does not necessarily follow the seven-year tribulation period strictly linearly. Instead, they might suggest that these judgments could overlap with or be condensed into a shorter timeframe within the seven-year period. In this view, the initial 3.5 years of tribulation might include some of the seal, trumpet, and bowl judgments, with the more intense or climactic judgments occurring in the latter 3.5 years leading up to the return of Christ. This interpretation allows for a compressed timeline while maintaining that the full seven years constitute the tribulation period, accommodating both the events leading up to the rapture and the pouring out of God's wrath.

The problem with proponents of the post-tribulation, pre-wrath perspective arguing for a condensed timeline for the trumpet and bowl judgments within the seven-year tribulation is significant when considering the nature of these judgments. The trumpet and bowl judgments in the book of Revelation are explicitly described as the "wrath of God" (Rev. 11:18; 15:1, 7, 16:1, 19). If the pre-wrath theory maintains that the church is raptured at the end of the tribulation but before the wrath, it raises a contradiction. By viewing the trumpet and bowl judgments as the wrath of God, the theory essentially places the church in the midst of God's wrath, which contradicts the core premise of being exempt from His wrath (1 Thess. 5:9). This contradiction highlights yet another challenge in reconciling the pre-wrath perspective with the biblical description of these judgments as divine wrath.

To summarise, upon examination, the post-tribulation, pre-wrath rapture theory raises theological questions and lacks biblical coherence. While it is one of four popular eschatological perspectives held by Christians, it faces significant hurdles when examined closely. The issue of the Holy Spirit's role and continuity during the tribulation remains a point of contention, especially in light of scriptural references to the Spirit's essential work in drawing people to faith. Additionally, the absence of the term "church" in Revelation after chapter 3:10 and the distinct promises made to the churches of Philadelphia pose challenges to the notion that the entire church will endure the tribulation without distinction.

The question of timing, particularly concerning the outpouring of God's wrath through the trumpet and bowl judgments, presents a significant issue, as reconciling a condensed timeline with the nature of these judgments raises theological contradictions. While the post-tribulation, pre-wrath view has its proponents, these challenges underscore the complexity and ongoing debate within eschatological discussions, ultimately raising questions about its viability as a comprehensive understanding of end-times events.

Another significant challenge to the post-tribulation, pre-wrath rapture theory emerges when we consider the recurring biblical motif of Jesus coming as a "thief in the night." This theme strongly aligns with the pre-tribulation rapture perspective, highlighting Christ's sudden and unforeseen return to gather believers before the commencement of the tribulation. This challenge gains further depth when we delve into the typology of the Galilean Wedding Feast, shedding light on this concept. Several pivotal verses bolster this argument. Firstly, 1 Thessalonians 5:2 underscores the element of unpredictability tied to the day of the Lord, drawing a parallel to a thief's unexpected arrival in the night. This reveals Christ's discreet return to rapture believers prior to the tribulation will catch the world, and many within the church, off guard. Moreover, Luke 12:39 echoes a similar theme, stressing the importance of readiness, as Christ may come unexpectedly, akin to a thief (cf. Lu. 21:34-36). Additionally, Revelation 3:3 imparts a stern warning to the church in Sardis, urging them to awaken and remain vigilant, as neglecting this could lead to Christ's arrival like a thief. This implies the danger of missing the rapture event and entering the tribulation unprepared. Importantly, proponents of the post-tribulation, pre-wrath rapture theory cannot claim Revelation 16:15 as supporting their position since it is situated within a chapter entirely dedicated to God's wrath, contradicting their belief in being spared from it.

These scriptural references and the Galilean Wedding typology reinforce the pre-tribulation rapture position, establishing a clear distinction between the rapture and the subsequent tribulation period in light of Christ's sudden return. Notably, the warning given to the church in Thyatira, which faces the prospect of being cast into the great tribulation unless they repent (Rev. 2:22), provides a poignant example of the significance of readiness and repentance in determining one's fate amidst the impending tribulation. If they heed the call to repentance and remain steadfast, they will be kept from the great tribulation, akin to the faithful within that church who are instructed to hold fast until Jesus comes (Rev. 3:25). This underscores the vital role of repentance and faithfulness in the context of the pre-tribulation perspective.

Historical Perspective

Historical evidence and early Christian writings have been cited by supporters of the post-tribulation, pre-wrath rapture theory to argue for an alignment with the post-tribulation view. Among the early church fathers, figures like Irenaeus and Justin Martyr wrote about believers enduring tribulation and then experiencing resurrection, a narrative that corresponds with the post-tribulation perspective. Additionally, texts such as the Didache offer insights into the early Christian experience, suggesting that the church faced tribulation and found salvation through it. However, it is essential to place these writings within their historical context. The early Christians indeed grappled with severe tribulation, enduring persecution from multiple sources, including the Romans, Jews, and fellow countrymen. Consequently, their writings primarily reflect the challenges they confronted rather than providing a rigid eschatological framework.

One vital point to consider is that early church fathers consistently stressed the importance of endurance and unwavering faith in the face of persecution. This emphasis on enduring through tribulation implies that the Holy Spirit played an active role within the church, providing sustenance and preserving those who remained faithful during trying times. This perspective poses a challenge for supporters of the post-tribulation, pre-wrath rapture theory, as they contend that the Holy Spirit, represented as "He," is taken out of the way before the tribulation begins. This apparent contradiction raises questions about how the early church fathers' emphasis on enduring through tribulation aligns with the notion of the Holy Spirit's removal before this period, presenting a theological dilemma for proponents of this particular perspective.

Modern Proponents

Distinguished theologians and scholars such as George Eldon Ladd, Douglas Moo, and Robert Gundry have played pivotal roles in advocating the post-tribulation perspective in contemporary theological discourse. Their contributions try to offer biblical exegesis in support of the belief that believers will undergo tribulation before experiencing the rapture. A more recent proponent of this view is Dr. Michael Brown, known for his book, "Not Afraid of the Antichrist." However, it is notable that Brown erroneously characterises the pre-tribulation theory as a recent invention, disregarding its historical roots.

In recent years, there has been a growing trend among critics of the pre-tribulation rapture theory to assert that this viewpoint had only been taught in 1820 A.D. As mentioned under the pre-tribulation argument, some have attempted to attribute the origin of this perspective solely to John N. Darby. However, Grant Jeffrey has unearthed an ancient reference from a sermon attributed to Ephraem of Nisibis, who lived between 306 and 373 A.D. In this sermon, Ephraem clearly expounds the belief that believers will be caught up and taken to Heaven before the onset of the tribulation. This sermon is regarded as one of the most intriguing apocalyptic texts from the early Middle Ages. Within this text, there is a passage that reads as follows: "For all the saints and Elect of God are gathered, prior to the tribulation that is to come, and are taken to the Lord lest they see the confusion that is to overwhelm the world because of our sins."

Originally titled "On the Last Times, the Antichrist, and the End of the World," this text exists in four Latin manuscripts attributed either to St. Ephraem or St. Isidore (the Parisinus, the Augiensis, the Barberini, and the St. Gallen). Some scholars speculate that an anonymous writer from the sixth century may have derived this text from the original Ephraem. The sermon outlines a sequence of events in the last days, commencing with the rapture, followed by a three 1/2-year Great Tribulation period under the rule of the antichrist, and concluding with the Second Coming of Christ. In Ephraem's work "The Book of the Cave of Treasures," composed around 370 A.D., he believed that the 69th week of Daniel's prophecy culminated with the rejection and crucifixion of Jesus, the Messiah.

Adding to Dr. Michael Brown's lack of historical knowledge, his perspective fails to adequately address the substantial challenges linked to the notion of the church enduring the tribulation, where, according to him, it must confront the formidable presence of the antichrist. This contradiction becomes apparent when considering the title and theme of his book, "Not Afraid of the Antichrist." The impracticality of relying on faith to mitigate the impending adversities becomes evident in light of the probable consequences. These include the vulnerability of the saints to being overcome by the antichrist (Dan. 7:21; Rev. 13:7). These challenges are underscored by biblical passages warning of false prophets and the deceptive nature of the antichrist, to lead astray, even the elect, if possible (Matt. 24:24), and depicting the devastating effects of God's wrath during the tribulation.

Additionally, Brown's approach neglects the fundamental principle that the church's primary focus should be the eager anticipation of the glorious return of Jesus Christ rather than becoming preoccupied with the identity of the antichrist. It underscores that the core message of Revelation revolves around a vigilant readiness for Christ's imminent arrival, aligning with the biblical teaching that Jesus will come for those who earnestly await His return. This perspective emphasises the church's need to maintain a watchful and expectant posture for the coming of their Saviour.

Symbolism and Types

The post-tribulation rapture perspective is argued to have support from various Old Testament narratives. For instance, the story of Joseph in Egypt, enduring seven years of famine, serves as an apt analogy for the seven years of tribulation. This parallel highlight the notion that believers may face earthly hardships while remaining under God's protective care. Additionally, other Old Testament accounts align with the post-tribulation view. The Israelites' slavery in Egypt, followed by their miraculous liberation, the three Hebrew youths preserved in the fiery furnace, and Daniel's safety in the lion's den all emphasise God's ability to safeguard His faithful in times of tribulation. These stories collectively underscore the idea that believers can expect to endure trials on earth but ultimately find divine deliverance and triumph in God's timing.

After considering the aforementioned factors, it is clear that we must not only address our understanding of future events but also heed the scriptural admonitions. Within the context of the rapture theory, proponents stress the importance of actively anticipating Jesus' imminent return for the church. Their conviction is grounded in the wisdom of biblical verses that underscore the utmost significance of being watchful and well-prepared. In Luke 21:34-36, Jesus lovingly cautions His disciples, urging them to "take heed to yourselves, lest your hearts be weighed down with carousing, drunkenness, and the cares of this life, and that Day come on you unexpectedly." This sobering reminder highlights the necessity of maintaining spiritual alertness and focus, ensuring we are prepared for His imminent return. Moreover, the message to the church in Sardis, found in Revelation 3:3, serves as a poignant warning to believers, encouraging them to "remember how you have received and heard; hold fast and repent." Neglecting this admonition will result in Jesus coming upon them as a thief, underscoring the grave consequences of being unprepared. When we combine these scriptural passages with the teachings of early church leaders, who similarly emphasised the importance of vigilance and readiness, it becomes evident that an active and expectant faith is indispensable for participation in the rapture event. From this perspective, those who are not diligently seeking Jesus' return will find themselves outside the gathering of believers when He calls them to meet Him in the air (1 Cor. 15:51-52; 1 Thess. 4:16).

In conclusion, the post-tribulation, pre-wrath rapture theory presents a far-reaching perspective on the timing of the rapture within the broader framework of eschatology. This theory, while advocated by notable theologians, faces significant theological and interpretive challenges. Key among these challenges is the question of the Holy Spirit's role during the tribulation and the apparent contradiction of the church being exempt from God's wrath while being present during the seal judgments, which are explicitly described as God's wrath in the Book of Revelation. This contradiction has led to the theory being sometimes humorously referred to as the "yo-yo theory," where believers are seemingly caught between heaven and earth without a clear scriptural basis.

Furthermore, the absence of the term "church" in Revelation after chapter 3:10, along with distinct promises made to various churches, raises questions about the role and presence of the church during the tribulation. For instance, the warning to the church in Thyatira suggests that they could be thrown into the great tribulation unless they repent

(Rev. 2:22). However, the faithful within that church are only instructed to "hold fast what you have until I come" (Rev. 2:25), implying an opportunity of being kept from the tribulation through faithfulness.

The post-tribulation, pre-wrath perspective also encounters difficulties in reconciling the timing of the trumpet and bowl judgments within the seven-year tribulation period, which some argue leaves little room for these extensive sequences of divine wrath.

In the end, the question of when the rapture will occur remains a topic of theological debate within the Christian community. While the post-tribulation, pre-wrath rapture theory offers a unique perspective, it continues to be met with substantial challenges and questions about its theological coherence and biblical alignment. The ongoing discussions and disagreements among scholars and theologians emphasise the complexity of understanding the intricacies of end-times events and the diverse interpretations within Christian eschatology.

THE "NO RAPTURE" ARGUMENT:

'Challenging Preterism and Examining Alternative Views'

As seen throughout the previous sections, in the realm of Christian eschatology, the concept of the rapture has been a subject of intense theological debate and speculation. While many Christians anticipate a future event where believers are caught up to meet Christ, there exists a perspective that firmly asserts there will be no rapture, as it is often depicted in popular evangelical teachings. This viewpoint is particularly embraced by those who approach the apocalyptic texts of the Bible through a more symbolic or allegorical lens. The following exploration will delve into the "No Rapture" argument, examining its biblical foundations, counterarguments, and alternative eschatological perspectives that challenge preterism.

Biblical Evidence and Symbolism:

The "No Rapture" argument draws heavily upon interpretations of biblical texts, particularly the Book of Revelation, as a symbolic work not to be taken literally. Proponents of this perspective often lean towards Preterist or Amillennial interpretations, both of which view Revelation as either primarily addressing the first-century context or symbolising the ongoing spiritual struggle between good and evil.

Preterist theory, a key component of the "No Rapture" argument, asserts that many end-times prophecies in the Bible, such as the return of Christ and the coming tribulation, were already fulfilled in the past, particularly during the first century A.D. The following sections will explore the origins of preterism, its scriptural support, contemporary proponents, implications for Christians, and its stance on the coming tribulation, millennium, and the Middle East conflict with a focus on Israel.

Origins of Preterist Theory:

The term "preterism" is derived from the Latin word "preter," meaning "past." While preterist interpretations of biblical prophecy were initially developed by early Christian theologians like Eusebius of Caesarea and Augustine of Hippo, the most significant development of preterism as a distinct eschatological theory took place during the Reformation period.

One of the early proponents of preterism was the 16th-century Spanish Jesuit scholar Luis de Alcazar. His work, "Vestigatio arcani sensus in Apocalypsi," aimed to interpret the book of Revelation as a symbolic and allegorical account of past events rather than a literal description of future events. Alcazar's ideas laid the foundation for later preterist thinkers and continue to influence this perspective today.

Key Scriptural Support for Preterism:

Preterism finds its primary support in certain passages from the New Testament, especially the writings of the apostles and the Book of Revelation. Preterists often cite several key verses to bolster their position:

1. Matthew 24:34 - "Truly, I say to you, this generation will not pass away until all these things take place." Preterists interpret

this verse as suggesting that the events described in Matthew 24, including the second coming of Christ, would occur within the lifetime of the generation Jesus addressed.
2. Revelation 1:1 - "The revelation of Jesus Christ, which God gave to John to show to the church the things that must soon take place." Preterists highlight the term "soon" to argue that the events described in the book of Revelation were imminent and would happen shortly after being revealed.
3. Revelation 22:6 - "And he said to me, 'These words are trustworthy and true. And the Lord, the God of the spirits of the prophets, has sent his angel to show His servants what must soon take place.'" This verse, akin to Revelation 1:1, underscores the idea that the events in Revelation were expected to occur shortly after being revealed.

Contemporary Proponents of Preterism:

Preterism is not a monolithic theory; various nuances exist within this perspective. Several contemporary theologians and scholars have championed preterism and contributed to its ongoing development. Prominent figures among preterist proponents include R.C. Sproul, N.T. Wright, and Gary DeMar. These scholars have added depth and insight to the preterist viewpoint, ensuring its relevance in contemporary theological discussions.

Application for Christians:

For Christians who embrace preterist views, their eschatological perspective has significant implications for their understanding of the Christian life and the end times. One notable implication is the belief that the end times are not a future event but have already transpired.

THE EVOLVING LANDSCAPE OF RAPTURE THEORIES

This perspective underscores the significance of living faithfully in the present and fulfilling one's Christian calling in the here and now rather than anxiously anticipating future apocalyptic events.

Dealing with the Coming Tribulation:

A pivotal element of preterist theory revolves around the great tribulation, as described in the Bible. Preterists contend that the Great Tribulation was a historical event that unfolded in the first century A.D., particularly during the Jewish-Roman War (66-73 A.D.) and the subsequent destruction of the Second Temple in 70 A.D. Preterists argue that this tribulation was not a global, end-of-the-world catastrophe but a localised event with a specific historical context.

Understanding the Coming Millennium:

Preterist perspectives on the millennium, as described in Revelation 20, exhibit diversity. Some preterists interpret Christ's thousand-year reign symbolically, signifying His spiritual reign in the hearts of believers throughout history, rather than a future, literal event. Others view it as a reference to the period between Christ's resurrection and the fall of Jerusalem in 70 A.D. when Christianity experienced significant growth and influence. Overall, preterism emphasises the spiritual aspect of Christ's rule and the growth of the Christian faith in the present age rather than focusing on a future, earthly millennial reign.

Response to the Middle East Conflict:

The Middle East conflict, particularly with Israel at its core, has been a topic of great significance and contention among Christian eschatologists, including preterists. The preterist interpretation of biblical prophecy significantly influences how it views Israel and its role in end times events.

Preterist interpretations generally do not foresee a future geopolitical restoration of Israel as a key element of eschatology. Instead, preterists argue that the New Testament redefines the concept of "Israel" to include all believers in Christ, regardless of their ethnic or national identity. Consequently, preterists often perceive the promises and blessings of the Old Testament as being spiritually fulfilled in the Christian church rather than awaiting a future national restoration of Israel.

This perspective can lead to a less fervent focus on the political and territorial aspects of the Middle East conflict. Preterists may advocate for a more peaceful and diplomatic approach to the region, emphasising reconciliation and cooperation among all parties rather than emphasising the fulfilment of specific biblical prophecies.

Countering the Preterist Perspective:

While preterism presents a distinct interpretation of biblical prophecy, it is essential to explore counterarguments and alternative eschatological perspectives that challenge its core tenets. These counterarguments touch upon various aspects of preterism theology, including its non-literal interpretation of prophecy, the perceived absence of historical evidence, unfulfilled biblical prophecies, potential ambiguity in New Testament writings, alignment with Replacement Theology, and compatibility with contemporary movements like the Seven Mountain Mandate.

Literal Interpretation of Prophecy:

One of the primary counterarguments against preterism concerns its departure from a literal interpretation of biblical prophecy. Critics contend that preterism often tends to allegorise or spiritualise passages that were originally intended to be understood in a straightforward, literal sense. For instance, the book of Revelation, which preterists often interpret symbolically, has traditionally been viewed by many theologians as a description of future, literal events. Detractors argue that preterism's symbolic interpretations can lead to strained and subjective readings of the text, deviating from the author's intended meaning.

Lack of Historical Evidence:

Another significant critique of preterism revolves around questions regarding historical evidence. Preterists assert that the biblical events prophesied were fulfilled in the first century A.D. However, sceptics argue that there is insufficient historical documentation to substantiate these claims. The contention is that if significant events such as the great tribulation, the return of Christ, and others indeed transpired during that time, there should be more widespread historical records and testimonies from that period, which appear to be lacking. Building upon this scepticism, further analysis of prophecies, particularly those in Revelation 17:9-14 alongside Daniel 7:11-12, raises additional doubts. Revelation describes seven kings with a temporal scope that extends beyond the first century, challenging the Preterist view that confines these figures to specific Roman emperors of that era. Daniel's vision of beasts, traditionally interpreted as successive empires, implies an ongoing historical process. The prophecy's culmination, with an eighth king symbolising a future king (beast) and system, aligns with a more expansive, futurist eschatology. This interpretation not only questions the historical adequacy of preterism but also posits a continuous, unfolding prophetic narrative, encompassing future events and powers yet to be realised, in stark contrast to the completed historical fulfilment preterism proposes.

Unresolved Prophecies:

As mentioned above, preterism encounters challenges in explaining unfulfilled prophecies in the Bible, particularly those related to the future restoration of Israel. Many passages in the Old and New Testaments describe a geopolitical and national restoration of Israel as a future event. Traditional interpretations of these passages suggest a literal and future restoration, whereas preterism often spiritualises or reinterprets them. Critics argue that preterism does not adequately address the unfulfilled elements of these prophecies, leaving significant gaps in its theological framework.

Ambiguity in New Testament Writings:

Preterism faces criticism related to perceived ambiguity in certain New Testament writings. For instance, the apostle Paul's writings in 1 Thessalonians 4:16-17 describe a future resurrection of the dead and the gathering of believers to meet the Lord in the air. Preterism's interpretation of such passages as referring to past events can be at odds with the plain reading of the text, leading to concerns about consistency in interpreting New Testament writings.

Alignment with Replacement Theology and the Influence of the Seven Mountain Mandate: In addition to the counterarguments, critics of preterism often express concerns about its alignment with Replacement Theology. This theological framework has strong ties to the controversial doctrine known as the Seven Mountain Mandate. Replacement Theology, also known as Supersessionism, posits that the church has supplanted Israel as the primary beneficiary of God's covenant promises found in the Old Testament. Within this context, the Seven Mountain Mandate gains prominence as it embraces Replacement Theology and espouses a specific vision for the world's future.

According to the Seven Mountain Mandate, the future of the world is the expectation that the earth will experience continuous and marked improvement, progressively becoming a more righteous and godlier place. In this view, Christians are tasked with ascending to positions of influence and control within seven key societal spheres, often referred to as "mountains." These spheres encompass various aspects of human society, including government, media, education, business, and more.

The proponents of this mandate envision a world where Christians wield significant authority within these societal domains, transforming the world into an ideal setting conducive to Jesus Christ's return. This perspective contrasts starkly with traditional eschatological beliefs that anticipate Christ's return within the context of a fallen and unredeemed world. Instead, the Seven Mountain Mandate envisions a linear and gradual improvement of global conditions driven by Christian influence and leadership in these spheres.

Critics contend that the Seven Mountain Mandate, by adopting Replacement Theology and claiming Old Testament promises for the church, distorts the biblical narrative and misinterprets God's covenant relationship with Israel. They argue that this teaching represents a departure from a literal interpretation of scripture and raises theological and interpretative concerns regarding Israel's role and the unique nature of God's covenant with them.

In summary, critics of preterism not only raise theological objections to its stance but also highlight concerns about its alignment with Replacement Theology and its connections to the controversial doctrine of the Seven Mountain Mandate. This mandate asserts the church's primacy in claiming Old Testament promises and envisions a world that steadily improves in preparation for the return of Jesus. This perspective departs significantly from traditional Christian eschatological beliefs. The debate surrounding these perspectives underscores the theological diversity within the Christian community and the various interpretations of biblical prophecy, Israel's role, and God's covenant promises.

Partial Preterism:

Within the Preterism realm exists a perspective called Partial Preterism or Moderate Preterism. Partial Preterism represents a theological standpoint within Christian eschatology that shares some commonalities with full Preterism while also maintaining crucial distinctions. Partial Preterists posit that certain prophecies concerning the end times were indeed fulfilled in the past, especially during the first century A.D. However, they do not subscribe to the belief that all end times events have already occurred. Instead, they anticipate future eschatological events, including the Second Coming of Christ and the final judgment. The following delineates the core tenets of Partial Preterism.

Partial Preterism: Fundamental Tenets:

1. Past Fulfillment of Some Prophecies: Partial Preterists acknowledge that specific biblical prophecies found their fulfilment in the first century A.D. They often point to historical events such as the destruction of the Second Temple in Jerusalem in 70 A.D. and the Jewish-Roman War as the contextual backdrop within which certain end-times prophecies, particularly those in the gospels and the Book of Revelation, were realised.

2. Future Eschatological Events: In contrast to full Preterism, Partial Preterism upholds the belief in future eschatological events. Partial Preterists eagerly anticipate the future return of Christ, a bodily resurrection of the dead, and the final judgment of all humanity. They assert that while some aspects of end-times prophecy found fulfilment in the past, other critical elements are still awaiting realisation.
3. Distinction Regarding "This Generation": Partial Preterists interpret passages like Matthew 24:34, where Jesus declares, "Truly, I say to you, this generation will not pass away until all these things take place," differently from full Preterists. They contend that "this generation" pertains to the contemporary audience Jesus was addressing, suggesting that some events He described would occur within their lifetime, though not necessarily all eschatological events.
4. Multiple "Comings" of Christ: Partial Preterism often makes a distinction between the "comings" of Christ. They posit that there was an initial coming of Christ in judgment upon Jerusalem and the Jewish religious system in 70 A.D. However, they anticipate a future, visible Second Coming that will signify the culmination of human history and the consummation of God's kingdom.
5. Final Resurrection and Judgment: Partial Preterists affirm the conventional Christian belief in the future resurrection of the dead and the final judgment. They view the resurrection as a forthcoming event in which both the righteous and the wicked will be raised, followed by a final judgment in which each person will be held accountable for their deeds.

6. Continuation of Spiritual Warfare: Similar to full Preterists, Partial Preterists often underscore the ongoing spiritual struggle between good and evil in the present age. They perceive the mission of the church as advancing the kingdom of God through spiritual warfare, even as they anticipate future eschatological events.

Counter to Partial Preterism:

The dating of the Book of Revelation presents a notable challenge to the Partial Preterist theory. While Preterists advocate for an early date of around A.D. 65, the prevailing consensus among scholars traditionally places its composition later, around A.D. 95. This later dating poses a significant obstacle to the preterist perspective since it positions the destruction of the temple and the sacking of Jerusalem approximately twenty-five years before the book's composition.

In the Book of Revelation, the author John refers to the events as being "soon to take place" (Rev. 1:1; 22:6) and asserts that "the time is near" (Rev. 1:3). If the prophecy were indeed fulfilled in A.D. 70, as preterism contends, it would cast doubt on the prevailing dating of the Book of Revelation, which situates its authorship around A.D. 95-96. Additionally, a significant challenge to the early dating argument arises from the establishment of the modern state of Israel in 1948. This development aligns with aspects of Matthew 24:32-35 and resonates with prophetic themes concerning end-times events in the Book of Revelation.

In conclusion, the "No Rapture" argument challenges conventional Christian eschatology, particularly the widely held belief in the rapture, by presenting alternative interpretations rooted in Preterism and related perspectives. These interpretations question the timing and nature of end-times events, emphasising the importance of understanding biblical prophecy within its historical and contextual framework. Preterism, a significant component of this argument, offers a distinctive viewpoint where many end-times events are believed to have been fulfilled in the past, primarily during the first century A.D. While Preterism introduces a unique perspective, it faces criticisms, including doubts about the dating of the Book of Revelation and concerns about non-literal interpretation. Additionally, within the Preterism realm, Partial Preterism or Moderate Preterism offers a nuanced approach by acknowledging both past and future fulfilment of prophecies. Ultimately, the ongoing theological debate among scholars underscores the diversity of interpretations within the Christian community regarding biblical prophecy, Israel's role, and God's covenant promises.

CONCLUSION: COMPELLING EVIDENCE FOR THE PRE-TRIBULATION RAPTURE THEORY

The following conclusion can be drawn after considering the Pre-, Mid-, Post-Tribulation, and No-Rapture positions. Among the various positions on the timing of the rapture, the pre-tribulation rapture theory holds a prominent place, asserting that believers will be taken up to meet Christ before the period of tribulation described in the Bible. The pre-tribulation rapture theory has been analysed against other popular positions using scriptural evidence, historical references, typology, and comparisons. While acknowledging other viewpoints, the pre-tribulation position is vastly superior over mid-tribulation, post-tribulation, and no-rapture theories.

One of the foundational pillars of the pre-tribulation rapture theory is the abundance of scriptural references that appear to support this perspective. Some key verses include:

1. Revelation 3:10: "Because you have kept My word about patient endurance, I will keep you from the hour of trial that is coming on the whole world, to try those who dwell on the earth." The

CONCLUSION: COMPELLING EVIDENCE FOR THE PRE-TRIBULATION RAPTURE THEORY

Greek word "ek" translated as "from" suggests a removal of the church before the tribulation.

2. **Revelation Absence of the Church:** After Revelation 3, the church is conspicuously absent from the narrative until its return with Christ in Revelation 19. This apparent absence aligns with the idea of a pre-tribulation rapture.
3. **Zephaniah 2:1-3:** "Gather together, yes, gather, O shameless nation, before the decree takes effect – before the day passes away like chaff." This Old Testament passage speaks of a gathering before judgment, consistent with the concept of a pre-tribulation rapture.
4. **John 14:2-3:** "In My Father's house are many rooms. If it were not so, would I have told you that I go to prepare a place for you? And if I go and prepare a place for you, I will come again and will take you to Myself, that where I am you may be also." This promise by Jesus implies a coming to gather believers before tribulation events unfold.
5. **1 Thessalonians 4:16-17:** "For the Lord himself will descend from heaven with a cry of command, with the voice of an archangel, and with the sound of the trumpet of God. And the dead in Christ will rise first. Then we who are alive, who are left, will be caught up together with them in the clouds to meet the Lord in the air, and so we will always be with the Lord." This passage describes a gathering of believers to meet Christ in the air, suggesting a pre-tribulation timing.
6. **2 Thessalonians 2:1:** "Now concerning the coming of our Lord Jesus Christ and our being gathered together to him…" This verse distinguishes between the coming of Christ and the gathering of believers, indicating a prior gathering.

7. 1 Thessalonians 2:6-7: "And you know what is restraining him (the antichrist) now so that he may be revealed in his time." He (the Holy Spirit) who now restrains it (the antichrist) will do so until he (the church indwelt with the Holy Spirit) is out of the way." These verses pose a significant dilemma for alternative viewpoints because they suggest that the antichrist cannot be revealed until the church is taken away. The "He" that is restraining the antichrist could potentially refer to either the Holy Spirit or the church. If the one being removed is indeed the Holy Spirit, leaving the church to endure the tribulation without the indwelling of the Holy Spirit, it would imply that the church, in this scenario, is no longer truly the church but rather an unsaved religious organisation.

Historical Evidence and Early Church Writings:

The pre-tribulation rapture theory is not a recent invention but has roots in early Christian thought. Ephraim the Syrian, a prominent Christian theologian and hymnographer from the 4th century, wrote a work titled "On the Last Times." While not explicitly formulating the doctrine of the rapture, Ephraim expressed the expectation of a gathering of the saints before the coming tribulation. This historical reference indicates that the concept of a pre-tribulation gathering predates modern interpretations.

Typology:

The Galilean Wedding provides a compelling typological argument for the pre-tribulation rapture. In this ancient Jewish custom, the bridegroom would come for his bride, take her to his father's house for a period of seclusion, and then return publicly with her. This pattern

CONCLUSION: COMPELLING EVIDENCE FOR THE PRE-TRIBULATION RAPTURE THEORY

mirrors the idea of Christ coming to gather His bride (the church), taking her to heaven for a period of tribulation on earth, and returning with her in glory. This typological parallel supports the pre-tribulation position.

Comparing with Other Rapture Theories:
Throughout this study, we have examined the pre-tribulation rapture theory against alternative viewpoints. The theory has been demonstrated to be superior based on the following summary.:

1. Mid-Tribulation Rapture Theory: This theory suggests that the rapture will occur halfway through the seven-year tribulation period. However, it faces challenges in explaining the absence of the church in Revelation from chapter 4 onwards and in reconciling this position with key biblical passages that support a pre-tribulation gathering.
2. Post-Tribulation Rapture Theory: This position argues that the rapture will take place at the end of the tribulation period. However, this view encounters difficulties when interpreting passages like Revelation 3:10, which promises to keep believers from the "hour of trial."
3. No-Rapture Theory: This theory boldly rejects the concept of a rapture and contends that there is no tribulation period. One of the key challenges it grapples with is the undeniable occurrence of Israel's rebirth in 1948.

Conclusion:

In conclusion, the pre-tribulation rapture theory presents a compelling case grounded in scriptural support, historical references, and typological parallels. The idea of gathering believers before the tribulation aligns with promises found in Revelation 3:10 and other key passages and early church writings like those of Ephraim the Syrian. Typological parallels, such as the Galilean Wedding, reinforce the pre-tribulation position.

Comparative analysis with other rapture theories reveals that the pre-tribulation rapture theory addresses these challenges more convincingly. While mid-tribulation, post-tribulation, and no-rapture theories have their adherents, they encounter scriptural and logical difficulties that the pre-tribulation position avoids.

Ultimately, the pre-tribulation rapture theory offers believers the hope and assurance of being spared from the wrath and judgment of the tribulation period, consistent with the promise that God will "keep you from the hour of trial." While this position may not be without its complexities and interpretations, it remains a compelling and historically supported perspective on the timing of the rapture.

THE DAY OF THE LORD WILL COME LIKE A THIEF IN THE NIGHT

'God Has Not Destined Us for Wrath'
1 Thess. 5:1-11

The passage of 1 Thessalonians 5:1-11 delivers a compelling message about the Day of the Lord's unforeseen arrival, metaphorically compared to a thief's surprise appearance at night. This section builds upon the foundations laid in 1 Thessalonians 4:13-18, further delving into eschatological themes, especially emphasising the importance of the Christian community being ready for the Lord's return.

The preceding section, "The Coming of the Lord," sees Apostle Paul address the Thessalonian Christians' concerns regarding the destiny of those who passed away prior to Christ's second coming. He provides solace and confidence through the concept of the rapture, a moment when both the living and deceased in Christ are united to greet the Lord in the air. This notion instils a sentiment of optimism, underscoring the unity and victory of believers at the time of Christ's return.

Moving forward, 1 Thessalonians 5:1-11 adopts a more cautionary note. It highlights the abrupt nature of the Day of the Lord, prompting believers to stay alert and uphold moral integrity, given the uncertain timing of these events. The 'thief in the night' analogy serves as a powerful reminder of the unforeseeable and inevitable nature of divine judgment.

The passage offers strong reassurance, specifically stating, "God has not destined us for wrath." This aligns with the concept of the pre-tribulation rapture, suggesting that believers will be exempt from the tribulation — a period marked by suffering and divine judgment before the final adjudication. This perspective suggests that the rapture will transpire prior to the tribulation, reinforcing a message of hope and salvation for those in Christ. Thus, 1 Thessalonians 5:1-11 plays a dual role as both an admonition and a source of comfort, urging believers to maintain a state of readiness and ethical vigilance while also confirming God's promise of redemption and safeguarding from the forthcoming tribulation. This dualistic message accentuates the themes of hope and preparation as integral to Christian eschatological beliefs.

In both 1 Thessalonians 4:13-18 and 5:1-11, Paul begins with a similar thematic tone, underscoring the Thessalonians' awareness of crucial Christian doctrines. In 4:13, his introduction, "We do not want you to be uninformed," addresses the fate of the deceased prior to Christ's return, laying the groundwork for his teachings on the rapture and resurrection of believers. Likewise, in 5:1, Paul notes, "Concerning the times and the seasons, you have no need to have anything written to you. For you are fully aware..." acknowledging their grasp of the Day of the Lord's unpredictability and emphasising the need for alertness and preparedness.

This approach confirms that the Thessalonian Christians were well-informed about these eschatological matters. Paul's method suggests they had received prior teachings or had an existing understanding within their community. Other New Testament scriptures reflect this notion of knowledgeable believers. For example, in Romans 13:11, Paul reminds the Romans that their salvation is closer now than when they first believed, encouraging them to live righteously, conscious of

CONCLUSION: COMPELLING EVIDENCE FOR THE PRE-TRIBULATION RAPTURE THEORY

the times. In 1 Corinthians 15:20-58, he discusses the resurrection, a key element of Christian eschatology, presumably familiar to the Corinthians.

In sum, Paul's intention in writing these sections to the Thessalonians is not to introduce new teachings but to clarify, console, and motivate the believers in their current knowledge. His goal in addressing them is to enhance their understanding, provide comfort concerning their deceased loved ones, and motivate them to live in a state of moral readiness for the Lord's return. His acknowledgment of their awareness serves as praise for their knowledge and faithfulness to date and as a foundation for additional teaching and encouragement.

In the early portion of this section, Paul swiftly introduces the phrase 'thief in the night' (1 Thess. 5:2b). This term, familiar to the Thessalonian church, required no further explanation, indicating their understanding despite the church's relatively young age of just over a year. This nascent church, which Paul founded during his journey through the region, as detailed in Acts 17:1-9, was already well-versed in these teachings.

The metaphor 'thief in the night' is used to convey the sudden and unexpected arrival of the Day of the Lord. This imagery is not unique to 1 Thessalonians but appears in various places in the Bible. It is found in Matthew 24:43, where Jesus uses it to describe the unforeseen nature of His return, urging vigilance. Similarly, in 2 Peter 3:10, Peter employs the phrase to emphasise the suddenness of the day of God's judgment. Revelation 3:3 and 16:15 also use this imagery, underlining the theme of unexpectedness and the need for constant readiness.

The term "thief in the night" is rooted in Jewish tradition and must be explored to fully grasp the depth of the idiom fully. This term is said to originate from a practice concerning the Jewish high priest, who unexpectedly visited the temple guards at night to ensure they were not asleep. This ritual held significant consequences; if a guard were found sleeping, the high priest would light the guard's garments with hot coals from the altar, forcing the sleeping guard to awake, discard their burning clothes, and run through the temple courts in search of new garments. Thus, in this context, the high priest acted as the 'thief in the night', a figure of sudden and unforeseen judgment for those found neglecting their duties.

When Jesus, Paul, and Peter used phrases like 'the thief in the night' in their teachings, they spoke to an audience familiar with this vivid and sobering image. This idiom powerfully conveyed the message of vigilance and readiness for an unannounced, significant event - a concept deeply ingrained in the Jewish consciousness.

In Matthew 24:43, Jesus employs this metaphor to illustrate the unpredictability of His return. The Jewish audience, familiar with the high priest's unexpected inspections, would have immediately understood the parallel - just as the temple guards needed to be alert to avoid the high priest's sudden appearance, believers must be spiritually vigilant for Christ's unforeseen return.

In 2 Peter 3:10, the apostle Peter echoes this sentiment, using the idiom to emphasise the suddenness of God's judgement. This reference would have resonated with a Jewish audience, underscoring divine intervention's immediacy and unexpected nature. Peter urges a lifestyle of godliness in anticipation of this day.

Similarly, the Book of Revelation (Rev. 3:3 and 16:15) incorporates this imagery to underline the theme of unpredictability and the essential need for constant readiness. Revelation 3:3's warning to the church of Sardis to stay awake and strengthen what remains directly appeals to the Jewish understanding of vigilance against unexpected events.

CONCLUSION: COMPELLING EVIDENCE FOR THE PRE-TRIBULATION RAPTURE THEORY

Likewise, Revelation 16:15 blesses those who stay awake and maintain their purity, aligning with the Jewish practice of remaining alert and prepared, akin to the temple guards on watch.

Thus, the 'thief in the night' metaphor, deeply embedded in Jewish tradition, is a compelling scriptural reminder of the need for perpetual spiritual vigilance. It highlights the importance of being prepared at all times for divine occurrences, mirroring the Jewish ethos of watchfulness and readiness in the face of life's uncertainties.

The term, "thief in the night" also parallels the pattern of a Galilean wedding, a cultural context familiar to the early Christian audience. In Galilean wedding customs, the bridegroom would come for his bride at an unexpected time, often at night. The bride and her attendants needed to be ready at all times, as they did not know when he would arrive. This practice served as an effective metaphor for the Christian anticipation of Christ's return. It highlighted the importance of being spiritually prepared at all times for the Lord's arrival, which, like the Galilean bridegroom, would be without warning and at an unanticipated hour. Thus, the 'thief in the night' metaphor, deeply rooted in Biblical tradition and cultural practices, effectively communicated the suddenness and unpredictability of the Lord's return, underscoring the necessity for constant vigilance and spiritual readiness among believers.

As mentioned previously, advocates of the pre-tribulation rapture view find support in verses like 1 Thessalonians 5:2, where the suddenness of the Day of the Lord is likened to a 'thief in the night.' This imagery indicates the rapture occurring before the tribulation, a time of great suffering and God's judgment on earth. The argument against this view often cites 2 Peter 3:10 and Revelation 16:15, which refer to Jesus' second coming, suggesting that the rapture and the second coming are simultaneous events at the post-tribulation. However, proponents of the pre-tribulation rapture counter this by emphasising the distinction between the unexpected nature of the rapture and the well-foretold events of the second coming. They argue that the sudden and unannounced nature of the rapture, as symbolised by the thief in the night metaphor, is fundamentally different from the second coming, which follows clear prophetic signs as described in the Book of Revelation. This distinction is crucial in the pre-tribulation framework, as it upholds the belief that believers will be taken up before the tribulation begins, thus being spared from the wrath and judgment that characterise this period. The pre-tribulation perspective views the rapture as an act of deliverance, separate from Christ's visible and triumphant return, which is to occur after the tribulation period.

In 1 Thessalonians 5:1, Paul's mention of the parousia is explicitly connected to a period of judgment, a theme deeply rooted in the historical use of "the times" within both the Old Testament and intertestamental Jewish literature. This concept is seen in texts such as Jeremiah (30:7, 46:10), Daniel (2:21, 7:12; 9:24-27, 12:1, 4, 9), Mark 13:33, Matthew 8:9, Luke 21:8, Acts 3:19–21, and Revelation 1:3, is often linked to divine intervention and judgment, particularly in the context of the end times. Paul's own use of "time" in 1 Corinthians 4:5 further emphasises this association with judgment. Additionally, the reference to "the times and seasons" in 1 Thessalonians 5:1 aligns with "the day of the Lord" in verse 2, underscoring the connection to a time of divine judgment.

This narrative in 1 Thessalonians 5:1-10 contrasts sharply with the themes presented in 1 Thessalonians 4:13-18. The latter passage focuses on the rapture, which is portrayed as a time of salvation and the gathering of believers to Christ, symbolising hope and deliverance. This distinction in Paul's writings points to two separate eschatological

CONCLUSION: COMPELLING EVIDENCE FOR THE PRE-TRIBULATION RAPTURE THEORY

events: first, the rapture, where believers are caught up to meet the Lord, embodying a time of rescue and hope; and second, the second coming of Christ, described in 1 Thessalonians 5:1-10 as a period of divine judgment and reckoning.

The separation of these events in Paul's discourse suggests a chronological progression: the rapture occurs first as a prelude to the tribulation period, followed by the second coming, which marks the culmination of divine judgment. This interpretation supports the notion of a pre-tribulation rapture, where believers are spared from the wrath and trials of the tribulation, again, underscoring the distinction between the deliverance of the church and the subsequent judgment of the world.

Preceding the term "thief in the night," Paul uses another: "The Day of the Lord." The concept of the "Day of the Lord," as outlined in 1 Thessalonians 5:2a, represents a significant period in future history when God's intervention in world affairs will be more direct and dramatic than at any time since the earthly ministry of Jesus Christ. This day, as prophesied by numerous Old Testament prophets (e.g., Isaiah 13:9–11; Joel 2:28–32; Zephaniah 1:14–18; 3:14–15; Zachariah uses the phrase 21 times), will encompass both judgment and blessing. It is marked to begin immediately after the rapture of the church and concludes with the commencement of the millennium, featuring prominently in biblical prophecy, particularly in Revelation 6–19.

As mentioned previously, like with the rapture, the suddenness of the "Day of the Lord" is likened to a thief's unexpected visit at night. This imagery, used in 2 Peter 3:10 and Revelation 16:15, emphasises the unpredictability of this period, underlining that it will catch many (most) off guard. However, the metaphor of the thief does not suggest that these events will occur specifically at night. Still, it underscores their unexpected nature, which will surprise people worldwide, regardless of their time zone.

In 1 Thessalonians 5:3, Paul explains that the "Day of the Lord" will begin amidst a time of apparent peace, which will be in stark contrast to the anticipated disasters. This deceptive calm is expected to be initiated by signing a seven-year covenant, as prophesied in Daniel 9:27. Notably, Paul distinguishes the target audience of this prophecy from those he includes in the discussion of the rapture (1 Thess. 4:15, 17). The term "them" refers to those who are not taken up in the rapture, essentially the non-Christians (including the lukewarm church) who will be left behind. These individuals, who are deceived by a false sense of peace and safety, a covenant of death (Isa. 28:15, 18), will face sudden destruction instead.

In the New Testament, particularly in 1 Thessalonians 5 and 2 Thessalonians 1:9, the term "destruction" (Greek: olethros) is used, but it should not be interpreted as complete annihilation. Instead, it conveys the idea of severe disruption and upheaval. This term, frequently found in the Septuagint (LXX), often carries the connotation of "eschatological destruction" in the prophetic texts. For instance, in Jeremiah 31:3, it is used in the phrase "destruction and great brokenness."

In the context of 1 Thessalonians, this destruction symbolises the disruption of a false sense of peace and security as a result of God's wrath, which will be unleashed during the Great Tribulation (Matt. 24:21). The onset of this eschatological destruction is likened to labour pains—a sudden, painful, and unavoidable occurrence (Matt. 24:8). Just as labour pains indicate the imminent arrival of birth and are impossible to evade, so too the signs of God's accumulating wrath become apparent, even though the precise moment of its onset remains unknown.

CONCLUSION: COMPELLING EVIDENCE FOR THE PRE-TRIBULATION RAPTURE THEORY

Once more, the coming inescapable and inevitable "destruction" refers to God's wrath. In 1 Thessalonians 5:9, Paul asserts that the church is not destined for wrath, a statement that forms a cornerstone argument against the post-tribulation theory. The use of a powerful Greek double negative (ou mē) by Paul (1 Thess. 5:3) in this context serves to highlight the inescapability of the divine judgment that will befall the earth during the "Day of the Lord." This wrath is not just a concluding event at the end of a seven-year period but is triggered when the peace treaty, prophesied in Daniel 9:27, is broken. This moment marks a dramatic shift from a semblance of peace to a time of unprecedented divine retribution.

The argument against the post-tribulation theory hinges on the timing and nature of this wrath. If the church is indeed not appointed to experience God's wrath, as Paul emphatically states, in that case, it follows that the church must be removed before the onset of these calamitous events, which aligns with the pre-tribulation rapture theory. This perspective posits that the rapture will occur before the tribulation, thereby sparing believers from the period of God's direct and severe judgment upon the earth.

Again, in 1 Thessalonians 5:4-5, Paul clearly differentiates between the state of the church and that of the rest of the world in relation to the end times. He emphasises that his readers, the church, are not ignorant or "in the dark" about these events; they have been previously taught and are well aware of what is to come. This awareness places them in a different category from those who will be surprised by the "Day of the Lord." Unlike the unsuspecting world, the church lives not in darkness but in light, as Paul also notes in Colossians 1:13. This distinction in understanding and expectation signifies that the church will not be caught off guard by the onset of God's judgment.

Moreover, Paul stresses that believers, as "sons of the light" and "sons of the day," inhabit a realm of spiritual illumination, warmth, and growth, contrasting sharply with non-Christians' state. This difference is akin to that between day and night, as further expounded in Ephesians 5:8. The implication here is profound: Christians, being of the light, are neither asleep nor inebriated with the ways of the world; they are alert and sober-minded, fully expecting the imminent return of Christ.

In this context, when Paul discusses the sudden and irrevocable changes that will engulf the world during the "Day of the Lord," he views the church as separate and distinct from those who will experience God's wrath. By virtue of being in the light and not in darkness, the church will not be subject to the catastrophic events that will unfold. The church will have already been united with the Lord, as described in 1 Thessalonians 4:13-18, indicating their removal from the earth prior to the tribulation. This understanding reinforces the idea that the church, being awake, alert, and not of this world, will not undergo God's wrath but will be raptured before these events, in line with the promise of deliverance and salvation.

For the above reasons, in 1 Thessalonians 5:6-7, Paul strongly encourages his readers to act according to their enlightened understanding of the end times. His exhortation is based on the duty to prepare for the Lord's return. Unlike those who are spiritually lethargic and insensitive, symbolised by sleep, and those who lack moral restraint, symbolised by drunkenness, Christians are called to be vigilant and self-controlled. This vigilance is not just a matter of being physically awake but also spiritually alert, ready for the imminent return of Christ (cf. 1 Cor. 1:7; Tit. 2:13; Heb. 9:28; 2 Pet. 3:12)

CONCLUSION: COMPELLING EVIDENCE FOR THE PRE-TRIBULATION RAPTURE THEORY

Paul uses the metaphor of sleep (katheudomen) to denote spiritual insensitivity, contrasting it with the state of believers who are 'sons of the light' and 'sons of the day.' This metaphorical sleep, indicative of the unsaved, represents a lack of awareness and moral turpitude. In contrast, believers must not behave as if they are part of this oblivious mass but should instead remain watchful and sober-minded, prepared for the divine judgment that will come upon those outside the faith.

Keeping with the call for readiness, in 1 Thessalonians 5:8-11, Paul employs the metaphor of a soldier (cf. Phil. 2:25; 2 Tim. 2:3, 4; Phil. 1:2) to illustrate the Christian's need for vigilance and self-control in anticipation of the Day of the Lord. He emphasises that as Christians belong to the day, they should live accordingly, especially when standing on the brink of an event that will lead to sudden translation for believers and sudden destruction for others.

In 1 Thessalonians 5:8, Paul presents the metaphor of a Roman soldier's armour to illustrate the spiritual protection afforded to believers. This imagery is not unique to this epistle but is a recurring theme in the Bible, symbolising the spiritual resources available to Christians. The breastplate, covering vital organs, represents faith and love in 1 Thessalonians 5:8. Faith offers inward protection, safeguarding the believer's heart and core beliefs against doubt and spiritual attack. In contrast, love provides outward protection, guiding interactions with others and reflecting Christ's love. This dual protection is crucial for those who are "of the day," as they live in anticipation of the Lord's return, safeguarded from the spiritual dangers associated with "the Day of the Lord" (1 Thess. 5:2, 4).

Additionally, the "helmet of salvation" guards the mind of the believer. In Ephesians 6:10-18, Paul expands on this armour concept, including the belt of truth, the shield of faith, the helmet of salvation, and the sword of the Spirit, which is the word of God. The helmet, representing salvation, protects the mind from false teachings and despair, focusing instead on the hope and assurance of deliverance from God's impending wrath.

The application of this armour is both defensive and offensive. Believers are called to stand firm in their faith, using truth, righteousness, and readiness from the gospel of peace, faith, salvation, and the word of God as their tools and weapons against spiritual adversity. Just as a Roman soldier would not go into battle without his armour, Christians are encouraged to equip themselves daily with these spiritual resources, ensuring their readiness for the challenges and spiritual battles they face, especially as they await the return of the Lord. This armour defends against spiritual harm and empowers believers to advance the gospel and live out their faith effectively.

In verse 9, Paul provides further motivation for this preparedness, stating that Christians are not appointed to wrath but to obtain salvation through Jesus Christ. This salvation is not a distant hope but a present reality, assured through Christ's death and promised deliverance from the tribulation's wrath. This perspective argues powerfully for a pre-tribulation rapture, suggesting that believers will be removed from the earth before the outpouring of God's wrath.

Verse 10 reinforces the comforting assurance to Christians that, regardless of their current spiritual state — whether they are "awake" and spiritually vigilant or "asleep" and less so — they are guaranteed life with Christ. This promise is deeply rooted in the purpose of Christ's death, which is to bring unity between believers and Himself, thereby overcoming the constraints of physical death. This concept ties in with the message in 1 Thessalonians 4:13-18, where Paul addresses concerns about those who have died before Christ's return. He assures

CONCLUSION: COMPELLING EVIDENCE FOR THE PRE-TRIBULATION RAPTURE THEORY

the Thessalonians that both the dead and the living in Christ will be caught up together to meet the Lord. Thus, the state of being "awake" or "asleep" extends beyond the metaphorical to include the literal physical state of believers, reaffirming that all who are in Christ, whether passed away or alive at His coming, will share in the eternal life with Him, transcending death through His redemptive sacrifice.

In 1 Thessalonians 5:11, Paul concludes with a call for mutual encouragement and edification among Christians, mirroring the closing encouragement of 1 Thessalonians 4:18. This consistent message of encouragement is crucial, especially in the context of the parousia, or Christ's return. Paul's exhortation reminds believers of the hope they share in Christ — a hope that transcends even death.

The encouragement found in these passages centres on two key assurances. First, there is the promise that believers who have died will not miss out on the resurrection when Christ appears in the air. As detailed in 1 Thessalonians 4:13-18, those who have passed away in Christ will be resurrected first, ensuring that they will be part of the glorious meeting with the Lord. This teaching offers profound comfort to those who have lost loved ones, affirming that death does not sever the believer's connection to Christ or their participation in His return.

Second, there is the reassurance for the living believers that they are not subject to God's wrath. This aspect supports the concept of a pretribulation rapture. The notion that believers are destined not for wrath but for salvation (1 Thess. 5:9) underlines the belief that Christians will be raptured or taken up to meet the Lord before the period of tribulation — a time characterised by God's judgment on the earth. This perspective offers hope and comfort to believers, assuring them that they will be spared from the trials of the tribulation period.

Together, these assurances in 1 Thessalonians 4:18 and 5:11 function as pivotal encouragements. They instruct believers on how to live in anticipation of the end times and provide deep-seated reassurance of their salvation and unity with Christ. This dual focus on the resurrection of the deceased believers and the deliverance of the living from divine wrath reinforces the community of faith, urging them to uphold moral and spiritual standards. At the same time, they await Christ's return with hope and assurance.

In sum, in 1 Thessalonians 5:1-11, Paul articulates a weighty message concerning the unexpected arrival of the Day of the Lord, likened to the unforeseen appearance of a thief at night. This teaching builds upon the foundations set in 1 Thessalonians 4:13-18, which focuses on the resurrection and rapture of believers, fostering optimism and assurance in the Christian community. As he transitions to a more cautionary tone in 5:1-11, Paul emphasises the need for vigilance and moral integrity in anticipation of the Day of the Lord, a time of divine judgment yet also of salvation for those in Christ.

The passage reassures believers that they are not destined for wrath, supporting the concept of a pre-tribulation rapture. This view posits that the church will be spared from the tribulation, with the rapture occurring before this period of suffering and judgment (cf. Rev. 3:10; 4:1). Paul's discussion in both 1 Thessalonians 4:13-18 and 5:1-11 highlights the Thessalonians' understanding of these eschatological events, affirming their preparedness and awareness.

1 Thessalonians 5:10-11 concludes with a powerful assurance: regardless of whether Christians are physically alive or have passed away (awake or asleep), they are guaranteed life with Christ, transcending physical death. This promise of unity with Christ aligns with the earlier teachings in 4:13-18, where Paul assures that both the living and the

CONCLUSION: COMPELLING EVIDENCE FOR THE PRE-TRIBULATION RAPTURE THEORY

dead in Christ will be caught up together in the rapture. This teaching provides comfort and hope, reinforcing the belief that deceased believers will not miss out on the resurrection and that living believers are not subject to God's wrath, further supporting the idea of a pre-tribulation rapture.

Paul concludes in 1 Thessalonians 5:11, echoing the encouragement found in 4:18, by urging mutual support among Christians. This encouragement to edify one another is vital for upholding the ethical and spiritual standards essential for living in anticipation of Christ's return. It reassures believers of their salvation and their promised unity with Christ, distinct from the impending divine wrath. This mutual support and assurance serve as a cornerstone for the Christian community, solidifying their hope and readiness for the parousia and further advocating for the pre-tribulation rapture viewpoint.

BE KEPT BLAMELESS AT THE COMING OF OUR LORD JESUS CHRIST

'Do Not Quench the Spirit'
1 Thess. 5:12-28

In the preceding passages of 1 Thessalonians, particularly chapters 4 and 5, Paul provides an exposition on the end times and the return of Jesus Christ. Building from 1 Thessalonians 5:1-11, where the suddenness of the Lord's return is likened to a thief in the night, the text emphasises the necessity of vigilance and preparedness. Paul's teachings in 1 Thessalonians 4:13-18 offer comfort and hope, detailing the pre-tribulation rapture where believers, both living and dead, will be caught up to meet the Lord in the air. This hope serves as a foundation for the exhortations in 1 Thessalonians 5:12-28. The passage underlines the imperative for Christians to be continuously alert, spiritually awake, and adorned in the armour of God. It stresses that at the moment of Christ's unexpected return, only those who are found blameless, vigilant, and ready—clothed in faith, love, and the hope of salvation—will be taken up, while others will be left behind. This section of the epistle, therefore, not only reassures believers of their ultimate redemption but also solemnly reminds them of the urgency to live in a manner worthy of this calling, consistently prepared for the Lord's imminent return.

In the latter sections of his first epistle to the Thessalonians, Paul transitions from eschatological themes to practical guidance for daily

CONCLUSION: COMPELLING EVIDENCE FOR THE PRE-TRIBULATION RAPTURE THEORY

Christian living, intertwining the expectancy of Christ's return with the immediate responsibilities of believers. This shift, evident in 1 Thessalonians 5:12-28, encompasses a series of succinct exhortations designed to foster a harmonious community life within the church. Paul addresses five key aspects:

1. Respecting and valuing church leaders for their spiritual leadership and dedication.
2. Offering support to those in need within the community.
3. Fostering positive personal relationships.
4. Adhering to the core practices of Christian life, such as constant prayer and thankfulness; and,
5. Maintaining spiritual vitality by embracing the Spirit's work and avoiding evil.

While specific, these instructions appear to address general concerns rather than particular crises within the Thessalonian church, perhaps influenced by the information Paul received about their condition. Similar exhortations are also found in Romans 12, suggesting a common pastoral approach in Paul's teachings. Overall, these verses aim to anchor the Thessalonians in the practical dimensions of their faith, effectively merging their eschatological hopes with the realities of communal and personal conduct, thereby reflecting the holistic nature of Christian discipleship as envisioned by Paul.

Throughout Paul's first letter to the Thessalonians, he articulates a vision of mutual ministry within the church, where both members and leaders bear responsibility for each other's spiritual welfare. This is particularly evident in 1 Thessalonians 5:14, where he outlines four continuous responsibilities for all Christians: warning the idle, encouraging the timid, helping the weak, and being patient with everyone. These tasks, embracing both correction and support, are essential for nurturing a thriving Christian community.

As listed above, in 1 Thessalonians 5:12, Paul emphasises acknowledging and respecting church leaders. He urges the Thessalonians to recognise those who labour among them, guiding and admonishing them. This recognition goes beyond mere awareness; it involves appreciating their toil and acknowledging their role as spiritual caregivers. Paul characterises these leaders through their hard work, leadership, and advisory roles within the community.

These leaders, possibly the church's patrons, play a crucial role in the church community's well-being, paralleling the function of patrons in Greco-Roman society and Diaspora synagogues. They are not just figures of authority but also caretakers who invest materially and spiritually in the church. Paul's instruction implies obedience to these leaders, mirroring his guidance to the Corinthians to respect Stephanas and his household for their patronage.

Furthermore, Paul's exhortation in 1 Thessalonians 5:15 against retaliation and for kindness reflects the Christian ethic of responding to wrongdoing with goodness. This approach demands conscious effort and continuous practice and starkly contrasts with the norms of retaliation in the surrounding culture.

In this section of the letter, Paul's teachings emphasise a non-egalitarian, functional form of leadership rooted in service and care. This framework is integral to the health and growth of the Thessalonian church, ensuring that all members, regardless of their role, contribute to and benefit from the communal life of faith.

Continuing with the same in 1 Thessalonians 5:13, Paul extends his guidance on church dynamics, emphasising the importance of high

CONCLUSION: COMPELLING EVIDENCE FOR THE PRE-TRIBULATION RAPTURE THEORY

regard for community leaders. He implores the Thessalonians to "esteem them highly in love on account of their work," linking this directive with the main verb "we implore" from the previous verse, creating a cohesive instruction set. The verb "esteem," from Greek, can imply "to consider in love" or "to esteem exceedingly," both carrying the sense of deep respect influenced by love and appreciation for the leaders' work. This respect is rooted not in the leaders' social status or personal qualities but in their spiritual commitment and service to the community.

The command in verse 13b, "Be at peace among yourselves," is a crucial call for harmony within the church, which may hint at existing tensions between different social groups. This directive, which can be found in various forms in early Christian teachings, suggests that Paul was addressing specific issues within the Thessalonian community, particularly around the acceptance of the de facto leadership of those who were socially and economically prominent. In this context, Paul's call for peace and respect is not just a general Christian principle but a specific appeal to support the community's existing social structure, fostering unity and respect among all members, regardless of their social or economic status.

In 1 Thessalonians, Paul addresses several key issues within the Thessalonian community, including the potential for discord and the serious threat of sexual immorality. This latter concern, highlighted in 1 Thessalonians 4:2-8, echoes Paul's earlier apprehensions in 1 Thessalonians 3:5, where he feared that his labour among the Thessalonians might have been in vain if they were led astray by the tempter, Satan. The parallel between these two concerns underscores the gravity with which Paul views the potential for discord, and Paul's solemn warning against sexual immorality is not merely a moral directive. However, it is deeply rooted in his understanding of the Christian's battle against spiritual forces. In Ephesians 6:12, Paul describes the struggle against "the rulers, against the authorities, against the cosmic powers over this present darkness, against the spiritual forces of evil in the heavenly places." In Paul's view, sexual sin and conflict are not just a matter of personal failing but a manifestation of spiritual warfare, where Satan seeks to undermine the unity, integrity, and holiness of the Christian community.

In 2 Corinthians 2:11, Paul warns against being outwitted by Satan, for "we are not ignorant of his designs." This suggests that Paul sees a pattern in Satan's strategies, where sexual immorality and discord within the church are among his primary tactics to destabilise believers. Similarly, in 1 Peter 5:8, believers are admonished to be sober-minded and watchful because "your adversary the devil prowls around like a roaring lion, seeking someone to devour." This imagery further emphasises the constant vigilance required to guard against spiritual threats, including moral and communal transgressions.

Thus, Paul's emphasis on sexual morality and unity in the church goes beyond individual behaviour to encompass a broader spiritual perspective. He sees these issues as part of the more significant spiritual battle every Christian and church community faces, highlighting the importance of steadfastness in faith and moral integrity in the face of such challenges. By addressing these issues head-on, Paul aims to fortify the Thessalonian believers not just in their personal lives but also in their collective spiritual resilience against the schemes of Satan.

Furthermore, Paul's teaching extends to how Christians should respond to offences. In 1 Thessalonians 5:15, he instructs believers not to retaliate but to show kindness, emphasising the need for proactive goodness rather than mere abstention from evil. This directive reflects a broader biblical principle against revenge, as seen in Matthew 5:38-48,

CONCLUSION: COMPELLING EVIDENCE FOR THE PRE-TRIBULATION RAPTURE THEORY

Romans 12:17-21, and 1 Peter 3:9 (vv. 9-12). Paul's exhortations are not isolated commands but part of a cohesive strategy to strengthen the church's internal bonds and present a united front in the face of external challenges.

In 1 Thessalonians 5:16, Paul commands believers to "rejoice always," recognising that true Christian joy transcends circumstances. Unlike worldly happiness, which fluctuates with external conditions, Christian joy is rooted in the permanent blessings of being in Christ. This joy is a deep, abiding state, reflecting trust in God's power, providence, and forgiveness. It is a commandment that challenges believers to maintain a joyful spirit even in trials, seeing God's hand in all situations and holding onto the hope of future salvation.

Continuing in verse 17, Paul urges "prayer without ceasing." This does not imply non-stop prayer but rather a continuous awareness and practice of prayer throughout daily life. Paul likens this to a persistent cough, suggesting that prayer should be as inherent and frequent in a believer's life as such involuntary actions. He views prayer as an essential discipline, both in private and corporate settings, for intercession and personal supplication.

In verse 18, Paul instructs believers to "give thanks in all circumstances." This command is grounded in the belief that God works in every situation for the good of those who love Him (Rom. 8:28). Thanksgiving, therefore, is not contingent upon favourable circumstances but a consistent recognition of God's sovereign work in all aspects of life.

These three exhortations – joy, prayer, and thanksgiving – are more than mere guidelines; they are expressions of God's will for those in Christ Jesus. By instructing the Thessalonians to embrace these practices, Paul enhances their spiritual disciplines and shapes their collective identity as a community anchored in gratitude, prayerfulness, and joy. He places significant emphasis on these behaviours, equating them with the will of God, thus elevating their importance to the same level as ethical conduct. For Paul, these practices are not optional add-ons to the Christian life but are essential elements that define it, integral to personal growth and communal health.

Flowing from Paul's emphasis on joy, prayer, and thanksgiving in 1 Thessalonians, again, these elements are crucial in the context of spiritual warfare, a theme Paul elaborates on in other parts of his writings. In Ephesians 6:10-18, Paul describes the "armour of God," which includes truth, righteousness, the gospel of peace, faith, salvation, and the Word of God as key components. This armour is vital for standing against the devil's schemes and evil's spiritual forces. In this spiritual battle, gratitude, prayerfulness, and joy are not just passive states of mind; they actively fortify the believer's spiritual armour. Gratitude keeps the helmet of salvation securely in place, reminding believers of their ultimate victory in Christ. Prayerfulness aligns with the shield of faith, enabling believers to extinguish the flaming darts of the enemy, as mentioned in Ephesians 6:16. Joy, rooted in the Holy Spirit (Gal. 5:22), acts like the shoes of peace, providing stability and readiness amidst spiritual battles.

Conversely, sexual sin and conflict within the church community will remove this spiritual armour. Sexual sin, as warned against in 1 Corinthians 6:18-20, defiles the body, which is the temple of the Holy Spirit, leading to a breach in the armour, particularly the breastplate of righteousness. Similarly, conflict and disunity, addressed in Romans 16:17-18, can disrupt the harmony and peace that the gospel of Peace—Shoes is meant to provide. These negative behaviours damage not only individual spiritual integrity but also the collective strength of the church in spiritual warfare.

CONCLUSION: COMPELLING EVIDENCE FOR THE PRE-TRIBULATION RAPTURE THEORY

Therefore, embracing gratitude, prayerfulness, and joy, as Paul emphasises, is crucial for maintaining the whole armour of God. These practices reinforce the believer's defences against spiritual attacks and contribute to the overall health and unity of the church. This unity is essential for standing firm in the face of spiritual challenges. The active cultivation of these virtues, alongside avoiding behaviours like sexual immorality and conflict, thus becomes a vital strategy in the Christian's spiritual warfare, ensuring readiness and resilience against the forces of evil.

In the context of 1 Thessalonians 5:19-22, Paul shifts focus from individual conduct to the dynamics within the church assembly, delivering a series of commands that underscore the collective responsibility in discerning and fostering the work of the Holy Spirit. The passage comprises a blend of negative and positive directives, with two admonitions followed by three affirmations, reflecting a balanced approach to spiritual life within the community.

Verse 19 cautions against quenching the Spirit, a metaphorical reference to resisting or suppressing the Holy Spirit's influence, likened to a flame that warms, enlightens and empowers (Isa. 4:4; Matt. 3:11; Acts 2:3-4). Paul warns that believers themselves can hinder the Spirit's work, emphasising the need for openness to the Spirit's movement. This verse sets the stage for understanding how the Spirit might have been stifled in Thessalonica.

In verse 20, Paul addresses the potential undervaluing of prophecy within the church. The gift of prophecy, crucial for the early church, involved receiving and conveying God's revelations, in context, about the future, but often concerning present guidance (Acts 11:28, 13:2). Paul suggests that personal interpretations or teachings, particularly about the Second Advent, might have led to a superficial evaluation of prophecy, hence the need to respect and uphold the authority of revelations preserved by the Holy Spirit in scripture.

Verse 21 expands on this by encouraging believers to test all teachings against the Word of God, a task requiring spiritual discernment (1 Cor. 2:14; cf. Heb. 6:14). This process involves sifting through teachings to identify what aligns with the divine revelation retaining what is good and true.

Finally, verse 22 broadens the scope of discernment, instructing believers to avoid every form of evil. This encompasses false teachings and any practice or belief contrary to Christian ethics. Paul acknowledges that while believers should avoid actions that knowingly cause offence, it is not always feasible to steer clear of everything that might appear objectionable to overly critical or limited perspectives.

These verses form a comprehensive framework for spiritual life within the Christian community, balancing the openness to the Holy Spirit's work with the responsibility to discern and uphold truth. This approach reinforces the collective role in maintaining doctrinal purity and ethical integrity, essential for a church engaged in spiritual warfare and committed to reflecting Christ's teachings.

In these final verses of 1 Thessalonians 5, Paul recognises the high standards outlined in his previous exhortations. He expresses a hope-filled prayer that God would enable the Thessalonians to meet these spiritual expectations. He shifts from emphasising individual responsibility to focusing on life within the community of believers, offering a series of commands that reflect the dynamic interplay of individual and communal spirituality.

In verse 23, Paul underscores God's role in fostering peace and sanctification within the church. He acknowledges the peace that the Thessalonian church experienced through the gospel and encourages

CONCLUSION: COMPELLING EVIDENCE FOR THE PRE-TRIBULATION RAPTURE THEORY

them by reminding them that the same God who brought them peace will continue to be their source of strength and sanctification. Paul's prayer for their sanctification (to be set apart for God) in every aspect of life is not an expectation of perfection but a desire for continual spiritual growth. He hopes their preservation is blameless at the Lord Jesus Christ's coming, emphasising the holistic nature of sanctification, encompassing spirit, soul, and body—each aspect representing different dimensions of their personhood and existence.

Verse 24 offers reassurance to the Thessalonians, reminding them of God's faithfulness in completing the work He has begun in them. This faithfulness is not just a one-time act but a continuous process where God calls and justifies by grace and sanctifies by the same grace. Paul assures them that their growth in sanctification is not solely dependent on their efforts but is also undergirded by God's faithful work through the Holy Spirit.

Paul concludes this section with a benediction summarising the letter's central themes, particularly the call to Christian living in anticipation of Christ's return. He reassures the Thessalonians that they are under God's protection and guidance, no matter their circumstances. This focus on God's faithfulness and ongoing call provides a foundation of hope and assurance for the believers, encouraging them to continue their faith journey confidently in God's sustaining grace. This emphasis on God's enabling power and faithfulness addresses the Thessalonians' concerns about meeting the high spiritual standards set forth. It affirms the communal aspect of their faith journey, where individual growth contributes to the health and maturity of the entire church community.

In the concluding part of 1 Thessalonians 5, Paul transitions from overarching spiritual teachings to more personal appeals and a final benediction. He makes three specific requests that strengthen the bond between him and the Thessalonian believers and reinforce the principles he has taught.

In verse 25, Paul asks the Thessalonians to "pray for us," a request commonly found in his letters (e.g., 2 Thess. 3:1-2; Rom. 15:30-32). This mutual intercession creates a deep connection between Paul and his readers and reflects the communal aspect of their faith journey. Understanding his own limitations and God's sufficiency, Paul values his fellow believers' prayers, knowing that much of his ministry's success can be attributed to their spiritual support.

Verse 26 encourages a physical expression of Christian love and unity: greeting one another with a holy kiss. This cultural practice, which is common in Paul's time, symbolises the familial bond within the church. The emphasis on the kiss being "holy" indicates that it should be a pure and genuine expression of fraternal affection, devoid of inappropriate connotations. This gesture, adaptable to different cultural contexts, is a tangible manifestation of the church's internal harmony and love.

In verse 27, Paul strongly urges that his letter be read aloud to the entire church. The term "I charge you" underscores the importance of his message to every member hearing it. This insistence might be due to specific issues within the church that Paul wanted to address or his recognition of the letter's spiritual significance as divinely inspired scripture.

The letter concludes with a benediction in verse 28, where Paul invokes the grace of the Lord Jesus Christ upon his readers. This grace, central to Paul's theology, encapsulates the totality of believers' salvation and blessings in Christ. Paul's desire is not just for the Thessalonians to possess this grace but to experience and enjoy it fully daily.

CONCLUSION: COMPELLING EVIDENCE FOR THE PRE-TRIBULATION RAPTURE THEORY

These closing verses of 1 Thessalonians serve as a personal and pastoral touch, binding the letter's teachings with specific, actionable practices and a prayerful wish for the Thessalonians. Paul's requests for prayer, affectionate greetings, and the communal reading of his letter, along with the invocation of Christ's grace, encapsulate his deep concern for the Thessalonians' spiritual welfare and his desire for their continued growth and unity in faith.

In this concluding passage of 1 Thessalonians 5:12-28, Paul intertwines the anticipation of Christ's return with Christian life's everyday responsibilities and dynamics. This section, with exhortations, aims to prepare the Thessalonian believers for the Lord's imminent return, emphasising the need for continuous vigilance, spiritual alertness, and a life adorned with the armour of God. It is a call to live blamelessly, with each member contributing to the church's overall health and unity.

Paul's guidance spans various aspects of church life, from respecting and valuing church leaders for their spiritual leadership, offering support within the community, fostering positive personal relationships, and maintaining spiritual vitality. These exhortations, while specific, are not just for the Thessalonian church but reflect a universal pastoral approach in Paul's teachings.

He emphasises the mutual ministry within the church, highlighting the shared responsibility for each other's spiritual welfare. This is evident in his detailed outline of the continuous responsibilities of all Christians: warning the idle, encouraging the timid, helping the weak, and being patient with everyone. Through these directives, Paul promotes a nurturing and supportive community, essential for facing spiritual challenges and anticipating their return.

Furthermore, Paul addresses the potential for discord and the threat of sexual immorality, recognising them as serious challenges that can undermine the community's spiritual integrity and unity. He situates these issues within the broader context of spiritual warfare, highlighting the necessity of maintaining the whole armour of God.

Paul's requests for mutual prayers, the exchange of a holy kiss, and the communal reading of his letter in verses 25-27 are not just practical actions but symbolic gestures that reinforce the teachings of the letter and the bond between him and the Thessalonian believers. These personal appeals, coupled with the final benediction invoking the grace of the Lord Jesus Christ, encapsulate his pastoral concern for the Thessalonians' spiritual growth and unity in faith.

In summary, 1 Thessalonians 5:12-28 serves as a comprehensive guide for Christian living in anticipation of Christ's return. It balances the theological with the practical, the individual with the communal, and the spiritual with the everyday, thereby encapsulating the holistic nature of Christian discipleship as envisioned by Paul. This passage, therefore, stands as a testament to the enduring relevance of Paul's teachings, offering timeless guidance for believers striving to live a life worthy of their calling in the present age and in preparation for the Lord's coming.

SECOND THESSALONIANS

INTRODUCTION

The apostle Paul, a pivotal figure in early Christianity, wrote the second letter to the church of Thessalonica. This letter was written under the inspiration of the Holy Spirit, follows the first letter, 1 Thessalonians (cf. 1 Thess. 1:1).

The consensus among conservative scholars places Corinth as the location from which 2 Thessalonians was written. This conclusion is drawn from the New Testament book of Acts, which records Paul, Silas, and Timothy being together in Corinth (Acts 18:5). Since 1 Thessalonians was also written from Corinth and given the similarity in the situations addressed in both letters, Corinth is deemed the logical site of composition for 2 Thessalonians.

The dating of this epistle is closely tied to that of 1 Thessalonians. It is believed to have been written shortly after the first letter, likely within a year, placing it in the early A.D. 50s. This makes 2 Thessalonians one of Paul's earliest canonical writings, following the letter to the Galatians.

The occasion for writing 2 Thessalonians arose from Paul's recent updates about the Thessalonian church. These updates likely came from the messenger who had delivered 1 Thessalonians and returned to Corinth and others familiar with the church's situation. The reports were mixed: while the Thessalonians were praised for their faithfulness and growth in the face of persecution, concerns were raised about false teachings regarding the day of the Lord, causing confusion and leading some believers to abandon their daily responsibilities in anticipation of the Lord's return. In response, Paul felt compelled to write this second epistle to commend the believers for their progress, correct doctrinal misunderstandings, and address the consequences of these errors.

The epistle's outline covers several main themes that are worth noting. Firstly, the salutation in verses 1:1-2 sets the tone for the letter, much like in 1 Thessalonians. Secondly, in verses 1:3-12, Paul expresses gratitude for the Thessalonians' spiritual growth and encourages them to endure in their faith during times of persecution while praying for their success. Thirdly, in verses 2:1-12, Paul addresses misconceptions about the day of the Lord and clarifies the beginning of this period while discussing the mystery of lawlessness. Fourthly, in verses 2:13-17, Paul gives thanks for the Thessalonians' calling and prays for their strength. Fifthly, in verses 3:1-15, Paul provides exhortations for future growth, including prayers for the apostles, confidence in the Thessalonians, guidance for dealing with disorderly members, and instructions for the idle and disobedient. Finally, the epistle concludes with a blessing and final greeting in verses 3:16-18.

In the context of Christian eschatology, 2 Thessalonians addresses the importance of perseverance under persecution, the future rapture, the revelation of the antichrist, and the return of Jesus Christ. These topics are essential for comprehending the early Christian eschatology and the obstacles encountered by the early church in upholding doctrinal purity and practical faithfulness amidst external pressures and internal confusion.

STEADFAST FAITH AS WE AWAIT HIS RETURN

'Enduring Persecutions and Afflictions'
(1:1-12)

The opening of 2 Thessalonians is different from that of 1 Thessalonians in one notable way: it refers to God as "our" Father. This term, which is often used in Paul's greetings (e.g., Rom. 1:7; 1 Cor. 1:3; Gal. 1:3), emphasises that Christians are part of God's metaphorical family. For this reason, the greeting in 2 Thessalonians is more elaborate than in the first letter, following the standard Pauline greeting format, except in cases like Colossians and possibly Galatians. The greeting's phrase "from God our Father and the Lord Jesus Christ" is consistent with Paul's typical style.

The second verse of the letter to 2 Thessalonians continues the greeting, where Paul implies the verb "be." He reminds them that they are the ones who have received God's grace and peace and expresses his desire for them to experience these blessings fully. "Grace" refers to God's unmerited favour, which is given freely to those who believe in Christ's sacrifice, offering blessings instead of judgment. "Peace" represents the end of hostility, made possible by Christ's death, which enabled reconciliation between God and humanity. This peace is not just a positional peace with God but also an experiential peace that believers experience in their lives. Paul wishes for the Thessalonians to remain peaceful even during trials and persecution. Both grace and peace are divine gifts that come through the Lord Jesus Christ. In 2 Thessalonians, Paul adds "from God the Father and the Lord Jesus Christ" to the greeting, emphasising the source of these blessings.

In this first section of the letter (3-12), Paul seamlessly transitions from one topic to another, beginning with gratitude for the Thessalonian believers' spiritual growth and encouraging their continued steadfastness while also praying for their spiritual success. Paul and his fellow missionaries had many reasons to thank God for the Thessalonian church. The church's faith grew remarkably, indicating a deepening trust in God. Similarly, their love for each other was also increasing, reflecting a strong sense of community and commitment. Paul often cited the Thessalonians' growth in faith and love as an example for other churches, especially their endurance in the face of persecution. The Thessalonians viewed their trials as part of God's will and relied on Him for strength. The reports of the Thessalonians' faith and perseverance, initially spread by Paul, were eventually widely known, as indicated in both letters.

In his letters to the Thessalonians, particularly highlighted in 2 Thessalonians 3-4, Paul extols the Thessalonian church for their steadfast endurance in the face of persecution, choosing a path of faithfulness over ease. This praise is deeply contextualised within both the first and second epistles, reflecting on their significant trials, including hostilities from both Gentile and Jewish communities, as narrated in Acts 17:5-9 and 1 Thessalonians 2:14-16. Their unwavering commitment to their faith amidst these adversities is a testament to their growing faith and love, a point Paul emphasises. He views their perseverance not as mere tolerance of suffering but as an active, faith-driven response to their situation, exemplifying the Christian life as one that embraces trials yet anchored in Christ's hope. Their resilience serves as a beacon to

INTRODUCTION

other Christian communities, illustrating that enduring hardships for the gospel is feasible through God's grace and a powerful demonstration of faith's transformative power. This aligns with the overarching New Testament teaching that followers of Jesus should anticipate trials as integral to their spiritual journey, with the assurance of God's deliverance and the hope of Christ's return (cf. John 16:33; Acts 14:22).

In 2 Thessalonians 1:5, Paul interprets the afflictions and persecution faced by the Thessalonians as indicative of God's righteous judgment. This view aligns with the first-century understanding of suffering, which considered adversities signs of divine selection and harbingers of future glory. Hence, the tribulations endured by the Thessalonians go beyond mere hardships; they serve as affirmations of their worthiness in God's kingdom, as ordained by His divine justice. Paul emphasises in this passage that these trials are not methods to achieve salvation but rather manifestations of their worthiness, granted by God's grace and solidified through their faith in Christ. This grace, which empowers believers to withstand overwhelming challenges, reinforces their rightful place in God's kingdom and their significant role under His sovereign rule. The Thessalonians' steadfastness in these trials thus becomes a crucial aspect of their contribution to God's overarching plan, enhancing His glory through their unwavering faith, affirming their position in His kingdom, and reflecting the unfolding of His righteous judgment.

Further, in 2 Thessalonians 1:6-7, Paul continues to illustrate how the Thessalonians' sufferings exemplify God's justice, which entails both retribution against their oppressors and relief for the oppressed. He reiterates a core Biblical principle: God's inherent justice, which ensures the balancing of justice's scales, promising retribution to those inflicting trouble upon the Thessalonians, as echoed in Galatians 6:7 and supported by Old Testament teachings like Isaiah 66:6, which promises recompense to God's enemies.

In verse 6, Paul declares it just for God to repay those who persecute the Thessalonians with affliction, a notion rooted in the lex talionis (the law of retaliation, whereby a punishment resembles the offence committed in kind and degree) associated with the day of the Lord. The oppressors, by afflicting God's people, inevitably set themselves against Him, facing eventual divine judgment leading to their destruction and eternal separation from God, as outlined in verse 9. This notion of divine retribution offers the Thessalonians a sense of eventual triumph over their current oppressors.

Conversely, Paul assures the Thessalonians of divine recompense in the form of rest and relief from their afflictions, to be bestowed upon Christ's glorious return (1:7). This positive facet of God's justice offers the afflicted a promise of rest, envisaged to occur at Jesus Christ's revelation, marked by His triumphant return with His angels. For the Thessalonians and all enduring similar hardships, this pledge of eventual relief validates their faith and is a testament to God's equitable and righteous judgment.

Building on Paul's message in 2 Thessalonians 1:6-7, where he assures the Thessalonians that God's justice will prevail both in punishing their oppressors and bringing relief to the oppressed, the apostle continues to elaborate on the divine judgment that will accompany the return of Christ.

Again, in his teachings to the Thessalonians, as seen in 2 Thessalonians 1:6-7, Paul assures them of the certainty of divine justice, promising that God will righteously balance the scales by punishing oppressors and bringing relief to the oppressed. This message, rooted in the principle of lex talionis, anticipates a future where God's judgment

INTRODUCTION

will prevail, as echoed in scriptures like Galatians 6:7 and Isaiah 66:6. However, Paul also imparts a crucial directive for the believers' conduct in the interim, as reflected in his earlier letter, 1 Thessalonians 5:14-18.

While it may be tempting to seek personal retribution, Paul counsels the believers to adopt a posture of prayer and patience. He urges them to be kind to everyone and avoid repaying evil for evil, as highlighted in 1 Thessalonians 5:15. Instead, they are encouraged always to seek good for each other and all people. This approach aligns with Jesus' teachings on loving enemies and praying for those persecuting you (Matt. 5:44).

Furthermore, Paul emphasises the importance of always rejoicing, praying, and giving thanks in all circumstances (1 Thess. 5:16-18). These actions are not mere suggestions but are declared as God's will for His people in Christ Jesus. This mindset fosters a spirit of resilience and hope, keeping believers focused on God's promises rather than being consumed by the desire for immediate justice or retaliation.

Therefore, the Thessalonians, and by extension, all believers, are called to live in a manner that reflects the character of Christ. While acknowledging the reality of suffering and injustice, they commit to a life of prayer, patience, and persistent pursuit of good, trusting that God's ultimate justice will be revealed in His time. This call to prayerful patience and kindness, even in the face of adversity, stands as a testament to the transformative power of the gospel and the believers' unwavering hope in the return of Christ.

In verse 8, Paul expounds on the specifics of this divine retribution. He categorises those who will face God's wrath into two groups: the ignorant of God, echoing Romans 1:18–32, and those who knowingly reject the gospel (cf. John 3:36). The latter, those who, having been granted greater knowledge and opportunity, bear heavier guilt for their wilful rejection of God's revelation. This principle is underscored in several biblical passages. Luke 12:48 articulates that greater responsibility accompanies greater knowledge, stating, "Everyone to whom much was given, of him much will be required, and from him to whom they entrusted much, they will demand the more." This verse highlights the increased accountability for those with more understanding and resources.

Similarly, the same chapter in Luke emphasises that the degree of punishment is proportional to one's understanding and opportunity, indicating that ignorance might mitigate, but not absolve, culpability. Moreover, 2 Peter 2:21 suggests that it is more grievous to have known the path of righteousness than to have turned away from it, illustrating the severe consequences of rejecting the truth after embracing it. These verses collectively stress the heightened responsibility and accountability before God for those blessed with more profound knowledge and greater opportunities. This delineation underscores God's perfectly just nature in dealing with human defiance and rejection.

Building on this understanding of divine judgment and accountability, the New Testament vividly illustrates the return of Jesus Christ, particularly in 2 Thessalonians 1:8, where it forewarns dire consequences through "flaming fire" and "vengeance" for those either ignorant of or disobedient to God. This dramatic portrayal finds resonance and expansion in other scriptural narratives. For instance, in Revelation 6:12-17 and 19:11-16, the imagery of Christ is powerfully drawn as a warrior king, majestically riding a white horse, donned in a blood-drenched robe, leading the armies of heaven. This cosmic and terrestrial upheaval theme is further explored in Matthew 24:29-31, which speaks of a darkened sun, falling stars, and the trembling of the heavens, all heralding Christ's return, a moment marked by global mourning.

INTRODUCTION

The Old Testament, too, contributes richly to this tapestry of eschatological imagery. In Daniel 7:13-14, a vision presents the "Son of Man" arriving with the clouds of heaven, bestowed with dominion, glory, and an eternal kingdom. Similarly, Isaiah 66:15-16 depicts the Lord's arrival with fiery grandeur, His chariots like a whirlwind, manifesting His wrath and rebuke with fiery flames. Collectively, these biblical passages weave a narrative of a momentous day of divine reckoning and splendour, instilling a sense of awe and trepidation, especially among those who have disregarded the divine call. This portrayal not only reflects the majestic and fearsome aspect of divine justice but also underscores the profound seriousness of the event for those unaligned with God's teachings.

In verse 9, Paul delves into the nature of the punishment awaiting these groups. The phrase "they will pay the penalty" emphasises the severity and eternity of their fate. Termed "eternal destruction," this punishment is not a temporary setback nor annihilation but a perpetual state of conscious suffering, starkly contrasting the concept of eternal life as presented in Matthew 25:46. The core of this eternal punishment lies in eternal separation from the Lord's presence, which, for believers, represents the ultimate joy and hope.

This separation juxtaposes the majestic display of Christ's power at His return, permanently barring the unbelievers from His presence and saving power. This notion of divine justice aligns with the promise of relief for the Thessalonians, offering them hope in their current trials.

Verse 10 shifts the focus to Christ's return, distinct from the rapture, marked by the revelation of Jesus Christ in power and glory and the establishment of His earthly kingdom. While not date-specific, this event is depicted as a day of judgment for the lost and a day of glorification for believers. Here, Christ's glory will be reflected in His saints. This includes the Thessalonian believers, who will share in this glorious day, affirmed by Paul's testimony. Such a vision, rich with hope and encouragement, strengthens believers, especially those like the Thessalonians, facing and enduring persecution and trials.

Paul's profound revelation about God's justice and the destiny of believers led him to pray fervently for his Thessalonian brethren. He desired that their lives align with their divine calling and destiny. Paul and his colleagues consistently interceded for the Thessalonians, their spiritual welfare deeply ingrained in the apostles' hearts. They prayed that God would deem the Thessalonians worthy of their calling through faith in Jesus Christ (cf. Rom. 8:30; Eph. 4:1; 1 Thess. 4:7), reflecting the Biblical principle that Christians live worthily not to earn salvation, but as a response to the salvation already granted.

Additionally, Paul hoped that God's will would be fully realised through the intention and action of the Thessalonians inspired by their faith. He understood that believers' motives and actions originate in God (Phil. 2:13) and are empowered by His strength. This prayer was not just about individual growth but also about how their lives would collectively glorify God. Paul's ultimate aim was for God's glory to be manifested in and through the Thessalonians, both in their present lives and at the future revelation of Jesus Christ. This would result in the believers themselves being glorified through their association with God.

In 1:11, Paul expresses a dual aspect of his prayer for the Thessalonians. He prays for their worthiness in God's calling, echoing the salvation theme discussed earlier in verses 7 and 10. This prayer also extends to their moral conduct, asking God to fulfil every good intention and act of faith among them. Here, Paul intertwines the concepts of divine enablement and human responsibility, emphasising that the

INTRODUCTION

Thessalonians' righteous actions are both a response to and a reflection of God's power at work in them.

In 1:12, Paul's prayer focuses on the mutual glorification of Christ and the believers. He envisions a reciprocal relationship where the glory of the Lord Jesus is reflected in the lives of the Thessalonians, and in turn, they are glorified in Him. This intertwining of divine and human glorification is rooted in God's grace, encompassing both God and the Lord Jesus Christ as the source of this unmerited favour. Through these prayers, Paul demonstrates a deep pastoral concern for the Thessalonians, desiring their endurance in the face of persecution and their spiritual growth and glorification in Christ.

Amid trials and persecutions, the Thessalonian church stands as a beacon of steadfast faith, exemplifying the endurance and faithfulness required of believers as they await the return of Jesus Christ. The opening of 2 Thessalonians vividly portrays their unwavering commitment to their faith despite the hostilities they faced. Paul's letters to them commend their spiritual growth and remind them of the divine justice that awaits. This justice, as Paul outlines, will bring retribution to their oppressors and relief to the oppressed at the glorious return of Christ.

Paul's fervent prayers for the Thessalonians, seeking God's declaration of their worthiness and the fulfilment of their good intentions and faith-driven actions, are deeply intertwined with this eschatological hope. The reciprocal glorification of Christ in the believers and of the believers in Christ is the cornerstone of Paul's vision for the Thessalonian church. This vision transcends their present sufferings, anchoring them in the promise of Christ's return, where eternal glory awaits those who have remained faithful.

The endurance of the Thessalonians, fuelled by their unwavering faith amidst trials, is a testament to the gospel's transformative power.

It vividly illustrates the Biblical teaching that trials are integral to the Christian journey, leading to ultimate deliverance and the fulfilment of God's righteous plan. As the church continues to face various forms of persecution and trials, the example of the Thessalonian believers remains relevant, encouraging steadfastness and faithfulness in anticipation of the day when Jesus Christ will return to repay each according to their deeds. In this waiting, the believers are called to live lives worthy of their calling, continually manifesting the grace and peace of God through their actions and relationships, thereby glorifying God and preparing for the day of Christ's triumphant return.

UNDERSTANDING THE SIGNS

'Preparing for Christ's Return'
(2:1-12)

During challenging times, the church in Thessaloniki stands as a model of unwavering faith and resilience, reminiscent of the churches in Smyrna and Philadelphia. Their shared experiences include enduring hardships and the promise of divine reward. Specifically, both the Thessalonian and Philadelphia churches were given the prophetic promise of the rapture, an event unseen in their time but expected in today's church era.

While sharing similarities, these churches differ from others mentioned in Revelation. Notably, the churches of Sardis and Laodicea received stark warnings: Sardis about the rapture and the risk of facing tribulation (Rev. 3:2-3), and Laodicea about the danger of mirroring worldly behaviours (Rev. 3:15-17), risking rejection from the promised salvation (via the rapture) and facing tribulation, like the warning to the church of Thyatira (Rev. 2:22). The warnings and commendations given to the seven churches point towards the Day of the Lord, and the millennial dispensation.

Paul, in his second letter to the Thessalonians, addressed their confusion and fear stemming from false teachings that they were in the "Day of the Lord," a belief fuelled by various sources including prophecies, reports, and a letter falsely claiming to be from Paul (2:2, 3:17). This misinformation led them to mistakenly think they were experiencing the prophesied tribulations, contradicting Paul's earlier teachings about the Lord's return and the promise of being spared from God's wrath (1 Thess. 1:10, 5:9).

In 2 Thessalonians 2:2, Paul addresses the Thessalonian believers' need for unwavering faith and discernment, cautioning against the influence of misleading teachings, including those claiming prophetic or apostolic authority. These deceptive teachings had led some in Thessalonica to incorrectly believe that their present trials were part of the 'Messianic woes', a Jewish eschatological concept describing a period of intense suffering preceding the Messiah's arrival. This erroneous belief parallels the misunderstanding evident among advocates of post-tribulation, mid-tribulation, and pre-wrath rapture theories.

However, Paul's teachings in 1 Thessalonians 4:15-17 and 5:9 present a different narrative for the church, distinct from the Jewish understanding of 'Messianic woes'. He emphasises that believers will be raptured, caught up in the air to meet the Lord, thus not appointed to endure the wrath of the tribulation period. The church's experience is clearly distinguished from that of Israel in Christian eschatology. According to this eschatology, Israel will undergo tribulation following the rapture of the church as described in Romans 11:25. During this tribulation, many will be conquered by the antichrist, as depicted in Revelation 13:7 and 10. Eventually, they will acknowledge Jesus as the Messiah, as shown in Matthew 23:39.

The revelation of the antichrist, a central figure in the tribulation period, is pivotal in understanding this distinction. Paul asserts that the antichrist will be revealed only after the church's removal (2:3, 6-7), aligning with the pre-tribulation rapture viewpoint. This teaching contrasts with the experiences of the Jewish people during the tribulation, highlighting a fundamental difference in the eschatological paths of

INTRODUCTION

the church and Israel. Thus, any teaching suggesting that believers will go through tribulation, like the future Jewish experience of 'Messianic woes', diverges from Paul's message and reflects a misinterpretation of his teachings.

As mentioned above, in his second letter to the Thessalonians, Paul addresses their concerns about the end times with a clear message to maintain their faith and not be misled by false teachings (2:3). He warns them against such deception, emphasising that they should not be swayed by any person or persuasive claims, even if they seem credible or claim apostolic authority. Paul, recognising the vulnerability of new Christians to deceptive teachings, emphasises the significance of basing oneself in the truth of God's Word (cf. 2 Tim 2:14). The author of the letter to the Hebrews also states that believers must develop discernment to distinguish truth from falsehood (Heb. 5:14).

In 2 Thessalonians 2:3, Paul outlines specific events that must occur before the day of the Lord's judgment. These include the great apostasy or rebellion within the church, a departure from the truth of God's Word, which Paul repeatedly spoke about (1 Tim. 4:1-3; 2 Tim. 3:1-5; 4:3-4). This apostasy is seen as a significant, future event, distinct from the ongoing apostasy in the church's history (cf. Jam. 5:1–8; 2 Pet. 2; 3:3–6; Jude).

Following the great falling away from sound biblical doctrine (2 Tim. 4:3-4), as mentioned earlier, another key event is the revelation of the "man of lawlessness" (2:3-4, 8), who will be revealed after the faithful church has been removed (2:7). This person, associated with and characterised by lawlessness, is also described as a man doomed to destruction. This man is the antichrist and will play a pivotal role in the end times, particularly in the latter half of the seven-year tribulation preceding Christ's second coming. This individual's identity will become apparent when he makes and then breaks a covenant with Israel, as prophesied in Daniel 9:27.

In sum, Paul's message in 2 Thessalonians 2 calls for vigilance and adherence to the truth, guiding the believers to discern the signs of the times without succumbing to fear or false teachings. His teachings serve as a reminder of the importance of steadfast faith in the face of confusion and misinformation about the end times.

In 2 Thessalonians 2:4, Paul further describes a man of lawlessness who opposes and exalts himself over Jesus Christ as the one worthy of worship. This description draws on the language from Daniel 11:36, which was originally referred to as Antiochus Epiphanes. It reflects the early Christian belief that a singular, arrogant figure would claim divine status and seek to replace true worship with his own. This man would even assert himself in the third temple, proclaiming himself to be God.

Again, Paul warns the Thessalonians and every believer throughout the ages not to be deceived by anyone, regardless of their credibility or claims of apostolic authority. Given the susceptibility of new and biblically illiterate Christians to being misled, Paul outlines three events that must occur before the day of the Lord:

- The apostasy or rebellion of the church (specific to lawless denominations that have departed from sound biblical doctrine).
- The revealing of the man of lawlessness.
- The removal of what restrains lawlessness.

As mentioned previously, the coming and current rebellion represents a significant departure from the truth within the church. Once again, this prophecy, predicting a future apostasy, is unfolding

INTRODUCTION

in contemporary times, paving the way for the emergence of the antichrist. The man of lawlessness, identified as the antichrist, is a genuine person who will masquerade as Christ, as indicated in passages like Matthew 24:23-26. His appearance will be a distinct and significant event in history.

In 2 Thessalonians 2:4, the Bible predicts the construction of the third temple, a significant event in the end-times prophecy. This temple is where the antichrist will assert his authority. Again, the antichrist's rise to power is prophesied to be marked by the signing and subsequent breaking of a peace treaty closely tied to the construction of this temple. When he takes his seat in the temple, committing the abomination of desolation as mentioned in Matthew 24:15-21 Daniel 9:27, and 12:21, he will declare himself to be God, an act of blasphemy that will further confirm his identity.

This period, known as the Great Tribulation, will see the antichrist's increasing demand for global allegiance. Revelation 13 describes him enforcing a mark known as 666, further identifying him to be received by everyone, symbolising his dominance and control. However, despite his attempts to establish himself as a world leader (as depicted in Daniel 2, 7, Revelation 13, and 17), he will only succeed in bringing a quarter of the world under his control, according to Revelation 6:8. This limitation in his power is evidenced by the resistance he faces from other nations, as detailed in Daniel 11:40-45 and Revelation 16:12-16.

This global resistance and conflict will culminate in the gathering at Megiddo for the Battle of Armageddon. This event signifies the tribulation period's climactic end and God's decisive intervention in human affairs. This battle, mentioned in Revelation 16:14-16, marks a turning point in eschatological events, leading towards the final defeat of evil and the establishment of God's kingdom. The third temple, the antichrist's blasphemous claims, and the global events of this period are central to understanding the prophetic narrative of the end times as described in the Bible.

Like with the first letter (1 Thess. 4:13; 5:1) in 2 Thessalonians 2:5, Paul reminds the Thessalonians of his earlier teachings about the Day of the Lord, teachings he had imparted during his time with them in Thessalonica (Acts 17:1-5). He uses this recollection to reinforce his message in his letter, asserting, "Do you not remember that while I was still with you, I used to tell you these things?" This appeal to their memory confirms that his readers were already familiar with the doctrine concerning the end time.

In sum, Paul's reference to these teachings serves two purposes. Firstly, it emphasises the truth and consistency of his message since he personally shared these teachings with them as an apostle of Jesus Christ in Thessalonica. This personal connection underscores the authenticity and importance of the message. Secondly, it highlights Paul's belief in the importance of prophetic truth for all Christians of all time. He did not view such teachings as too complex, insignificant, or contentious but rather as an integral part of God's overall plan and counsel, deserving of clear communication without hesitation or reservation.

In 2 Thessalonians 2:6-7, Paul elaborates further on the enigmatic figure of the "man of lawlessness" and the removal of what currently restrains this embodiment of evil. For many, these verses are challenging due to their cryptic nature and presuppose knowledge not explicitly outlined in the text. Based on his oral teachings, Paul indicates that his original readers would have been familiar with this concept, as he states in verse 6, "and now you know." The primary interpretative challenge lies in understanding the meaning of the terms "the one who now restrains"(2:7a) and "the one who will do so" (2:7b).

INTRODUCTION

The identity of this restrainer, a subject of much debate, needs clarification. Preterist theories suggest that it references the Roman Empire or a particular emperor, as some early interpretations suggest. However, many modern scholars see this view as less likely due to the apocalyptic and mythical nature of Paul's imagery, which aligns differently from the civil and political contexts of the Roman Empire.

Another, more acceptable interpretation of 2 Thessalonians 2:6-7 proposes that the entity restraining the "man of lawlessness" is the Holy Spirit, operating within the church. This perspective suggests that the Holy Spirit, dwelling in believers, acts as a force of righteousness and truth, effectively holding back the antichrist's emergence.

According to this view, the church, indwelt by the Holy Spirit, plays a crucial role in this restraining process. If the Holy Spirit were removed, leaving the church behind to endure the tribulation, it implies that it would be devoid of the Holy Spirit's presence. By definition, such a scenario would mean that the entity left behind could not be considered the church in its proper, Spirit-filled form. Instead, the entity left behind would better resemble the harlot church or religious system, as described in Revelation 17. Therefore, it is argued that the Holy Spirit, residing in the church, is the primary force countering the rise of the antichrist.

This theory further posits that when the church is raptured, it is not the Holy Spirit that departs from the earth but rather the church as the vessel of the Holy Spirit's work. The revelation of the antichrist follows this event. However, the Holy Spirit's influence persists on earth, as evidenced by the sealing of the 144,000 Jewish evangelists and the mass revival described in Revelation 7. This continued presence of the Holy Spirit during the tribulation is vital, as it enables the significant spiritual revival prophesied in these eschatological events.

Thus, in this interpretation, the Holy Spirit, through the church, currently acts as a restrainer against the antichrist until the church is taken away by way of the rapture. After the rapture, while the church is absent from the earth, the Holy Spirit remains active, working in different capacities during the tribulation. This interpretation underscores the integral role of the Holy Spirit in God's redemptive plan throughout all end-times events.

In 2 Thessalonians 2:8, Paul speaks about the future disclosure of the "man of lawlessness," a figure who will emerge following removing what currently restrains evil. Empowered by Satan himself (2:9), this individual will be known for performing deceptive signs and wonders, ultimately leading to his downfall at the hands of Jesus Christ during His Second Coming (Rev. 19:20). This phase in biblical eschatology will cover the seven-year period following the rapture, known as the tribulation (Dan. 9:24-27).

This prophecy aligns with visions described in Daniel 7, where diverse beasts symbolise different empires and a little horn emerges, speaking boastfully, depicting a ruler who will oppose God and oppress His people. Similarly, in Matthew 24, Jesus says of false prophets performing great signs and wonders to deceive, if possible, even the elect, warning of the rise of deceptive, influential figures in the end times.

In Revelation 13, the imagery of a beast rising from the sea is a compelling metaphor often interpreted as symbolising the emergence of a powerful, end-times empire. Again, this beast, which is empowered by Satan (the dragon), is described as performing astonishing signs and leading people around the world into deception. The sea often represents chaos, tumult, or a vast expanse of nations and peoples in biblical symbolism. For instance, in Isaiah 17:12-13, nations are likened to the roaring seas. In Daniel 7:2-3, Daniel has a vision of four beasts

INTRODUCTION

coming up from the sea, each different from the others, representing successive empires.

Many scholars and theologians thus see the beast's description in Revelation 13 as a symbol for a revived form of the Roman Empire. This interpretation draws from the vision in Daniel 7, where Daniel sees four beasts traditionally interpreted to represent the Babylonian, Medo-Persian, Greek, and Roman Empires. The fourth beast, terrifying and powerful with iron teeth, is often associated with the Roman Empire. Therefore, the beast from the sea in Revelation 17, with its ten horns and seven heads, is seen as a revival or continuation of this fourth empire, signifying a future resurgence of a Roman-like empire in the end times.

This interpretive framework aligns with the understanding of many eschatological perspectives that see a revived form of the Roman Empire playing a significant role in end-times events. These interpretations often point to the European Union or a similar confederation of nations as a potential fulfilment of this prophecy, seeing it as a modern-day equivalent to the ancient Roman Empire in terms of influence and reach.

In 2 Thessalonians 2:9-11, Paul delves into the sinister nature of the antichrist, emphasising his dependence on Satanic power to perform deceptive miracles. This deception targets those who have turned away from the gospel's truth, leading them to spiritual ruin. This starkly contrasts with the fate of those who acknowledge and cling to the truth and thereby attain salvation. This dichotomy underscores the necessity of steadfastness in the gospel amidst end-time deceptions and powerful misleading forces.

Revelation 14:1-12 provides a further layer to this narrative by introducing a heavenly warning against worshipping the antichrist and receiving his mark. This warning from the angels is a direct contrast to the deceptive allure of the antichrist described in Revelation 13, where he performs great signs and misleads and deceives many. The angels' message in Revelation 14 serves as a divine call to reject the antichrist's allure and to remain faithful to God, even in the face of great deception and pressure.

Reinforcing the theme of opposition to the antichrist's deceptions are the two witnesses featured in Revelation 11. These individuals are formidable adversaries to the antichrist, displaying miraculous powers that eclipse the antichrist's fraudulent signs. With the ability to call down fire to consume their adversaries, halt rain from the sky, transform water into blood, and unleash various plagues upon the earth at will, they starkly contrast the antichrist's counterfeit miracles. Their role and actions not only confront the antichrist's false claims to divinity but also call for repentance and urge the rejection of his deceitful ways. During the tribulation and the rise of the antichrist, these witnesses' persistence and prophetic work shine as a beacon of hope and truth. They guide and inspire those committed to maintaining their faithfulness in these challenging and chaotic times.

In 2 Thessalonians 2:10, Paul again warns of a widespread spiritual decline leading into and during the tribulation, where many, including those within the church, will face destruction due to their lack of commitment to truth and obedience. Again, this period will be marked by a significant departure from sound biblical teaching, as mentioned in 2 Thessalonians 2:3, which signifies a falling away within the church. The era, referring to today, is already witnessing an escalation of antichrist-like behaviours and deceptions within the church, characterised by a counterfeit gospel, false prophecies, and deceptive signs (2:7).

INTRODUCTION

It is important to reiterate that a key sign of the end times, as foretold in the scriptures, is the deviation of those who claim to be followers of Christ from authentic biblical teachings. Engaging in spurious spiritual practices and being misled by false miracles, these individuals will not be part of the church that is raptured at Christ's return. As mentioned earlier, this mirrors the church's situation in Sardis, as depicted in Revelation 3:1-6, which outwardly seemed alive but was, in reality, spiritually dead. Leading into and during the tribulation period, many will stubbornly refuse to accept the truth, instead becoming ensnared by the profound deceit of the antichrist. This figure, whom they unintentionally embody, represents the culmination of their rejection of gospel truth. Their decision to yield to this grand illusion signifies their spiritual downfall and is a stark reminder of the severe consequences of abandoning the truth as revealed in the gospel.

In 2 Thessalonians 2:11-12, Paul continues the theme from previous verses, elaborating on the grave consequences of rejecting the truth. These verses, forming a cohesive thought, emphasise the judgment that befalls those who deliberately turn away from the truth. Paul asserts that when individuals choose falsehood over truth, God permits them to follow the path of delusion. This divine judgment, manifesting as a powerful delusion, arises from their decision to embrace error, specifically the lie that the man of lawlessness is God.

In verse 12, Paul explains that God's intention is to execute justice. Those who refuse to accept the truth and find pleasure in unrighteousness will be condemned eternally, which shows the consequences of spiritual choices. This principle of divine judgment applies to all ages and is everlasting.

Regarding the fate of those present during the revelation of the man of lawlessness, Paul highlights a particularly severe judgment.

The 'powerful delusion' sent by God indicates that post-rapture salvation might be exceptionally rare, particularly for those who had prior knowledge and yet rejected the gospel. This aligns with the Book of Revelation, which mentions many saints during the tribulation, likely referring to individuals who had not previously encountered or rejected the gospel (cf. Rev. 7:4).

Summarising this passage, Paul reassures the Thessalonians that their current tribulations are not indicative of them undergoing the judgments of the day of the Lord. The rapture has not been missed; certain events must precede it, including widespread apostasy, the removal of the Restrainer – the Holy Spirit working through the indwelling church – and the revelation of the antichrist, revealed through the signing of the peace treaty. As these events had not yet transpired, the Thessalonians were not amid the judgment of the day of the Lord.

Adding to this, Paul's teachings clarify that the church, indwelt by the Holy Spirit, is crucial in restraining the antichrist. The Holy Spirit's presence through the church is a bulwark against the full manifestation of evil. This understanding aligns with the Biblical narrative that believers will not endure the tribulation, supported by passages such as 1 Thessalonians 4:15-17, where Paul vividly describes believers being caught up in the air to meet the Lord, and 1 Thessalonians 1:10, and 5:9, which affirms that the church is not destined for wrath. According to this perspective, theories proposing a mid-tribulation, post-tribulation, or pre-wrath rapture are divergent from Paul's teachings and the broader Biblical narrative.

INTRODUCTION TO MILLENNIALISM

While on the topic of the end times, as expounded in 1 Thessalonians 2:1-12, where Paul speaks of his ministry and the coming of the Lord, it is essential to take a layby to define what Millennialism is in the context of eschatology. Millennialism, or millenarianism, is a Christian belief rooted in the Book of Revelation 20:1-6, which envisages Christ establishing a kingdom on earth for 1,000 years. This belief, derived from the Latin term "millennium" (meaning "one thousand years"), varies significantly among Christian denominations and even within denominations. Some believe Christ's return precedes the millennial kingdom (premillennialism), while others view it as following it (postmillennialism). Premillennialism considers Christ's return as a divine intervention to break away from a wicked world, inaugurating the millennial kingdom. In contrast, postmillennialism sees Christ's return after a millennium established through Christian influence in culture and politics. Amillennialism symbolically interprets the millennium as the church's existence on earth between Christ's first coming and return, with the actual kingdom of God being in heaven.

These interpretations, despite their differences, agree on the earthly nature of the millennial kingdom, aligning with God's promise to Abraham about giving him "this land" (Gen. 12:7; 17:8). The diversity in millennial views reflects various biblical interpretations, with key debates over the timing of Christ's return relative to the millennium.

Origins of millennialism trace back to Jewish apocalypticism during the tumultuous inter-testamental period, including texts like Enoch, Jubilees, and 2 Esdras, which prefigure a messianic figure establishing a millennial kingdom. Christian millennialist thinking, primarily based on Revelation 20:1-6, evolved from Jewish beliefs.

In Christian history, millennialism has gone through various phases:

1. Early Church: Premillennialism, or "chiliasm," was prominent in early Christianity, with leaders like Papias, Justin Martyr, and Irenaeus supporting it.
2. Medieval Period: Amillennialism, popularised by Augustine, became dominant, with the church sceptically viewing a literal thousand-year kingdom.
3. Reformation and Seventeenth Century: Reformers like Luther and Calvin upheld amillennialism, while Anabaptists and other radical groups revived premillennialism.
4. Modern Millennialism: Postmillennialism gained ground in the eighteenth century, influencing movements like the Great Awakening. Dispensationalism, a form of premillennialism, rebounded in the nineteenth century and became prominent in the United States.

Non-Christian forms of millennialism have also appeared, such as the Taiping Rebellion and Nazism, which borrowed millennial concepts. The Taiping Rebellion in 19th century China, led by Hong Xiuquan, showcased a unique blend of Christian millennialism infused with distinctive Chinese cultural and religious elements. This movement envisioned a radical transformation of society, driven by a conviction in Hong's 'divine' mission. Similarly, Nazism in 20th-century Germany also adopted millennial concepts, albeit in a radically different context. Under Adolf Hitler, Nazism framed its ideology around a millenarian vision of a "Thousand-Year Reich," promising a utopian future through

INTRODUCTION

a racially purified and globally dominant German empire. Both these examples reflect how millennialist thought can be adapted to diverse cultural and political contexts, often merging with existing beliefs and ideologies to create unique movements that, while rooted in transformative change, diverge significantly in their interpretation and implementation from traditional Christian millennialism.

For the purpose of this study, we will be examining four prominent eschatological viewpoints within Christian theology: Pre-tribulation (Dispensational) Pre-Millennialism, Post-Tribulation Pre-Millennialism, Post-Millennialism, and Amillennialism. These views offer diverse interpretations of the end times, the millennium, and the Second Coming of Christ, each with unique theological nuances and scriptural interpretations.

INTRODUCTION TO PRE-TRIBULATION (DISPENSATIONAL) PRE-MILLENNIALISM:

Pre-Tribulation (Dispensational) Pre-Millennialism is a perspective within Christian eschatology that interprets the end times with a specific sequence of events leading up to the Second Coming of Christ. The belief in a pre-tribulation rapture characterises this view. Christians are taken to heaven before tribulation on earth, followed by Christ's return and a literal thousand-year reign.

To gain insight into pre-tribulation (dispensational) pre-millennialism, examining the connections between Genesis 3, Genesis 12, and Revelation 20 is beneficial. Genesis 3 details the fall of man, introducing sin and the resultant estrangement of humanity from God. This pivotal chapter lays the groundwork for the Bible's redemption story, underscoring the need for human salvation, divine intervention, and restoration.

Adding to this narrative, Genesis 12 introduces the Abrahamic Covenant, where God promises Abraham land, descendants, and blessing. This covenant plays a crucial role in unfolding Biblical history and the dispensational framework, where God's dealings with humanity are seen through distinct periods or dispensations. The promises to Abraham in Genesis 12 are often viewed in pre-tribulation (dispensational) pre-millennialism as foundational to understanding God's plan for humanity and the eventual establishment of Christ's kingdom.

Revelation 20, conversely, depicts the culmination of this redemptive arc. It describes Satan being bound for a thousand years, the reign of Christ with his saints, and the final judgment. In the context of

INTRODUCTION

Pre-tribulation (Dispensational) Pre-Millennialism, this chapter is critical as it illustrates the ultimate vanquishing of evil and the establishment of Christ's millennial kingdom, viewed as a literal fulfilment of God's promises of restoration and peace, including those made to Abraham, and his offspring, which includes the church (Rom. 4:16-17; 9:6-8; Gal. 3:7-9, 29; Eph. 2:11-13).

It is important to note the distinction between the church being a spiritual descendant of Abraham and the concept of replacement theology. While scriptures such as Romans 4:16-17, 9:6-8, Galatians 3:7-9, 29, and Ephesians 2:11-13 illustrate the church's spiritual lineage from Abraham, this does not equate to the church replacing Israel in God's plan. Romans 11 swiftly debunks the notion of the church replacing Israel. It emphasises Israel's ongoing and distinct role in God's salvific plan. This distinction is particularly crucial in Pre-tribulation (Dispensational) Pre-Millennialism, which underscores the literal fulfilment of God's promises of restoration and peace, including those made to Abraham and his offspring. This perspective views Israel and the church as integral parts of God's redemptive narrative, each with its unique role and purpose in unfolding God's eschatological plan.

In sum, pre-tribulation (dispensational) pre-millennialism, God's comprehensive plan for redemption, interprets the relationship between Genesis 3, Genesis 12, and Revelation 20. The fall in Genesis 3 sets the need for redemption in motion, further developed through the covenantal promises in Genesis 12. The narrative reaches its climax in Revelation 20, where the consequences of the fall are rectified through Christ's end-time victory and reign. This perspective emphasises God's sovereignty and the fulfilment of Biblical prophecy, viewing human history as a dispensational journey towards the final restoration of creation as depicted in Revelation.

Dispensationalism is a theological framework for understanding the Bible that divides God's relationship with humanity into distinct periods or dispensations. God's manner of relating to and governing humanity varies in each dispensation. Dispensationalism is particularly noted for its eschatological focus, distinctive views on the church and Israel, and literal interpretation of prophetic scriptures.

Typically, dispensationalists divide history into seven dispensations, although the exact names and durations can vary slightly among different teachers:

1. Innocence (Creation to the Fall): This era extends from creation to Adam and Eve's fall in the Garden of Eden. Humanity is in a state of innocence, without sin, until the fall.
2. Conscience (Fall to Noah): After the fall, humanity lives by the dictates of their conscience, leading up to the great flood in Noah's time.
3. Human Government (Noah to Abraham): Starting with Noah and the flood's aftermath, humans are responsible for governing themselves and upholding justice, as seen in the establishment of capital punishment.
4. Promise (Abraham to Moses): Begins with God's covenant with Abraham, focusing on the promises made to Abraham and his descendants, the Israelites.
5. Law (Moses to Christ): Covers the time from Moses receiving the Law at Sinai to the birth of Jesus Christ, characterised by Israel living under the Mosaic Law.
6. Grace (Christ to the Rapture): The current era, initiated by Christ's death and resurrection, where salvation is offered

INTRODUCTION

through grace. This dispensation is believed to end with the Rapture.

7. **Millennial Kingdom (Second Coming to the Eternal State):** A future thousand-year reign of Christ on earth following His Second Coming, leading to the final judgment and the eternal state.

While often associated predominantly with the church era or the Dispensation of Grace in Christian theology, grace is not exclusive to this period alone. In reality, the concept of grace is a continuous thread woven throughout all the dispensations, each ultimately culminating in judgment.

In the Dispensation of Innocence, grace is evident in God's merciful response to Adam and Eve's sin. Instead of immediate death, they are clothed and promised a future Redeemer (Gen. 3:15, 21). This period ends with the judgment of expulsion from Eden.

From Adam to Noah, grace is seen in God's patience with increasingly wicked humanity during the Dispensation of Conscience. However, this era concludes with the judgment of the Flood (Gen. 6-8).

In the Dispensation of Human Government, following the Flood, God's covenant with Noah (Gen. 9:11) is a display of grace, promising never to destroy the earth with a flood again. However, the Tower of Babel incident (Gen. 11:1-9) shows humanity's unified rebellion against God, leading to the judgment of language confusion and dispersion.

The Dispensation of Promise, initiated with Abraham, is marked by God's gracious covenant to bless all nations through Abraham's seed (Gen. 12:1-3). However, the Egyptian bondage and eventual conquest of Canaan serve as judgments upon both the Israelites (for their failures) and the Canaanites (for their iniquity).

In the Dispensation of Law, grace is seen in God's provision of the sacrificial system as a means to atone for sin (Leviticus). However, this dispensation ends in judgment with the Babylonian captivity due to Israel's continual disobedience and idolatry (2 Chron. 36:15-21).

The Church Age, also known as the Dispensation of Grace, is fundamentally characterised by the ultimate act of grace: Christ's death and resurrection. However, this era is not exempt from the prophesied conclusion marked by judgment. Biblical passages such as Jeremiah 30:7, Daniel 12:1, and Matthew 24:21 foretell a period of unparalleled tribulation and judgment, signalling this dispensation's intense and unique culmination. This forthcoming judgment, unprecedented in its severity, aligns with the creation narrative, which suggests a timeline where the Church Age spans 2000 years. Thus, by this interpretation, the current age, blessed in exceeding grace, moves inexorably towards a destined period of trial and judgment as it reaches its two-millennia mark.

The Millennial Reign, often called the Millennial Kingdom, is a prophetic era distinguished by the physical reign of Jesus Christ on Earth, succeeding the Church Age or the Dispensation of Grace. This period, vividly described in biblical passages such as Zechariah 14 and Revelation 20, is characterised by a harmonious blend of divine governance and grace, with Christ ruling as a just and benevolent monarch. This era stands in contrast to the previous age, primarily defined by Christ's sacrificial death and resurrection, which offered salvation and grace to humanity.

During the Millennial Reign, the world will experience unparalleled peace and righteousness, as prophesied in Zechariah 14. The Lord's rule will extend from Jerusalem, transforming the world into a place of justice and holiness. This epoch represents the fulfilment of numerous prophecies. It is seen as a time when the earth is restored to

INTRODUCTION

its Edenic state, with humanity living in harmony under Christ's direct lordship and leadership.

However, this time of grace and divine rule does not negate the ultimate conclusion of judgment. As Revelation 20 illustrates, following this thousand-year reign, a final judgment occurs, known as the Great White Throne Judgment. This event marks the end of human history as we know it and the beginning of a new, eternal order. All humanity, both living and resurrected, face this final judgment, where deeds and faith are weighed, resulting in eternal destinies being sealed.

The transition from the Millennial Reign to the Great White Throne Judgment underscores the biblical theme of divine justice balancing grace. While the Millennial Reign exemplifies Christ's merciful and righteous rule, the Great White Throne Judgment embodies the final act of religious adjudication, ensuring that justice prevails. This sequential unfolding from grace to judgment reflects the biblical narrative of redemption, judgment, and the eventual restoration of all things under God's sovereign plan.

Building upon the theological framework presented earlier, it is intriguing to delve into how specific interpretations, especially within dispensationalism, draw parallels between the biblical account of creation and the timeline of human history. The Genesis narrative describes God creating the universe in six days and resting on the seventh. In dispensationalist thought, these days are seen as literal 24-hour periods and symbolic of a more expansive timeline. Each "day" in the creation story is equated with a thousand years, thus framing human history within a grand 7,000-year plan.

This interpretation adds a layer of depth to the understanding of the Millennial Reign and the subsequent Great White Throne Judgment. If the six days of creation correspond to 6,000 years of human history, followed by a seventh day of rest, this mirrors the thousand-year reign of Christ as a time of peace and restoration, akin to a Sabbath rest for the earth. This perspective reinforces the cyclical nature of biblical narratives. It emphasises the harmony and continuity between the creation account and the eschatological vision of the future, where history moves towards a divinely ordained climax and resolution.

Under this framework, the six days of creation represent 6,000 years of human history, segmented into various dispensations. Each dispensation is seen as a distinct phase in God's plan, with specific purposes and characteristics. Notably, the Church Age, also known as the Dispensation of Grace, is often attributed to 2,000 years. This interpretation aligns with the "a day is like a thousand years" principle in 2 Peter 3:8 and Psalm 90:4.

Following this, the final or seventh day, God's Day of rest, is paralleled with the Millennial Kingdom, a period of 1,000 years where Christ reigns on Earth, as described in Revelation 20. This millennial period is seen as a time of peace and restoration, mirroring the rest and sanctity of the Sabbath in the creation account.

Again, in the framework of dispensationalism, which often uses the principle "a day is like a thousand years", as found in 2 Peter 3:8 and Psalm 90:4, each of the biblical ages or dispensations is typically associated with a specific time frame. As mentioned previously, this perspective views human history as divided into distinct epochs, each with a unique role in the divine plan. The following is an overview of the time frames typically attributed to each of the preceding ages:

1. The Age of Innocence: Not specifically timed but considered brief.

INTRODUCTION

2. The Age of Conscience: Approximately 1,600 years (from Adam to Noah).
3. The Age of Human Government: Around 400 years (from Noah to Abraham).
4. The Age of Promise: About 430 years (from Abraham to the Exodus).
5. The Age of the Law: Roughly 1,500 years (from the Exodus to Christ's crucifixion).
6. The Church Age (Dispensation of Grace): Approximately 2,000 years (from Christ's crucifixion to the present).
7. The Millennial Reign of Christ: Predicted to last 1,000 years.

Adding these together:

- 1,600 (Conscience) + 400 (Human Government) + 430 (Promise) + 1,500 (Law) + 2,000 (Church Age) + 1,000 (Millennial Reign) = 6,930 years.

This total is less than 7,000 years. However, the specific duration of the Age of Innocence is sometimes defined in years, which could account for the difference to reach 7,000 years. The exact duration of each age is based on interpretations of biblical genealogies and events, and scholars and theologians vary in their interpretations.

By aligning the days of creation with this theological timeline, each "day" or thousand-year period becomes emblematic of a significant phase in God's overarching plan for humanity, from creation to the culmination of history in the Millennial Kingdom. This interpretation allows for a structured understanding of human history and eschatology within the dispensational framework, providing a comprehensive narrative from the creation of Genesis to the prophetic visions of Revelation.

Adding to the Creation story is the parable of the Good Samaritan, hinting at the timing of Jesus' Return. The parable of the Good Samaritan found in Luke 10:25-37, is traditionally understood as a lesson on loving one's neighbour. However, dispensationalists interpret it symbolically in the context of God's plan for the ages. In this interpretation, the injured man represents humanity, the priest and Levite represent the inability of the Law and the Old Covenant to provide ultimate salvation, and the Good Samaritan symbolises Jesus Christ providing salvation. The two days the Samaritan spends at the inn illustrate the two thousand years of the Church Age (based on the principle of "a day is like a thousand years" from 2 Peter 3:8), after which Christ would return.

PRE-TRIBULATION (DISPENSATIONAL) PRE-MILLENNIALISM

Millennial thought is critical in eschatological studies as a pivotal element that influences and determines one's stance on the rapture. This is evident when examining various millennial perspectives and their corresponding views on the rapture. For instance, in Pre-tribulation (Dispensational) Pre-Millennialism, the belief is that the rapture occurs before a seven-year tribulation period, reflecting an interpretation of an imminent return of Christ and a clear distinction between the church and Israel in God's plan. In contrast, Post-tribulation Pre-Millennialism posits that the rapture and the Second Coming of Christ are singular events after the tribulation. This view emphasises the church's perseverance through trials, aligning with the notion of the church experiencing the tribulation before Christ's millennial reign.

On the other hand, post-millennialism typically does not emphasise a specific rapture event before the millennium, as it envisions Christ's return after the church has influenced a significant transformation of the world. Finally, Amillennialism views the rapture symbolically or as coinciding with the final judgment rather than as a separate event, in line with its non-literal interpretation of the millennium. These millennial perspectives directly shape adherents' conception of the rapture, demonstrating millennial thought's integral role in the broader framework of Christian eschatology.

As mentioned earlier, the pre-tribulation, pre-millennial view, deeply rooted in dispensational theology, offers a comprehensive interpretation of biblical prophecy and eschatology, particularly concerning the end times. This perspective organises human history into distinct periods or dispensations, each characterised by God's unique interactions with humanity. At the heart of this theology lies the pre-tribulation rapture concept, suggesting that the church will be raptured or 'caught up' with Christ before a period of intense global tribulation begins.

Again, in the dispensational framework, these eras include innocence (from creation to the fall), conscience (from the fall to Noah), human government (Noah to Abraham), promise (Abraham to Moses), law (Moses to Christ), grace or the Church Age (Christ to the rapture), and the Millennial Kingdom (following the rapture). The current dispensation, known as the Church Age or Age of Grace, is marked by Christ's death and resurrection, offering salvation through grace. This age is seen as a unique period in which the church is central to God's divine plan, distinctly separate from His dealings with Israel or the rest of humanity.

The pre-tribulation rapture theory posits that the Church Age will end with the church being raptured, initiating the final dispensation leading to Christ's millennial reign. This view is supported by New Testament scriptures such as Luke 21:34-36, which discuss the possibility of escaping the impending tribulation (the possibility refers to those remaining free from the world), and John 14:2-3, 1 Thessalonians 4:16-17, and 1 Corinthians 15:51-52, which depict the sudden gathering of believers with Christ. Revelation 3:10 further reinforces this perspective by promising protection from a global trial.

This doctrine, far from being a modern concept, is firmly grounded in early Christian teachings. Throughout Christian history, the anticipation of Christ's return and the church's deliverance from forthcoming wrath have been recurrent themes. Prophetic events like the rise of the antichrist and the Middle Eastern peace treaty referenced in Daniel

INTRODUCTION

9:24-27, along with the progression of the tribulation, are understood to take place after the rapture in the dispensationalist view.

For believers, this perspective emphasises the importance of vigilance and preparedness for the imminent rapture. It also provides a lens through which to interpret current and future global events in light of biblical prophecy. While some critics challenge the pre-tribulation rapture view as escapist or lacking explicit scriptural backing, it is arguably consistent with the overall narrative of redemption and God's historical pattern of rescuing His people before periods of judgment, as demonstrated in Old Testament examples like Noah and Lot.

Within the pre-tribulation (dispensational) pre-millennial view, a fascinating school of thought draws parallels between biblical figures and groups to illustrate the rapture and tribulation concept. This interpretation uses the stories of Enoch, Noah, and Lot as typological representations of different groups in the end times. Enoch, whom God took up before the Flood (Gen. 5:24), is seen as a symbol of the church, which will be raptured or 'caught up' before the tribulation. This aligns with the pre-tribulation rapture theory, suggesting that the church, like Enoch, will be removed from the earth before the outpouring of God's wrath.

Noah, on the other hand, is viewed as representing Israel. Though he lived through the Flood, he was kept safe in the ark, mirroring the belief that Israel would endure the tribulation, but a remnant would be somewhat preserved. This is paralleled in Revelation 12, where a portion of Israel finds refuge during the tribulation. However, Zechariah 13:8-9 foretells that two-thirds of the people in the land will be cut off and perish. Nevertheless, a third will be left in it, suggesting significant suffering for Israel during this period.

The world at large, enduring the full brunt of the tribulation, is often likened to the figure of Lot. Lot's experience in Sodom and Gomorrah (Genesis 19) – living through the destruction, yet ultimately being saved – represents those who will live through the tribulation without the protective removal experienced by the Church. Despite being surrounded by judgment, Lot's deliverance is a typological representation of those who turn to faith during the tribulation, surviving its horrors and witnessing the Second Coming of Christ.

This interpretation weaves a compelling narrative that supports the pre-tribulation rapture theory. It suggests a clear distinction between the Church, Israel, and the rest of the world in the end times, each experiencing God's plan for the tribulation differently, aligning with the segmented approach of dispensationalism. These typological parallels offer an insightful perspective into the dispensational understanding of end-time events, emphasising different groups' unique roles and destinies as God's eschatological plan unfolds.

Significantly, Paul's letters to the Thessalonians contribute to the foundational understanding of this theory within dispensationalism. In these epistles, Paul addresses the Thessalonian church's concerns about the fate of believers who had died before Christ's return. In 1 Thessalonians 4:15-17, he assures them that the deceased in Christ will rise first at Jesus' return, followed by the living believers being raptured. This teaching was intended to provide comfort and hope, affirming that the living and the dead in Christ would partake in His triumphant return.

Further, Paul clarifies in 1 Thessalonians 5:9 that the church is not destined for God's wrath, suggesting its removal before the tribulation. This aligns with the dispensationalist view that the church is meant for

INTRODUCTION

salvation through Christ, not for enduring the divine judgment of the tribulation.

In 2 Thessalonians, Paul delves into the sequence of end-time events, discussing the revelation of the 'man of lawlessness' or the antichrist and indicating that this figure cannot be revealed until a restraining force, often interpreted as the Holy Spirit operating through the church, is removed. This supports the idea that the rapture of the church must occur before the tribulation can begin.

Paul also acknowledges the presence of evil during the Church Age but notes that its full manifestation is restrained by the church, empowered by the Holy Spirit. This suggests that the church's role is to limit the full emergence of lawlessness until its removal at the time of the rapture.

In essence, the pre-tribulation (dispensational) pre-millennial view, focusing on the imminent rapture of the church, seamlessly integrates into the larger dispensational framework. This perspective shapes believers' understanding of end-time events. It influences their spiritual lives, emphasising the urgency of Christ's return and the importance of living in a state of readiness and faithfulness.

Adding to the abundance of scriptural support, as mentioned under the topic referring to the pre-tribulation nature, of the pre-tribulation (dispensational) pre-millennial view, supported by the teachings of early church fathers, lends substantial weight to the pre-tribulation rapture theory. As mentioned earlier, this doctrine, suggesting believers will be taken to heaven before a period of tribulation, is not merely a construct of modern theology but has deep roots in Christian thought, dating back to the church's earliest centuries.

In the 1st century, documents such as Clement of Rome's First Epistle to the Corinthians and Polycarp's The Epistle to the Philippians, along with The Didache, contain allusions to the gathering of the faithful, hinting at a pre- or post-tribulation rapture. These texts reveal an early Christian anticipation of Christ's return and a gathering of believers, indicative of a developing understanding of the rapture.

The 2nd century further enriches this eschatological perspective. In his seminal work 'Against Heresies,' Irenaeus explores themes related to the church being caught up, potentially before a tribulation period. Similarly, Tertullian's "A Treatise on the Soul" delves into the bodily resurrection and translation of the saints, alluding to a pre-tribulation event.

The 3rd century saw Victorinus' Commentary on the Apocalypse and Methodius of Olympus' writings, which support the notion of a pre-tribulation rapture with references to believers being spared from tribulation. These early interpretations present a compelling case for the rapture before the tribulation period, resonating with the dispensational pre-millennial framework.

The 4th-century contributions from Ephraim the Syrian, notably in his work "On the Last Times" and the sermon "Sermon on the End of the World," attributed to Pseudo-Ephraem, further fortify this doctrine. These texts discuss the gathering of saints and the elect before the tribulation, showcasing an early Christian expectation of a pre-tribulation rapture.

However, from the 5th to the 17th centuries, there was a notable silence on detailed eschatological theories, including the rapture. This gap can be attributed to the church's focus on establishing orthodoxy and surviving political turmoil rather than developing intricate end-time scenarios. The pre-tribulation rapture theory regained prominence in the 18th and 19th centuries. It was significantly influenced by John

INTRODUCTION

Nelson Darby and popularised through C.I. Scofield's annotations in the Scofield Reference Bible.

From Clement to Ephraim, the early Christian texts collectively present a tapestry of thought that supports the pre-tribulation rapture theory. These writings, infused with anticipations of Christ's return and the gathering of believers, lay a foundational understanding of the rapture that aligns with the dispensational pre-millennial view. They underscore an early recognition of critical themes such as Christ's sudden and imminent return, the importance of holiness and vigilance among believers, and the church's role in the broader eschatological narrative.

This historical lineage of the rapture concept demonstrates its deep-seated roots in Christian theology. The teachings of early church fathers, coupled with scriptural evidence, provide a robust argument for the pre-tribulation rapture. They affirm that this doctrine is not an afterthought or a modern innovation but an integral part of the Christian eschatological tradition, tracing back to the church's earliest days.

In conclusion, Pre-Tribulation (Dispensational) Pre-Millennialism presents a comprehensive and historically grounded view of eschatology that resonates deeply with scriptural teachings and the early church's doctrines. This perspective, which interprets human history as divided into distinct dispensations culminating in Christ's millennial reign, is anchored in a pre-tribulation rapture theory. The theory posits that the church will be raptured, or 'caught up,' with Christ before a period of great tribulation, supported by a thorough examination of scriptures from Genesis to Revelation.

The foundational pillars of this view are found in the critical connections among key biblical chapters: the fall of man in Genesis 3, the Abrahamic Covenant in Genesis 12, and the prophetic visions in Revelation 20. These chapters collectively trace the narrative arc of sin, covenantal promises, and ultimate redemption through Christ's second coming. They form the basis of the dispensationalist approach, emphasising God's sovereignty and the fulfilment of biblical prophecies across different eras of human history.

The biblical narrative, and the historical evidence from the early church fathers to contemporary theologians, underscores the legitimacy and depth of the pre-tribulation (dispensational) pre-millennial view. It affirms that the rapture doctrine and its timing relative to the tribulation has been a subject of contemplation and belief among Christians for centuries. These layers of scriptural interpretation and historical theology provide a solid foundation for believers who subscribe to this perspective, encouraging the church to live in a state of preparedness and faithfulness while anticipating Christ's imminent return. Thus, Pre-tribulation (Dispensational) Pre-Millennialism stands as a compelling and well-substantiated viewpoint within Christian eschatology, offering insights into the nature of God's plan for humanity and the ultimate destiny of the church and Israel.

POST-TRIBULATION, HISTORICAL, AND PRE-WRATH PRE-MILLENNIALISM

In the diverse landscape of Christian eschatology, the concept of Pre-millennialism has significantly impacted theological discourse. This doctrine, which divides principally into Dispensational Pre-millennialism and Historic Pre-millennialism, is centred on the belief that the second coming of Christ will precede a thousand-year reign, commonly referred to as the Millennium. Each of these strains offers nuanced and distinct perspectives, particularly in their views on the timing and nature of the rapture and the interplay between the church and Israel.

While the post-tribulation rapture theory has been previously addressed, this section will serve as a refresher and an introduction to Historic Pre-millennialism. We will be taking another look at the pre-wrath interpretation, focusing on its distinct characteristics.

Pre-millennialism, a significant viewpoint in Christian eschatology, is broadly categorised into Dispensational Pre-millennialism and Historic Pre-millennialism. Both theories share the belief that the return of Christ will precede a thousand-year reign, known as the Millennium. However, they diverge significantly in their interpretations of this period's events, particularly their views on the rapture and the relationship between the church and Israel.

The pre-millennial post-tribulation rapture theory, integral to Historic Pre-millennialism, argues that the rapture and the second coming of Jesus will occur simultaneously. Proponents of this view believe believers will meet Christ in the air following the tribulation, returning to earth to begin the millennial reign. This interpretation contrasts sharply with Dispensational Premillennialism, which supports a pre-tribulation rapture theory. According to this view, believers are raptured to heaven before the tribulation, thus avoiding the associated troubles.

Historic Pre-millennialism's roots are said to extend back to the early church, making it one of the earliest forms of pre-millennial thought. This view was prevalent until the rise of Augustine of Hippo (354–430 AD), who was instrumental in the development of Amillennialism. Early church figures, such as Papias of Hierapolis, Justin Martyr, and Irenaeus of Lyons, were known proponents of the pre-millennial stance. Despite its early origins, Historic Pre-millennialism was overshadowed by Amillennialism and Post-millennialism, particularly after Augustine's influential works. However, the 19th and 20th centuries saw a revival in interest towards Historic Pre-millennialism, mainly due to the efforts of theologians like John Nelson Darby, C.I. Scofield and George Eldon Ladd (1911–1982), whose work "The Blessed Hope" played a pivotal role in this resurgence.

One of the key differences between Historic and Dispensational Pre-millennialism lies in their respective views of the church and Israel. Historic Pre-millennialism views the church and Israel as part of a continuous narrative of God's people. This perspective is supported by passages like Galatians 3:26-29 and Ephesians 2:11-13, which emphasise the unity of Jewish and Gentile believers in Christ. Conversely, Dispensational Pre-millennialism maintains a clear distinction between the church and Israel, each having distinct roles in God's plan.

As mentioned earlier, another significant divergence is seen in the timing of the rapture. Dispensationalists believe in a pre-tribulation rapture, where the church is taken from the earth before the period of intense suffering begins. In contrast, Historic Pre-millennialism posits

INTRODUCTION

that the rapture and Christ's return are post-tribulation events, implying that believers will experience the tribulation period and be raptured at Christ's return.

The approach to biblical prophecy also differentiates these perspectives. Historic Pre-millennialists often adopt a more allegorical and liberal interpretation, open to varied fulfillments of prophecies. They acknowledge that the specifics of end times may be beyond current understanding, reflecting the unexpected ways in which Old Testament prophecies were fulfilled by Christ's first coming. Dispensational Pre-millennialists, however, generally favour a more literal and structured interpretation of prophecy, closely aligning New Testament revelations with Old Testament prophecies.

Historic Pre-millennialism's post-tribulation view of the rapture significantly influences its adherents' understanding of suffering and tribulation as integral to the Christian experience. It encourages believers to endure trials as part of their spiritual journey, anticipating ultimate redemption at Christ's return. This perspective promotes a holistic reading of scripture, emphasising the continuity between the Old and New Testaments and the shared heritage of Jewish and Christian believers.

The post-tribulation, pre-wrath rapture theory represents a unique standpoint within the spectrum of eschatological interpretations. This theory seeks to bridge traditional post-tribulation and pre-tribulation views by proposing that the rapture occurs post-tribulation but before the full manifestation of God's wrath, as depicted in the Book of Revelation, commencing from the sixth seal in chapter 6. It suggests that the seven-year tribulation, linked to Daniel's 70th Week, begins with a significant event like signing a peace treaty in the Middle East. This period is bifurcated into the first 3.5 years as the tribulation phase and the latter half as the Great Tribulation. Scriptural passages from

Matthew (24), Daniel (7, 9), and Revelation (11, 12, 13) support this division, particularly emphasising the intensified tribulation in the latter 3.5 years.

The post-tribulation, pre-wrath view maintains that the church will experience tribulation but be spared from God's wrath, unleashed following the rapture. This interpretation aligns with the belief that believers will endure persecution and hardship during the tribulation but will be shielded from the divine judgment reserved for the unrepentant. The church, facing trials from satanic, antichristian, and worldly sources, is not subject to God's wrath, as affirmed in 1 Thessalonians 5:9. This theory distinguishes the initial seal judgments in Revelation 6 from God's wrath (6:17), viewing them as resulting from satanic or antichristian forces (12:17).

However, the post-tribulation theories encounter several challenges. A key issue is the interpretation of the "elect" in Matthew 24:22, 31, which refers to Israel and new believers saved during the tribulation rather than the church. The understanding that the first seal judgments are not God's wrath is contested since Christ, as the Lamb, initiates and orchestrates these judgments (Rev. 5-6:1). This challenges the premise that the church will not experience God's wrath when going through any part of the tribulation.

Another contentious point is the role of the Holy Spirit during the tribulation, as suggested in 2 Thessalonians 2. If the Spirit is removed, it raises questions about the church's existence and effectiveness during this period. Additionally, the conversion of people during the tribulation, traditionally attributed to the Spirit's work, becomes problematic.

The absence of the term "church" in the narrative of Revelation from chapters 3:10 to 22:16 complicates the post-tribulation view, especially

INTRODUCTION

if the church is to endure the tribulation. This notable absence raises questions about the church's role and presence during this period.

Furthermore, the promise to the church of Philadelphia in Revelation 3:10 suggests a form of protection or preservation distinct from enduring the tribulation, contrasting with the message to the church in Smyrna, which does not receive the same assurance.

The timing of the trumpet and bowl judgments within the seven-year tribulation presents particular difficulties for the pre-wrath theory. If the tribulation encompasses the entire period, there is little room for these extensive judgments (sixth and seventh seals, the seven trumpets, and the seven bowls) described in the Book of Revelation 6:12 to 16:21.

Lastly, the post-tribulation theory struggles to reconcile the promise in John 14:2 of a place prepared in the Father's house, traditionally understood as heaven, with the rapid return of believers to earth for Christ's millennial reign. This apparent contradiction gives rise to the "yo-yo" theory critique, suggesting a swift transition of believers between heaven and earth.

In conclusion, while the post-tribulation and pre-wrath rapture theories offer a nuanced view of end-times events, they face substantial theological and interpretative challenges. The theories attempt to bridge traditional post-tribulation and pre-tribulation views but encounter obstacles in scriptural interpretation, the role of the Holy Spirit, and the timing and nature of God's wrath.

In stark contrast, as discussed previously, the pre-tribulation, pre-millennial position presents several compelling arguments more closely aligned with biblical prophecy and eschatology. This perspective maintains a clear distinction between the church and Israel, which is vital for understanding their different roles in God's plan, especially during the tribulation. The tribulation, referred to as "Jacob's Trouble," is seen as primarily directed towards Israel, supported by the absence of the church in the tribulation narratives of the book of Revelation.

The doctrine of Christ's imminent return is central to the pre-tribulation theory, in line with New Testament teachings that encourage believers always to be ready for Christ's return. This sense of imminence is less compatible with post-tribulation views, which necessitate certain tribulation events before Christ's return.

The pre-tribulation interpretation also emphasises believers' deliverance from God's wrath, which is consistent with God's historical pattern of sparing His people, as evidenced in the deliverances of Enoch, Noah, and Lot. Furthermore, scripture portrays the tribulation as a period of divine judgment distinct from the general trials faced by Christians, not intended for the church but for the judgment of the world and the fulfilment of prophecies concerning Israel.

The role of the Holy Spirit, as discussed in 2 Thessalonians 2:6-7, is interpreted by pre-tribulationists as the Holy Spirit in the church. This interpretation supports the view that the church must be removed before the revelation of the antichrist, further bolstering the pre-tribulation stance.

In conclusion, the pre-millennial, pre-tribulation rapture theory offers a coherent narrative encompassing scripture's teachings on the end times. It maintains the distinction between Israel and the church, the imminence of Christ's return, the church's exemption from God's wrath, and the continuous role of the Holy Spirit. While Historic Premillennialism and the pre-wrath theory provide alternative perspectives, the pre-tribulation, pre-millennial position offers a more consistent and scripturally aligned interpretation, giving hope and comfort to believers in Christ's protective providence and imminent return.

POST-MILLENNIALISM

Post-millennialism is another Christian doctrine that offers an optimistic view of the end times. It focuses on the thousand-year reign of Christ as described in the Book of Revelation (Rev. 20:1-7). This doctrine differs from premillennialism, which suggests that Christ's return will initiate a literal thousand-year reign. In contrast, postmillennialism suggests that the Second Coming of Christ will occur after a period of Christianisation of the world (cf. Matt 24:14). This period, metaphorically referred to as 'the Millennium,' is envisioned as a time when the gospel will bring about global peace, justice, and prosperity. It symbolises a prolonged phase of Christian ascendance and societal transformation rather than a literal period of a thousand years.

Building on the concept of post-millennialism, it is important to contrast this with amillennialism, another Christian eschatological view. While post-millennialism envisions a future golden age of Christian dominance leading to Christ's return, amillennialism offers a different perspective. It interprets the Millennium mentioned in Revelation not as a future, literal thousand-year reign on earth but as a current, symbolic period. In the amillennial view, the Millennium is seen as the ongoing reign of Christ, primarily in a spiritual sense, which commenced with His first coming and will continue until His second coming. This perspective does not anticipate a specific era of global Christian dominance before Christ's return. Instead, it views the present church age as fulfilling the prophesied Millennium, symbolising Christ's spiritual reign with His followers rather than anticipating a distinct, earthly utopian period.

Post-millennialism's development within Christian theology follows a nuanced historical trajectory. The earliest seeds of this eschatological viewpoint can be found in the rise of Christendom, particularly significant after Emperor Constantine declared Christianity as the Roman Empire's official religion in A.D. 313. This event led to a dramatic growth in the Christian population and a transformation within the Empire, fostering a victorious and optimistic outlook among Christians. However, this optimism was later challenged by various historical setbacks.

As Christian thought progressed, Augustine, a key figure in early Christian theology, played a crucial role in shaping eschatological views. Augustine interpreted the millennium as the period between Christ's first and second comings, a view more in line with amillennialism due to its lack of post-millennial optimism.

The Reformation era brought a different perspective. Protestant reformers like Luther and Calvin had a predominantly bleak view of history, which contrasted sharply with the optimistic outlook of post-millennialism. Calvin's theology, while somewhat progressive, did not align with post-millennial ideas.

In the post-Reformation era, post-millennialism began to gain more clarity and refinement. This period saw a shift in eschatological perspectives, influenced by changing cultural, social, and religious landscapes. Daniel Whitby (1638-1725) emerged as a key figure. Recognised for refining systematic post-millennialism, Whitby's work synthesised existing post-reformation elements into a coherent system, marking a significant evolution from amillennialism and profoundly impacting post-millennial thought.

Post-millennialism peaked in the seventeenth century, focusing on the successful preaching of the gospel and the conversion of Jews.

INTRODUCTION

However, its influence waned after the French Revolution and during the World Wars, partly due to its association with the Social Gospel and Liberalism. The doctrine saw a resurgence in the 1970s through the reconstructionist movement but remains a minor position in modern eschatological thought.

Following the historical context of post-millennialism development, contemporary figures like Kenneth L. Gentry Jr. have furthered the doctrine in modern times. Gentry, a prominent figure in Reformed theology and an ordained minister in the Reformed Presbyterian Church and General Assembly, is known for his advocacy and scholarly contributions to orthodox preterism and post-millennialism. He is also a strong supporter of theonomy and a fervent proponent of reconstructionism, a theological stance characterised by seven fundamental principles. These principles emphasise the onset of God's kingdom with Jesus' earthly ministry, highlighting its redemptive and spiritual nature and potential for significant societal transformation.

Kenneth L. Gentry Jr.'s understanding of post-millennialism aligns with contemporary theological movements like "Kingdom Now" theology and the "Seven Mountain Mandate." Movements such as the New Apostolic Reformation (NAR) are key proponents of Kingdom Now theology, urging the church to participate actively in societal reform. Influenced by figures like R.J. Rushdoony (1916–2001), these modern approaches to post-millennialism call for a proactive Christian engagement in societal affairs, emphasising the church's role in transforming various aspects of life. Additionally, this theology is often referred to as dominionism, a belief highlighted by leaders like Bill Johnson, which holds that the church is destined to dominate the earth by spreading the gospel and bringing heaven's ruling principles down to earth. This concept extends the post-millennial vision that anticipates a world increasingly shaped and enhanced by Christian values and teachings.

Prominent leaders, such as Lance Wallnau and the above-mentioned Bill Johnson of Bethel Church, Redding, California, are at the forefront of promoting the "Seven Mountains of Culture" concept today. As mentioned earlier, they believe that it is essential for the church to engage with culture by actively shaping society according to Christian principles and values. Wallnau refers to himself as a 'futurist', claiming to be the first to introduce this fresh template to explain how Christians must engage with culture in the 21st century.

Subscribers of the Seven Mountain Mandate use Revelation 17:8-12 as a key scriptural reference. Traditionally, this passage is interpreted as revealing the final earthly kingdoms before the return of Jesus, highlighting the revived Roman Empire under the rule of the antichrist (the seventh kingdom), followed by a New World Order and a One World Leader, identified as the antichrist (the eighth kingdom). However, subscribers to the Seven Mountain Mandate employ this passage symbolically. They view the "beasts" and "kings" mentioned in these verses not as literal end-time kings and figures but as representations of contemporary societal structures and powers. This symbolic interpretation is applied to their mission of influencing and transforming various sectors of society - including government, media, and education - to reflect Christian values. In this way, the Seven Mountain Mandate diverges from a traditional eschatological view, focusing instead on Christians' present and active role in shaping societal "mountains" according to their faith.

While post-millennialism has garnered support and advocacy from notable figures within Christian theology, it has not been without its share of criticism, especially from those who align themselves

INTRODUCTION

with premillennial perspectives. One of the primary critiques towards post-millennialism revolves around its perceived overestimation of humanity's capacity to establish the kingdom of God on Earth, ostensibly without the necessity of a literal return, rule, and reign by Jesus Christ.

In examining the optimistic outlook of post-millennialism, which foresees a world gradually improving before the second coming of Jesus Christ, Scripture presents a contrasting narrative. The Bible depicts a reality of escalating wickedness in a world distanced from God, challenging the utopian vision of post-millennialism. This divergence begins with humanity's expulsion from Eden in Genesis 3:22-24, setting a stage where self-centeredness, greed, and hedonism prevail, as described in 2 Timothy 3:1-5.

The Book of Ecclesiastes delves deeper into this theme. It reflects on the futility of trying to recreate Eden's paradise through earthly efforts, culminating in the realisation that life without God is meaningless. This sentiment resonates in the New Testament, particularly in Romans 8:18-25, where Paul speaks of a creation groaning for redemption and Christians eagerly awaiting Christ's return and the renewal of all things.

Contrasting sharply with the challenges of today's world, the prophecy in Isaiah 65:17-25 imagines a transformed reality where joy and peace replace sorrow. In a different vein, the Gospel of Matthew (24:6-8) and passages from Jeremiah 30:7, Daniel 12:1-2, Joel 2:2, and the Book of Revelation depict a future escalating into chaos and tribulation as Christ's return approaches. This foretold future is marked by widespread global strife, a period of extraordinary difficulty following the church's departure, as revealed through Luke 21:34-36, 1 Corinthians 15:51-52, 1 Thessalonians 4:15-17, 5:9, 2 Thessalonians 2:1, 3, 6-7, and Revelation 3:10, 4:1; cf. 11:12.

When considering the tribulation period (Rev. 6-19) following the removal of the church, an analysis based on the current global population, estimated at 8 billion, paints a striking picture. This analysis includes roughly 1.9885 billion children, per the United Nations Population Fund's 2023 data, who are envisaged as part of the raptured population. With an initial population of 8 billion, this group of children is taken away first. The analysis further estimates that 1% of the remaining adult population is also raptured (cf. Matt. 71:3-14, Lu. 13:22-30).

During the unfolding of prophetic events described in the Book of Revelation, including the Seal (Rev. 6), Trumpet (Rev. 8-15), and Bowl Judgments (Rev. 16), followed by the climactic battle marking the return of Jesus Christ (Rev. 19), the global population undergoes dramatic shifts. Initially, approximately 2.049 billion people, comprising both children and adults, are taken away in the rapture, leaving around 5.951 billion behind. The Seal Judgments lead to a 25% decrease in this number, resulting in a population of about 4.463 billion. This figure is further diminished to approximately 1.3225 billion following the first three Trumpet Judgments and then to around 955.5 million after the 4th to 6th Trumpet Judgments. The proposed impact of the Bowl Judgments is assumed to be a 50% reduction, reducing the remaining population to about 663.9 million. The series of events culminates with the final battle, potentially seeing a further 90% reduction, leaving an estimated 66.4 million people to enter the Millennial Kingdom. This final population represents a mere 0.83% of the original 8 billion, illustrating the profound and catastrophic changes prophesied for the end times.

When the above-mentioned scenario is compared to historical tragedies such as the Roman siege of Jerusalem in 70 AD and the Holocaust

INTRODUCTION

during World War II, the magnitude of human suffering and loss becomes even more apparent. The Jewish-Roman War, culminating in the siege of Jerusalem as recounted by Flavius Josephus, is estimated to have resulted in around 1.1 million deaths, though this number is subject to debate. Additionally, about 97,000 people were captured and enslaved. This event, particularly marked by the destruction of the Second Temple, was a pivotal moment in Jewish history, signifying substantial cultural and religious upheaval.

Dwarfing the Roman siege of Jerusalem in 70 AD was the Holocaust during World War II, which led to the systematic extermination of approximately 6 million Jews, an atrocity on an unimaginably vast scale. This genocide, executed with chilling efficiency and brutality, stands as one of the darkest chapters in human history.

When comparing these historical events to the catastrophic scenarios depicted in the Book of Revelation, such as the massive global population reductions through the Seal, Trumpet, and Bowl Judgments, there is a clear disparity in scale. Revelation outlines that the tribulation period suggests an apocalyptic decline in the global population, from an initial 8 billion to a mere 66.4 million survivors. Again, this represents a reduction to only about 0.83% of the original population, a level of devastation far exceeding anything recorded in human history, including the tragic events of 70 AD and the Holocaust.

This comparison brings into question the preterist, post-millennial interpretation of the Book of Revelation, which posits that its prophecies were fulfilled in the first century, particularly with the fall of Jerusalem in 70 AD. The sheer magnitude of the prophesied tribulation, as envisioned in Revelation, dwarfs even the horrors of the Holocaust.

The analysis concludes that the events described in Revelation, when taken literally, anticipate a scale of global catastrophe far beyond what has been historically experienced, including in World War II. Therefore, from this perspective, the preterist view needs to be revised in accounting for the prophetic scope and scale outlined in the Book of Revelation.

As mentioned earlier, the concept of post-millennialism paints a picture of a consistently improving world. However, the scriptural narrative tells a different story, depicting a chaotic and complicated world during the end times. It highlights the deep yearning for redemption and renewal in a world that is affected by the fall, culminating in the promise of a new creation. The Bible perspective emphasises that true hope and restoration can only be achieved through a restored relationship with God, which can be obtained by accepting Jesus Christ. It stresses that a life without God and the actual, physical return of Jesus Christ is ultimately doomed (cf. Matt 24:22).

Another contentious aspect of postmillennial thought is the concept of supersessionism, or the notion that the church has assumed the role and the promises initially made to Israel in the Bible. This school of thought is directly challenged by passages like Romans 11:1-2a, 29, which articulately state, "I ask, then, has God rejected His people? By no means! ... for God's gifts and the calling God are able." These verses affirm the unending nature of God's covenant with Israel, indicating that the church has not supplanted Israel in God's overarching plan. This scriptural evidence points towards continuity in God's relationship with Israel, coexisting with the church's role in the broader narrative of salvation history instead of replacing one with the other.

Further addressing the issue of supersessionism, the Bible presents two poignant metaphors that elucidate the relationships between God, Israel, and the church. Paul portrays the church as the bride of Christ in his epistles to the Corinthians (2 Corinthians 11:2) and

INTRODUCTION

Ephesians (Ephesians 5:25-27). Paul likens his role to preparing a bride – the church – for her one husband, Christ, symbolising a relationship marked by purity, devotion, and anticipation. This allegorical imagery is echoed in Ephesians, where Paul parallels a husband's love for his wife and Christ's sacrificial love for the church. In this analogy, Christ is shown as sanctifying the church, purifying her to present her spotless and unblemished.

In stark contrast, the Old Testament frequently depicts Israel as the wife of God, signifying a profound covenant relationship yet one that is tarnished by Israel's spiritual infidelity, as exemplified in the books of Jeremiah (Chapter 3) and Ezekiel (Chapter 16). This portrayal forms a striking contrast to the devoted imagery of the church as the bride of Christ. Nonetheless, the narrative concerning Israel does not conclude with alienation. As per Romans 11:25 and subsequent verses in the New Testament, there is an anticipated future restoration, wherein Israel's spiritual hardening is prophesied to last only until the full number of the Gentiles has been realised – a moment often associated with the rapture of the church. Following this pivotal event, Israel is predicted to experience a significant spiritual reawakening during the tribulation, as delineated in Revelation 7, leading a multitude to faith.

The Book of Revelation further elaborates this overarching theme of the relationship between God, Israel, and the church. Revelation 19:7-9 articulately describes the "marriage supper of the Lamb," where the bride, the church, is depicted as having prepared herself for Christ. Adorned in fine, clean linen, the church is shown rejoicing in fulfilling its divine union. Additional 21:2, 9-10 also presents a prophetic vision of the New Jerusalem descending from heaven, portrayed as "a bride beautifully dressed for her husband." This imagery encapsulates the culmination of God's plan for Jews and Gentiles, unified in the bride, the wife of the Lamb – a representation of the ultimate fulfilment of divine promises and the harmonious unification of the narratives of both the Old and New Testaments.

In conclusion, post-millennialism presents an optimistic outlook on Christian eschatology, focusing on a metaphorical millennium symbolising a period of Christian dominance and societal transformation. This doctrine, significantly shaped by figures like Daniel Whitby and Kenneth L. Gentry Jr., contrasts with premillennialism by placing Christ's Second Coming after a period of global Christianisation. While post-millennialism peaked in the seventeenth century and experienced a resurgence in the 1970s through the reconstructionist movement, it remains a less dominant view in Christian eschatology, facing criticism for its optimistic view of human progress and issues like supersessionism.

The doctrine's association with modern movements like "Kingdom Now" theology and the "Seven Mountain Mandate" reflects its enduring influence and the continued efforts of leaders like Lance Wallnau and Bill Johnson to promote active Christian societal engagement. However, the critical perspective highlights a potential overestimation of humanity's capacity to establish God's kingdom on earth and conflicts with sound scriptural teachings.

Furthermore, as illustrated through biblical metaphors, the relationship between the church, Israel, and God presents a more complex narrative. While the church is depicted as the bride of Christ, symbolising purity and devotion, Israel was portrayed as God's wife, marked by a covenant relationship and spiritual infidelity. Nevertheless, the narrative anticipates a future reconciliation and restoration of Israel, signifying the inclusive nature of God's plan for both Jews and Gentiles.

AMILLENNIALISM

Amillennialism and postmillennialism represent divergent paths within Christian eschatology, each interpreting biblical prophecy distinctively. Postmillennialism is optimistic about the future, envisaging a world where Christian principles increasingly prevail, leading to Christ's return. Conversely, amillennialism interprets the millennium mentioned in Revelation symbolically, seeing the current church age as this period, focusing on Christ's spiritual reign rather than a future earthly Christian dominance.

This view contrasts with postmillennialism and Kingdom Now theology (Dominionism), which anticipates a future era marked by Christian dominance. Amillennialism underscores Christ's ongoing spiritual authority, reflected in the church and believers' lives, focusing on the present rather than a utopian pre-Second Coming society.

Understanding eschatology correctly is crucial, with debates centred on the scriptural support for amillennialism and postmillennialism. These views are argued to lack robust biblical backing, shaped more by external influences than scriptural exegesis, contrasting with premillennialism. Premillennialism, rooted in a consistent literal interpretation of the Bible, aligns with the biblical narrative and provides a coherent end to history. It emphasises the importance of scriptural fidelity in eschatological understanding, asserting its historical and theological precedence over amillennial and postmillennial interpretations.

The evolution of amillennialism within Christian theology marks a notable shift from the victorious and optimistic perspective that became prominent with the rise of Christendom, especially following Emperor

Constantine's embrace of Christianity. It introduces an alternative understanding of the end times, downplaying the concept of a triumphant earthly reign to highlight the spiritual influence of Christ and His church. This amillennial perspective is principally shaped by interpreting key scriptural passages, especially Revelation 20:1-7. In this scripture, which proposes the idea of a thousand-year reign, amillennialists interpret the millennium symbolically. As mentioned earlier, they see it not as a future, tangible thousand-year reign of Christ on earth but as an enduring spiritual reign. This approach is consistent with amillennialism's focus on Christ's present spiritual authority and influence, forming a clear juxtaposition with postmillennialism's emphasis on a future-oriented Christian dominance.

This amillennial interpretation is further supported by several other key biblical passages. In Matthew 28:20, Christ assures His disciples of His presence "to the very end of the age." Amillennialism interprets this as affirming Christ's perpetual spiritual reign and His continuous presence with believers. According to amillennialism, this verse is evidence that Christ's kingdom is not just a future expectation but a present reality, with Christ actively reigning in the lives of believers and guiding the church throughout all ages.

According to its subscribers, 2 Peter 3:8 also reinforces the amillennial perspective: "With the Lord, a day is like a thousand years, and a thousand years are like a day." Amillennialists interpret this as a poetic expression of God's timelessness, suggesting that the 'thousand years' mentioned in Revelation should not be understood in literal human terms but rather as a symbolic expression of God's eternal nature and the transcendent aspect of Christ's reign.

Another supporting passage, according to subscribers, is found in 1 Corinthians 15:22-26, where Paul discusses Christ's victory over death

INTRODUCTION

and the subjugation of all enemies, including death itself. Amillennialists view this as indicative of the current spiritual triumph of Christ over sin and death, demonstrating that Christ's kingdom is already manifesting its power and influence, primarily through the church's witness and the transformative experience of salvation among believers.

John 18:36 is said to provide further theological grounding for amillennialism, where Jesus states, "My kingdom is not of this world." This declaration reinforces that Christ's kingdom is primarily spiritual, countering notions of a literal, physical kingdom on earth. It underlines the belief that Christ's reign is centred on the hearts and lives of believers rather than on earthly political or territorial dominance.

These scriptures form the foundation of amillennial thought, portraying the kingdom of God as both a present reality and a spiritual entity, transcending traditional notions of time and space. The amillennial interpretation of scripture urges believers to view Christ's reign as a current, dynamic force influencing the world through the spiritual life and mission of the church. Amillennialism thus shifts the eschatological focus from awaiting a future earthly reign to recognising and participating in the ongoing spiritual kingdom of Christ.

In the amillennialist reading of scripture, passages from 1 and 2 Thessalonians are also viewed through a symbolic and spiritual lens rather than as literal descriptions of future events. For example, 1 Thessalonians 4:15-17, which portrays Christ's return and the gathering of believers, is interpreted symbolically as representing Christ's ultimate victory and the spiritual union of believers with Him. This passage conveys assurance of redemption and Christ's eternal kingdom, emphasising spiritual realities over specific end-time events. Similarly, 1 Thessalonians 5:1-9, addressing the day of the Lord, is seen as a call for spiritual vigilance and righteousness, reminding believers of the unpredictability of Christ's final manifestation and the importance of living in faith, love, and hope. The discussion in 2 Thessalonians 2 about the rebellion and the "man of lawlessness" is interpreted as symbolic of ongoing spiritual opposition to God and apostasy rather than as a literal antichrist figure. This passage underscores the church's continuous moral and spiritual challenges, emphasising the need for steadfast faith and resistance to false teachings.

Overall, the amillennial perspective highlights the current spiritual reign of Christ, the ongoing struggle between good and evil, and the importance of living faithfully under Christ's rule, awaiting the ultimate realisation of God's kingdom.

The development of amillennialism in Christian theology has unfolded as a fascinating narrative of evolving interpretations and influences, extending from the early church to the contemporary era. This eschatological perspective, which centres on a spiritual understanding of the millennium, has been significantly shaped by various theological figures and historical contexts.

Tracing its roots, amillennialism found early proponents among the church fathers, who generally favoured a spiritual approach to biblical prophecy and eschatology. Key among these early influencers was Origen (AD 184 – AD 253), an esteemed theologian and scholar from Alexandria. Known for his allegorical interpretation of Scripture, Origen's approach laid the groundwork for subsequent amillennial thought, interpreting eschatological passages, including those in Revelation, as symbols of spiritual battles rather than as predictors of literal earthly events.

Another pivotal figure in early Christianity, Tyconius, who lived in the late 4th century and whose works influenced Augustine, also contributed to the amillennial viewpoint. Tyconius interpreted the Book

INTRODUCTION

of Revelation symbolically, seeing the millennium as representing the church age, which spans the period between Christ's first and second comings.

Augustine of Hippo (354-430), a famous theologian in Christian history, played a crucial role in shaping the millennial perspective. His extensive writings, most notably in "The City of God," present the millennium as a symbolic era between Christ's ascension and His second coming, a time characterised by the church's spiritual reign. Augustine's perspective marked a stark departure from the then-prevailing premillennialism and set the stage for the broad acceptance of amillennialism in later Christian thought.

During the Medieval period (5th to 15th Century), the influence of Augustine's interpretation made amillennialism the dominant eschatological view in Christian theology. The millennium was a continuous reality, with Christ spiritually reigning through His church. This period saw minimal focus on apocalyptic speculation or anticipation of a future earthly reign of Christ, aligning with the medieval era's emphasis on the spiritual realm and the authoritative role of the church.

The Reformation era (16th Century) further cemented amillennialism as a significant theological stance. Key reformers like Martin Luther (1483-1546) and John Calvin (1509-1564) maintained amillennial views, with Luther critiquing speculative end-times theories and emphasising Christ's spiritual presence in believers' lives. Calvin, too, symbolically interpreted eschatological passages, highlighting the ongoing reign of Christ in the church. This emphasis on scriptural authority and spiritual realities during the Reformation solidified amillennialism's place in Christian theology.

Historically, amillennial thought has been championed and propagated by a diverse group of influential theologians and preachers, spanning various eras and traditions. Figures such as John Gill, a renowned 18th-century Baptist theologian, and Charles Spurgeon, a prominent 19th-century Baptist preacher, have been instrumental in promoting amillennialism. Contemporary voices like John Piper and Albert Mohler also contribute to the ongoing discourse on this perspective, resonating with a broad Christian audience.

Influential modern theologians and scholars have further enriched this perspective. James Montgomery Boice, a prominent Reformed theologian, and George Eldon Ladd, known for his significant contributions to evangelical understandings of the kingdom of God, have been key figures in promoting amillennialist thought.

Contemporary Christian leaders, including Francis Schaeffer, Carl F. H. Henry, Harold Lindsell, D. A. Carson, Robert Schuller, and Rick Warren, have significantly impacted the amillennial perspective. Although Rick Warren's contribution is more indirect, he promotes millennial thought by dismissing eschatology. Their collective work and contributions from pastors and authors such as Bryan Chapell and Gordon Clark have expanded and deepened the understanding of amillennialism within the Christian community.

As mentioned earlier, subscribers of amillennialism promote a focus on Christ's spiritual reign and offer a lens through which believers can view their engagement in the world. This perspective discourages an overemphasis on end-time speculation, directing believers to live out their faith in the present, guided by the teachings of Christ. It motivates Christians to engage actively in societal and cultural realms, not to establish a utopian society but to be agents of God's transformative work on earth. This engagement is characterised by demonstrating kingdom values such as justice, peace, and love in everyday life.

INTRODUCTION

In the context of the interpretations mentioned above, amillennialism faces challenges from premillennialism, which presents several key arguments focusing on scriptural interpretation and the nature of end-time events. Premillennialists advocate for a literal reading of prophetic texts, particularly those in Revelation, criticising amillennialism for its reliance on allegorical interpretations. They argue for a distinct future millennium, envisioning a literal thousand-year reign of Christ on earth, contrasting with the amillennial view of a current spiritual reign.

A significant point of contention lies in the role of Israel in God's plan; premillennialists emphasise Israel's ongoing significance, which is diminished or spiritualised in amillennial thought. Differences in understanding Christ's Second Coming are also highlighted, with premillennialists pointing out that amillennialism may need to pay more attention to tangible events like the resurrection and final judgment. They often claim historical precedence for their view, asserting that it aligns more closely with early church beliefs and fosters a greater sense of eschatological urgency and emphasis on evangelism. Premillennialists also critique amillennialism for potentially underestimating human depravity and overvaluing the church's role in improving the world, emphasising the need for Jesus to literally rule and reign on the earth with an iron rod (Rev. 2:27) rather than gradual societal transformation through the church.

In conclusion, amillennialism represents a theological stance emphasising Christ's current spiritual reign, interpreting eschatological scriptures symbolically rather than literally. This perspective resonates with figures like Robert Schuller, who advised young church leaders to prioritise a long-term vision and focus on spiritual leadership over a narrow concentration on eschatological predictions. Similarly, in his influential book "The Purpose Driven Life," Rick Warren advocates for emphasising present Christian practices and spiritual growth over concerns and speculation about the end times.

However, this approach, while focusing on the immediate spiritual aspects of Christianity, is critiqued for potentially underplaying the importance of prophetic signs and events that are significant in Christian eschatology, such as the increasing prevalence of evil in the world and the concept of the rapture. Critics of amillennialism argue that deprioritising these aspects will result in a lack of understanding regarding these crucial theological events among believers. This criticism points to a need for a balanced approach that recognises the importance of present spiritual engagement and an awareness of future prophetic fulfilment in Christian theology.

CONCLUSION: COMPELLING EVIDENCE FOR PRE-MILLENNIAL DISPENSATIONALISM

Pre-millennial dispensationalism, particularly the pre-tribulation viewpoint, presents a compelling and comprehensive framework for understanding Christian eschatology. This perspective is rooted in a literal interpretation of biblical prophecies and an organised view of history through distinct dispensations, each reflecting God's unique interaction with humanity.

Central to this view is the pre-tribulation rapture theory, which posits that the church will be raptured before a seven-year tribulation period, a belief supported by scriptural references such as Luke 21:34-36, John 14:2-3, and 1 Thessalonians 4:16-17. This perspective is not a modern invention but is deeply rooted in early Christian teachings, with prophetic events like the rise of the antichrist and the Middle Eastern peace treaty in Daniel 9:24-27 serving as key indicators.

The dispensational framework divides history into eras such as innocence, conscience, human government, promise, law, grace, and the Millennial Kingdom, each characterised by God's unique dealings with humanity. The current Church Age is seen as a time of salvation through grace, distinct from God's dealings with Israel.

Furthermore, the Pre-Tribulation rapture theory is enriched by typological interpretations using biblical figures such as Enoch, Noah, and Lot, representing different groups in the end times. Enoch symbolises the church, raptured before the tribulation; Noah represents Israel, preserved through tribulation; and Lot signifies those who turn to faith during the tribulation.

The writings of the early church fathers, including Clement of Rome, Polycarp, and Irenaeus, provide additional historical support for the Pre-Tribulation perspective, hinting at an early Christian understanding of the rapture. This doctrine, reaffirmed by figures like John Nelson Darby and C.I. Scofield, has a rich lineage in Christian theology, demonstrating its long-standing place in eschatological thought.

In contrast, post-tribulation, Historical, and Pre-Wrath Pre-Millennialism offer different interpretations but face several theological and interpretive challenges. The post-tribulation view, for example, struggles with scriptural interpretations regarding the role of the Holy Spirit during the tribulation and the absence of the term "church" in key Revelation chapters. While attempting to bridge the post-tribulation and pre-tribulation views, the Pre-Wrath theory encounters difficulties in reconciling the timing and nature of God's wrath and the sequence of end-time events.

Post-millennialism, with its optimistic view of a world progressively influenced by Christian principles before Christ's return, contrasts with the scriptural depiction of a world descending into chaos and tribulation. This view, influenced by figures like Daniel Whitby and Kenneth L. Gentry Jr. and movements like the New Apostolic Reformation, faces criticism for its overestimation of humanity's capacity to establish God's kingdom and for potentially superseding Israel in God's plan.

CONCLUSION: COMPELLING EVIDENCE FOR PRE-MILLENNIAL DISPENSATIONALISM

Amillennialism, advocating for a symbolic interpretation of the Millennium and focusing on Christ's current spiritual reign, offers an alternative to the more literal approaches. This view emphasises Christ's ongoing spiritual authority, influenced by early church fathers like Origen and Augustine and modern theologians such as John Piper and Albert Mohler. However, premillennialists critiqued it for its allegorical interpretation of prophetic texts, potential underestimation of human depravity, and the necessity of Christ's literal reign.

In summary, Pre-Millennial Dispensationalism, particularly the Pre-Tribulation perspective, offers a coherent, historically rooted, and scripturally supported framework for understanding Christian eschatology. It underscores the imminent return of Christ, the distinction between the church and Israel, and the church's deliverance from God's wrath, aligning closely with the narrative of redemption throughout the Bible. While other eschatological views provide valuable insights, the clarity, historical continuity, and scriptural fidelity of the Pre-Tribulation Pre-Millennial perspective are compelling.

FIRM / HOLD FAST

'Ready and Waiting for Jesus'
(2:13-17)

In the midst of a world filled with uncertainty and spiritual challenges, the message of 2 Thessalonians 2:13-17 emerges as a beacon of hope and a call to steadfastness for believers. Paul, addressing the Thessalonian church, presents a theme that is as relevant today as it was in the first century: "Standing Fast, Ready and Waiting for the Return of Jesus." This passage serves as a crucial reminder to Christians to remain firm in their faith, anchored in the gospel's truth, and vigilant in their anticipation of Christ's return.

The purpose of Paul writing the two letters to the Thessalonians is to clarify misconceptions and provide a comforting assurance about the future by writing to a community of believers beset by confusion and fear regarding the end times (cf. 1 Thess. 4:13; 5; 2:1-3). He juxtaposes the grim fate of those who reject the truth (1 Thess. 5:1-11; 2 Thess. 2:1-12) with the blessed assurance for those who have embraced the gospel (1 Thess. 1:10; 2:19; 3:13; 4:15-17; 5:9; 2 Thess. 2:1). As with the letters combined, this next section of Paul's letter (2 Thess. 2:13-17) is a blend of warning and encouragement designed to fortify the believers' resolve in the face of adversity and deception.

The introduction of this "standing fast" theme in the context of 2 Thessalonians 2:13-17 is particularly poignant. It acknowledges the

CONCLUSION: COMPELLING EVIDENCE FOR PRE-MILLENNIAL DISPENSATIONALISM

trials and tribulations that Christians may face while stressing the importance of perseverance and faithfulness. Paul's exhortation to stand fast is not merely a call to endure passively but an active charge to engage with the present reality with hope and confidence in the promise of Christ's return.

Paul's epistles consistently emphasise the theme of steadfastness amid trials, particularly in the context of suffering and persecution for the gospel's sake. His words resonate as a source of strength and guidance, urging believers to maintain their resolve until the end. Within this framework, Paul highlights the crucial need for vigilance and firmness in faith rooted in the teachings they have received. This is especially poignant considering Paul's deep concern for the believers in Thessaloniki, as he feared they might succumb to Satan's temptations (1 Thess. 2:17-3:5). Such steadfastness is not merely an individual pursuit but a collective effort, shared among believers as they unite in anticipation of Jesus Christ's triumphant return.

Building on the theme of divine judgment in 2 Thessalonians 2:12, where Paul sternly warns of eternal condemnation for those who reject truth and righteousness, he shifts focus in verses 13–15 to offer comfort and assurance to the Thessalonians regarding their spiritual standing. In stark contrast to the grim fate of those destined for God's wrath, Paul underscores the Thessalonians' divine selection for salvation, emphasising their chosen status and call to Christ's glory. This affirmation is especially significant against the severe consequences outlined for those who turn away from the gospel.

Paul's message resonates with the distinctions he makes in 1 Thessalonians 5:1-11 between those in Christ and those of the world, using stark contrasts such as "you and us" versus "them and they." He paints a vivid picture of believers as being in the light, sober, awake, and shielded from God's wrath, in contrast to the non-believers who are depicted as enveloped in darkness, intoxicated with worldly pleasures, spiritually asleep, and ultimately destined for wrath. This vivid dichotomy reinforces the message of hope and salvation for the Thessalonians and all believers, juxtaposing their secure position in Christ with the perilous state of those outside the faith.

Thus, Paul's teachings in these passages provide guidance, encouragement, and a clear demarcation of the differing destinies awaiting believers and non-believers. For the Thessalonians, and by extension all Christians, these teachings are a call to remain vigilant and steadfast in their faith, comforted by the assurance of their salvation and the promise of Christ's glory, while bearing witness to the starkly different path that lies ahead for those outside of Christ's saving grace.

Building on the previous passage (2 Thess. 2:1-12), Paul's encouragement is set against the backdrop of the severe judgment highlighted in the context of the revelation of the man of lawlessness, the antichrist. He suggests that salvation will be exceedingly rare post-rapture, especially for those who previously had the opportunity to embrace the gospel but chose to reject it (2 Thess. 2:10-11, cf. Heb. 6:1-8; 10:23--39). This notion is echoed in the Book of Revelation, which alludes to the emergence of saints during the tribulation, presumably those who had not previously encountered or dismissed the gospel message (cf. Rev. 7:4).

In summarising, Paul assures the Thessalonians that their current sufferings do not signify that they are experiencing the judgments of the day of the Lord. He explains that the rapture has yet to occur. He outlines the sequence of events that must precede it: a period of widespread apostasy (1 Thess. 2:3), the cessation of the restraining influence of the Holy Spirit through the church (2 Thess. 6-7), and the revelation

CONCLUSION: COMPELLING EVIDENCE FOR PRE-MILLENNIAL DISPENSATIONALISM

of the antichrist (2 Thess. 2:8). As these events have not yet unfolded, the Thessalonians can be confident that they are not in the tribulation, and the midst of the day of the Lord's judgment.

In this light and context, Paul emphasises the pivotal role of the church, indwelt by the Holy Spirit, in restraining the antichrist. The Spirit's presence within the church is a defence against the full emergence of evil. This concept is consistent with the Biblical narrative, suggesting believers will be spared from the tribulation. Again, passages like 1 Thessalonians 4:15-17 and 1 Thessalonians 1:10, 5:9 reinforce the idea that the church is not destined for wrath, lending weight to the pre-tribulation rapture view and challenging alternative interpretations such as mid-tribulation, post-tribulation, or pre-wrath rapture theories.

In the above-mentioned context, where Paul highlights the critical role of the church, empowered by the Holy Spirit, in holding back the antichrist and countering the rise of evil, he continues in verse 14 to expand on the divine calling of the Thessalonian believers. This calling initiated through the gospel preached by Paul and his apostolic companions in Thessalonica (Acts 17:15) aligns with the broader Biblical narrative of believers being spared from tribulation and wrath.

The phrase "to which," or "to this" at the beginning of verse 14 encompasses the complete concept of "salvation by the sanctification of the Spirit and belief in the truth," underlining that it was God Himself who called the Thessalonians to this experience of salvation. This calling is portrayed not as a distant, predetermined choice but as an immediate act of God realised during Paul's missionary work.

The calling through the gospel is both a divine initiative and realised through missionary preaching, which is essential for the call to exist (cf. Rom. 10:8-15). The ultimate aim of this calling is to enable the believers to share in the glory of the Lord Jesus Christ, a central theme in Paul's theology. The transformation of God's people into a form that resembles the divine existence of Christ, which is described as the eschatological transformation, is a return to the brilliance and glory of God's presence. This transformation ultimately culminates in the resurrection, as noted in other Pauline writings like 1 Corinthians 15:43 and Philippians 3:21.

In the larger context of the Holy Spirit's role in the church and the expected rapture, Paul's message to the Thessalonians is not only about their current state of salvation. It emphasises the hope of sharing in Jesus Christ's honour and glory, which He currently enjoys at the Father's right hand (cf. Eph. 2:6). This message reinforces the belief that the church, which the Holy Spirit indwells, is not meant for wrath but for deliverance and glory. Again, it supports the pre-tribulation rapture viewpoint and challenges other rapture theories.

Following the theme of divine calling and the crucial role of the church in countering evil, as outlined earlier, Paul in 2 Thessalonians 2:15 further addresses the Thessalonian believers, shifting from reassurance about their salvation to an exhortation on living their Christian lives in adherence to the apostolic tradition they have received. The phrase "so then" marks this transition, indicating an inference drawn from the previous discussion. Paul implores the Thessalonians, referred to affectionately as "brothers [and sisters]," to "stand firm". This imperative, often accompanied by an object in other contexts (e.g., 1 Corinthians 16:13, Philippians 4:1), implies standing firm against false teachings or prophecies about the day of the Lord, harking back to concerns expressed in verse 2.

Paul, in his letter to the Thessalonians, strongly encourages them to "hold fast" to the traditions that they have been taught, both through oral instruction and through his epistles. These traditions embody a range of Paul's teachings, which include kerygmatic (the core message

CONCLUSION: COMPELLING EVIDENCE FOR PRE-MILLENNIAL DISPENSATIONALISM

of the Gospel), ecclesiastical (guidelines for church practices), and ethical (standards for Christian conduct) elements. Specifically, in this passage, Paul emphasises the kerygmatic traditions regarding the parousia of Christ (the rapture and the Second Coming), highlighting their critical significance for the Thessalonians' salvation.

Given their divine calling, the Thessalonians are exhorted to unwaveringly sustain their faith in God, show care for fellow believers, and eagerly anticipate the imminent return of Jesus Christ, mirroring the ethos presented in 1 Thessalonians 1:3. Christians, including the Thessalonians, are continually confronted with the challenge of countering the influences of a non-Christian culture and avoiding apathy in their faith and relationship with God. The call to fervently adhere to the teachings imparted by God's messengers is paramount, particularly as the Thessalonians grapple with the possibility of straying from these apostolic teachings. They are at risk of backsliding in their spiritual journey due to the trials they encounter and the constant negative influences of the world, the flesh, and the devil. This persistent theme of steadfastness and adherence to apostolic traditions in Paul's writings stresses the essential need for resilience and dedication in the Christian life.

Building upon the earlier discussion of the Thessalonians' need for steadfastness in their faith, Paul extends his guidance through prayer, seeking divine encouragement and strength for them, as he previously did in 1 Thessalonians 3:2, 13 and 2 Thessalonians 3:3. In 2 Thessalonians 2:16, he reflects on the unity of the Son and Father, perceiving them as one entity, with God's love and grace serving as the foundation for eternal encouragement amidst temporary present distress. This divine love extends hope for the future, a beneficial hope and reassures believers of the return of their victorious Saviour.

In verse 17, Paul expresses two specific desires for the Thessalonians: firstly, the need for comfort and encouragement in light of their anxiety caused by false information about the day of the Lord, and secondly, the need for God's grace to make them firm and stable in every good deed and word, defence and confirmation of the gospel.

As seen through verses 16-17, many addresses in Paul's letters take the form of prayers, which some described as a wish-prayer. This type of prayer, as a peroration, requests that God and the Lord Jesus Christ fulfil in the lives of the Thessalonians what Paul's arguments in the preceding verses aimed to persuade them to believe and act upon.

In verse 16 of this prayer form, the wish-prayer starts with Jesus Christ, "Himself," which is an important structural element. Interestingly, Christ's name appears before God's in this prayer. The participial phrase explains how God saves us and identifies Paul and his readers by using the pronoun "us." This emphasises God's love as the reason for divine favour. The gospel message highlights how God's saving grace provides eternal encouragement.

Verse 17's wish-prayer for the Thessalonians combines the encouragement of their hearts with strengthening their resolve in every good deed and word. The distinction between inward encouragement and outward behaviour underlines Paul's desire for their internal fortitude to be matched by godly behaviour. This connection with verse 15 highlights Christians' need for stability in both thought and behaviour.

This wish-prayer in 2 Thessalonians echoes Paul's intentions in sending Timothy to the Thessalonians as described in 1 Thessalonians 3:2. The intention behind Timothy's mission – to establish and encourage the Thessalonians in their faith amidst persecution – is precisely reflected in the prayer of 2 Thessalonians 2:17.

CONCLUSION: COMPELLING EVIDENCE FOR PRE-MILLENNIAL DISPENSATIONALISM

In conclusion, Paul's message to the church of Thessaloniki, in 2 Thessalonians 2:13-17, is a blend of eschatological teaching and pastoral care, emphasising the necessity for Christian steadfastness amidst a world rife with spiritual challenges. This section of his letter, as relevant today as in the first century, urges believers to stand firm in their faith, grounded in the truth of the gospel and vigilant in anticipation of Christ's return.

Throughout the letters, Paul delineates a stark contrast between the destinies of believers, portrayed as vigilant and secure in God's grace, and non-believers, who are depicted as ensnared in darkness and destined for wrath. He emphasises the importance of holding fast to apostolic teachings as a collective effort among the faithful, uniting in readiness for their wait for Jesus Christ.

The concluding wish-prayer encapsulates Paul's pastoral concern, seeking divine encouragement and strength for the Thessalonians, highlighting the need for internal fortitude to be complemented by godly behaviour. Overall, this passage stands as a powerful reminder of the hope, assurance, and commitment central to the Christian journey as believers await the glorious return of Jesus Christ.

FAITHFUL AND STEADFAST IN THE LIGHT OF HIS COMING

'Enduring Persecution'
(3:1-5)

Building upon Paul's message to the Thessalonians in 2 Thessalonians 2:13-17, where he intertwines eschatological insights with pastoral guidance, the subsequent section of the epistle, 2 Thessalonians 3:1-5, marks a transition into practical exhortation. After establishing the foundational principles of Christian perseverance and doctrinal adherence, Paul shifts his focus towards the practical implications of these teachings in the lives of believers.

As the letter progresses, Paul's concern for the Thessalonian church becomes increasingly evident. He underscores the duality in the destinies of believers and non-believers, painting a vivid contrast between the faithful, who live in the light of Christ's imminent return, and those who remain outside the grace of God. This dichotomy reinforces the urgency of maintaining a steadfast faith rooted in the apostolic tradition and collective vigilance.

Entering 2 Thessalonians 3:1-5, Paul extends this theme into a call for communal support and intercessory prayer. Understanding the challenges the believers face, he emphasises the necessity of mutual encouragement within the body of Christ. This passage not only reiterates the need for personal spiritual strength but also highlights the communal

CONCLUSION: COMPELLING EVIDENCE FOR PRE-MILLENNIAL DISPENSATIONALISM

aspect of the Christian journey. Paul's call for prayer underlines the interdependence of believers, urging them to actively participate in God's work through prayer, especially for the spread of the gospel and the well-being of its messengers.

This letter section seamlessly continues Paul's earlier teachings, blending doctrinal instruction with practical guidance. It serves as a compelling reminder of the communal responsibilities of believers, encouraging them to support one another through prayer and action as they collectively await the triumphant return of Jesus Christ.

At the start of 2 Thessalonians 3:1, shifting from Paul's prayer for the church (2:16-17), he launches into an appeal for prayer for himself and his missionary companions. This call for prayer, mirroring a similar but broader one in 1 Thessalonians 5:25, centres on the advancement and honour of the gospel, diverging from personal needs. Paul employs the vivid metaphor of the "word of the Lord" rapidly spreading, possibly drawing on Psalm 147:15, to illustrate the swift propagation of the Christian message. This metaphor underscores the need for the gospel's effective communication, reception, and distinction from diluted interpretations.

The comparison of God's Word to rain and snow in Isaiah 55:10-11 complements Paul's thoughts in 2 Thessalonians 3:1, emphasising the efficacy and purposefulness of God's Word, much like the life-sustaining natural water cycle. This parallel, alongside Psalm 147:8, (15), 16-18, accentuates God's Word's commanding and prevailing nature.

God's Word's transformative power, akin to the earth-altering impact of rain and snow, is highlighted, emphasising its inherent strength and intention. It serves various roles – enlightening, correcting, and directing lives, as seen in 2 Timothy 3:16-17. God's sovereignty is evident in His Word, achieving His purposes, even if they diverge from human expectations.

The scripture passages collectively present God's Word as a potent, deliberate force in the world and believers' lives, consistently realising God's plans. The phrase "as indeed with you" in 2 Thessalonians 3:1 (NKJV, NIV) has allowed for multiple interpretations, suggesting Paul encouraged the Thessalonian believers to ponder their own gospel experiences. The ESV translates it as "As happened among you," referring to Acts 17:1-5.

Addressing the dangers of relying solely on personal interpretation of scripture and experiences, particularly when out of context, is crucial for Christians, as mixed interpretations of 2 Thessalonians 3:1 highlight the importance of cautious and contextual interpretation of the Bible.

In 1 Corinthians 14:33, Paul emphasises that God is not a source of confusion. This suggests that misusing and misinterpreting God's word, whether through prophecy or scripture, particularly through those who are not appointed to teach and preach (cf. 1 Cor. 14:34-25, 1 Tim. 2:11-14), can cause confusion and discord in the church. Therefore, while personal reflection on scripture is valuable, it should be balanced with contextual understanding, communal discernment, and reliance on the Holy Spirit to prevent misinterpretation and misapplication of God's Word.

Alongside communal understanding and agreement on God's words, the letter's progression highlights the need for prayer among the Thessalonians and the apostles, portraying prayer as a tool for mutual support. Paul's acknowledgment of their dependency on God's assistance for their missionary success and their recognition of the gospel's spread and acceptance as divinely orchestrated motivate the Thessalonians to pray earnestly for others to accept the gospel similarly.

CONCLUSION: COMPELLING EVIDENCE FOR PRE-MILLENNIAL DISPENSATIONALISM

In 2 Thessalonians 3:2, Paul broadens his plea for prayers, emphasising the advancement of the gospel and seeking protection from adversaries hindering their missionary work. This situation was not unfamiliar to the Thessalonians, as Acts 17:5-9 vividly recounts their struggles against those actively impeding Christianity's growth. Paul paints these adversaries as illogical in their rejection of God's gracious offer and as harmful to the spiritual health of others, dubbing them as "wicked" and "evil." This condemnation underscores the profound moral corruption of those who resist God and His emissaries. Furthermore, these "evil men" mentioned in 2 Thessalonians 3:2 can be seen as a manifestation of the "evil one" referenced in 2 Thessalonians 3:3, foreshadowing the antichrist as mentioned in 2 Thessalonians 2. In this latter passage, the evil nature of the antichrist is evident, as he is described as opposing and exalting himself above all that is called God or that is worshipped. He is sitting in the temple of God, showing himself that he is God (2 Thessalonians 2:4). This portrayal aligns with the overarching theme of wickedness and opposition to divine truth, further exemplifying the stark moral contrast between the Christian message and its detractors.

Paul seeks divine intervention for protection against these adversaries, indicating his reliance on God for deliverance, akin to the divine salvation mentioned in 1 Thessalonians 1:10 and 5:9. This plea for rescue from human forces opposing the Christian mission is also reflected in 2 Corinthians 1:8-11 (read verses 3-11), where Paul again seeks communal prayer for his deliverance.

The second verse's final part indicates that faith is not universally embraced. This absence of faith in God, and the prevalence of self-belief, is the fundamental cause of the persecution faced by Christian missionaries and, as a result, the Thessalonian believers. This interpretation links to verse 3, which focuses on the idea of fidelity in the gospel's context.

In 2 Thessalonians 3:3, Paul shifts the focus from the challenges posed by non-believers to a strong affirmation of the Lord's unwavering faithfulness. This transition, while abrupt, bridges human faith with divine fidelity, underscoring a central theme in Paul's letters to the Thessalonian church. He moves from discussing his own adversities to addressing the concerns of his readers, reassuring them of God's protective presence amidst the malice of their adversaries. This juxtaposition between human faithlessness and divine faithfulness emphasises the assurance of God's guardianship over his believers.

Paul's message in this verse (3:3) aligns with the broader New Testament narrative, acknowledging the inevitable suffering in a Christian's life while offering hope and assurance of God's steadfast support. Revelation 2:10, for instance, exhorts believers to remain faithful through trials, promising the crown of life, reflecting the Christian journey's confrontation with suffering underpinned by God's faithfulness.

The statement made in verse 3 about the Lord's faithfulness to safeguard and empower believers against evil does not imply that they will not face difficulties. Rather, it assures them that God will always support them throughout their trials. This verse emphasises the Lord's faithfulness in difficult times, which is a recurring theme in the New Testament. The Christian journey is full of challenges, but believers can always count on God's unwavering presence and protection. This understanding is essential when we consider early Christians' experiences during Emperor Nero's reign from 54 to 68 A.D.

Although the church in Thessalonica may not have directly faced Nero's intense persecution, their fellow Christians in Rome certainly did. Post-Paul's letters to the Thessalonians, the Christian community

CONCLUSION: COMPELLING EVIDENCE FOR PRE-MILLENNIAL DISPENSATIONALISM

endured one of its most severe trials. Following the Great Fire of Rome in 64 A.D., Nero targeted Christians for horrific persecution to deflect blame from himself. The methods of torture and execution employed were ruthless, designed both to punish and to serve as a public spectacle. Christians were subjected to unimaginable brutality, including being torn apart by dogs, crucified, and burned alive as human torches.

The suffering endured by Christians during Nero's reign is a poignant illustration of the trials forewarned in the New Testament. Despite the terror of these persecutions, the enduring faith and resilience of the Christian community were remarkable, reinforcing the message of God's sustaining faithfulness amidst trials. As expounded by Paul, the gospel acknowledges the inevitability of suffering but concurrently offers hope and assurance of God's enduring presence. This period of persecution, rather than diminishing the Christian faith, fortified it, as the steadfastness of the martyrs laid a foundation for the future growth and spread of Christianity.

While the Thessalonians, situated in present-day Greece, dealt with persecution from local sources such as Jewish opponents and Roman authorities, the widespread hostility and suspicion towards Christians, exacerbated by Nero's actions, would have also impacted them. Though varying in intensity, this shared experience of persecution united early Christian communities in their common struggle and steadfast faith (1 Cor. 12:26a).

The believers in Thessalonica, who faced challenges from both external opposition (as recounted in Acts 17:5-9 and 1 Thessalonians 2:14-16) and spiritual attacks from Satan (1 Thessalonians 3:5), would have found great solace in Paul's emphasis on the Lord's faithfulness. This emphasis served as a source of comfort and reflected Paul's firm conviction in divine justice which would be fully realised at the second coming of the Lord Jesus (cf. 2 Thess. 2:5-12). This belief provided a foundation of strength for the early Christians, enabling them to endure persecution.

In 2 Thessalonians 3:4, Paul expresses his trust in the Thessalonians' commitment to practising and continuing the teachings he has imparted to them. This conviction stems from his belief in the transformative power of Christ working within them, shaping their actions and decisions. This perspective aligns with Paul's overarching themes of divine guidance and care in his letters.

Delving into Paul's letters to the Thessalonians, there are various commands and instructions that he expects his reader to follow, which include:

1. Leading a life of quietness and working with their own hands (1 Thess. 4:11).
2. Abstaining from sexual immorality (1 Thess. 4:3).
3. Loving one another (1 Thess. 4:9).
4. Staying alert and sober (1 Thess. 5:6).
5. Respecting and acknowledging those who work hard among them (1 Thess. 5:12).
6. Warning the idle, encouraging the disheartened, helping the weak, and being patient with everyone (1 Thess. 5:1 and 2 Thess. 3:6).
7. Work and earn your own living (2 Thess. 3:10-12).
8. Stand firm and hold to the traditions (2 Thess. 2:15).
9. Do not grow weary in doing good (2 Thess. 3:13).

Paul's focus on his directives underlines his commitment to the Thessalonian congregation's spiritual development and ethical

CONCLUSION: COMPELLING EVIDENCE FOR PRE-MILLENNIAL DISPENSATIONALISM

uprightness. He sees their compliance with these instructions as crucial to their Christian walk, showcasing Christ's transformative power in their lives. While recognising the hazards brought by deceitful and selfish individuals, as highlighted in his other epistles (1 Tim. 4:1-2; 2 Tim. 3:1-8; 4:3-4), Paul's chief concern is still the affirmative conduct and attitudes he anticipates from the Thessalonians. This includes the warning from 2 Thessalonians 3:13-15, where Paul advises not to grow weary in doing good and to take note of those who do not obey his instruction in the letter, admonishing them as brothers but not regarding them as enemies. This guidance adds a layer of accountability and community responsibility to his teachings, encouraging the Thessalonians to actively engage in good deeds while being vigilant about maintaining the purity and discipline of their fellowship. This dual approach of fostering positive actions and being cautious of negative influences exemplifies Paul's holistic concern for the well-being and integrity of the church.

In verse 5, Paul offers another prayer wish (cf. 2:16-17), desiring the Lord to guide the Thessalonians' hearts towards a deeper appreciation of God's love and Christ's example of perseverance. This is more than a simple call to obedience; it is an encouragement to find strength and endurance through meditation on God's love and Christ's steadfastness amid trials. This focus on God's love and Christ's endurance is a compelling motivator for the Thessalonians to remain faithful in their Christian walk, aligning their actions with the gospel's teachings.

Paul's approach in these verses, while indirectly expressing his confidence, is strategic. He prepares the believers for forthcoming directives by highlighting the importance of proper conduct within the community. The concluding prayer in verse 5 reinforces the call for obedience, guiding believers to reflect on God's love and Christ's perseverance, inspiring them to emulate these virtues in their lives. This combination of divine love and Christ's example is a powerful impetus for enduring trials and maintaining fidelity to the apostle's teachings.

In conclusion, in this section, titled "Faithful and Steadfast in the Light of His Coming", Paul builds upon his earlier messages to the Thessalonians, combining eschatological insights with practical pastoral guidance. He transitions from foundational teachings on Christian perseverance and doctrinal adherence to focusing on the practical implications for believers. This shift underscores the contrast between the destinies of the faithful and non-believers, emphasising the urgency of steadfast faith in anticipation of Christ's return. Paul calls for communal support and intercessory prayer, recognising the necessity of mutual encouragement within the Christian community. His message on the interdependence of believers highlights the collective aspect of the Christian journey, urging active participation in God's work, especially in praying for the gospel's spread and the well-being of its messengers.

Paul's appeal for prayer at the start of 2 Thessalonians 3:1 centres on advancing the gospel, employing the metaphor of the rapidly spreading "word of the Lord." He parallels God's Word and natural elements like rain and snow, emphasising its efficacy and purposefulness. This imagery underlines the power of God's Word to impact and transform lives, serving roles of enlightenment, correction, and guidance.

While the Thessalonian believers, facing opposition from their community and spiritual attacks from Satan, would find reassurance in Paul's emphasis on the Lord's faithfulness, they were also part of a larger narrative. The early Christian church, particularly during Nero's reign, experienced severe persecution. Though the church in Thessalonica may not have faced Nero's atrocities directly, their fellow Christians in Rome did. Instead of weakening the faith, this period of intense persecution fortified Christianity, as the endurance of martyrs laid a foundation for its future growth. Though varying in intensity, this shared experience of suffering united the early Christian communities in their struggle and faith, exemplifying the reality of suffering and the assurance of God's enduring presence.

Concluding his message, Paul emphasises the transformative work of Christ in believers, fostering obedience and endurance amidst trials. He strategically prepares the Thessalonians for upcoming directives, underscoring proper conduct within the community and reinforcing the call for obedience through the example of God's love and Christ's perseverance. This dual focus is a powerful motivator for enduring trials and adhering to apostolic teachings, illustrating the essence of being "Faithful and Steadfast in the Light of His Coming."

IMITATE US AS WE WAIT FOR THE RETURN OF JESUS CHRIST

'Faithful and Steadfast in the Light of His Coming'
(3:6-15)

In this section of the second letter to the church of Thessaloniki, titled "Imitate us as we wait for the return of Jesus Christ" (3:6-15), Paul exhorts the Thessalonians to follow his example of hard work (1 Thess. 2:9; 2 Thess. 3:7-8; cf. Acts 18:3; 1 Cor. 4:12) and avoid idleness. Following his prior encouragements and teachings, Paul delves into practical advice, urging the church community to remain diligent, disciplined, and devoted in their Christian walk, especially as they anticipate the Lord's return (1:7b, 2:1; cf. 1 Thess. 4:15-17). This section (3:6-15) is particularly significant as it bridges the thematic elements of enduring persecution introduced in 2 Thessalonians 3:1-5 with a concrete call to action. Having laid a foundation of prayer, mutual support, and the importance of spreading the gospel, Paul now emphasises the necessity of living out one's faith through work, conduct, and community responsibility.

The urging by Paul for his followers to "imitate us" (3:7, 9) transcends a simple appeal to emulate apostolic behaviours broadly; it is deeply anchored in the anticipatory context of Christ's second coming (1:7b, 2:1). By this, Paul highlights the essential equilibrium between the hope for the future and the duties of the present. Such equilibrium is

CONCLUSION: COMPELLING EVIDENCE FOR PRE-MILLENNIAL DISPENSATIONALISM

pivotal as the Christian community manoeuvres through the challenges of balancing immediate realities with future aspirations. Therefore, the guidance to distance oneself from individuals who are idle and not living according to the passed-down traditions (3:14-15; 2:15; 1 Cor. 11:2) serves as a tangible way to uphold community integrity and motivate every individual to make a meaningful contribution to the collective body of Christ.

In this section (3:6-15) of the letter, Paul emphasises the issue of idleness and stresses the importance of Christians working while they wait for the return of Jesus (Luke 19:13b). In other passages such as 1 Thessalonians 4:11-12, 5:14, and Ephesians 4:28, Paul instructs the Christian community to engage in manual labour. These passages encourage Christians to work and earn their own living (2 Thess. 3:12b), promoting the importance of combining faith with action and engaging with the world by promoting and proclaiming the gospel in our daily lives (cf. 3:1).

In 2 Thessalonians 3:6, Paul emphasises the gravity and sinfulness of being idle by instructing the Christian community to distance themselves from those who do not engage in manual labour (cf. 3:14), which is part of the apostolic traditions (3:14-15; 2:15; 1 Cor. 11:2). Paul's instruction highlights the importance of accountability in communal life. This teaching is given with the authority of Jesus Christ (3:1a), making it a theological mandate rather than just Paul's advice. Idleness is considered as a serious violation of communal ethics that can lead to departing from the gospel tradition and being dependent on others. In verse 11, Paul highlights how some people have deviated from the gospel by being idle and engaging in gossip. He uses the term "busybodies" to describe these individuals. This warning is repeated in 1 Timothy 5:13, where Paul cautions against being drawn away from Christ and abandoning the faith due to idle behaviour and gossip. The presence of such behaviour can harm the reputation and integrity of the church. Therefore, a disciplinary measure of social distancing is prescribed for those who refuse to work. This act symbolises the spiritual separation that idle and gossiping behaviour can cause.

Paul is concerned not only about an individual's ethical and moral values but also about the reputation and sustainability of the Christian community. The appeal to withdraw from idle members is a call to uphold the values of diligence and mutual support intrinsic to the Christian faith, mirroring broader Greco-Roman virtues of work while distinctly framing them within the Christian narrative. This action, intended to realign the community with apostolic teaching, carries implications for both internal cohesion and external perception, asserting the Christian commitment to responsible living as a testament to their faith.

In incorporating a reference to earlier admonishments to "warn those who are idle" (1 Thess. 5:14), the text reveals a progression in Paul's approach to church discipline, moving from a warning to more tangible forms of correction. This escalation, necessitated by persistent idleness and its disruptive effects on community life, reflects a deep pastoral concern for the spiritual well-being of the individuals involved and the collective witness of the church. By invoking the name of Jesus Christ (3:1a), Paul elevates the directive to obedience to the Lord, reinforcing the seriousness of the issue.

In verse 3:7, Paul presents a compelling reason for his instruction to avoid idleness within the Christian community. He bases this rationale on his own exemplary conduct and that of his missionary colleagues during their time in Thessalonica. He underlines his instruction with the words "for you (already) know," providing a solid foundation for

CONCLUSION: COMPELLING EVIDENCE FOR PRE-MILLENNIAL DISPENSATIONALISM

rejecting any brother or sister living in idleness, thus breaking the established traditions within the community. Paul also reminds his readers of his example as an ethical imperative, a tradition of self-sufficiency and diligence intended to serve as a concrete model for all believers, then and now.

In 2 Thessalonians 3:8, Paul elaborates on this apostolic commitment to self-sufficiency during their mission in Thessalonica (cf. 1 Thess. 2:9), highlighting their deliberate effort to not rely financially on others. Paul clarifies that while they did not outright reject gifts or meals, they fundamentally sustained themselves, embodying a work ethic that earned them their daily bread. This approach, rooted in a Semitic idiom of self-maintenance and independence, was part of Paul's broader missionary strategy to set a positive example for the community and to distinguish their genuine apostolic mission from the practices of itinerant preachers who exploited their listeners for material gain (1 Thess. 2:5-6).

Paul's insistence on not eating bread "without payment" underscores a principled stance against imposing a financial burden on the Thessalonians. This stance was not merely theoretical but was put into practice through "toil and exertion, working night and day," ensuring that their ministry did not financially strain any church or its members. This expression of diligent labour, mirroring language used in 1 Thessalonians 2:9, signifies the depth of Paul's commitment to a self-supporting ministry to reduce dependency and foster a culture of mutual respect and independence within the Christian community.

The repetition of the phrase about working "night and day" in both letters (1 Thess. 2:9; 2 Thess. 3:8) to the Thessalonians suggests a consistent thematic concern across Paul's correspondence, intended to serve as an exemplar for the Thessalonian believers to emulate, thus reinforcing the ethical imperative of hard work and financial independence within the Christian community. Paul's concern for his followers is also expressed through his prayers for them "day and night" (1 Thess. 3:10; cf. 2 Tim. 1:3).

In 2 Thessalonians 3:9, Paul distinguishes between the apostolic right to receive support and their actual practice, serving as a model for their followers. He clarifies that their decision not to claim this support ("not that we did not have the right") was intentional, aiming to set a precedent for self-reliance and to avoid any suspicion of preaching for personal gain. This approach is underscored by references to the law of Moses and temple practices in 1 Corinthians 9:4–18, where Paul asserts his and his colleagues' entitlement to material support for their spiritual work. Nevertheless, he notably refrains from exercising this right with the Corinthians, setting himself apart from other apostolic missionaries. This self-imposed restraint was motivated by a desire to offer themselves as an example ("in order that we might give ourselves as an example to you for imitation"), encouraging their converts towards self-sufficiency.

This lifestyle choice was also intended to demonstrate self-sacrificing love and diligence, as reflected in 1 Thessalonians 1:7, where the apostles' sacrifice for the benefit of others is highlighted. While Paul acknowledges the legitimacy of receiving support for spiritual ministry, as detailed in 1 Corinthians 9:3–14 and affirmed in 1 Timothy 5:18 and Galatians 6:6, his primary message here is self-support. By forgoing their rights, the apostles taught that Christians should not rely on others for their upkeep but should strive to be as self-supporting as possible, thus embodying the principles of self-sacrificing love in their daily lives.

In 2 Thessalonians 3:10, Paul underscores the principle of self-reliance and industriousness as foundational to the Christian ethic, emphasising not only through his and his fellow missionaries' exemplary conduct but also through explicit instruction. The phrase "for indeed" signals the introduction of a clear directive regarding the obligation of believers to be self-supporting. Paul recalls the command given during his time with the Thessalonians, highlighting its repeated emphasis on the necessity of work for one's provision. This teaching is encapsulated in the maxim "If anyone does not wish to work, neither let that person eat", which targets not those unable to work but those who choose not to, distinguishing unwillingness from incapacity.

The command, characterised by its straightforwardness and practicality, reflects a deeper understanding of community responsibility. It asserts that those who are capable yet refuse to work should not benefit from the efforts of others who do. This approach encourages personal responsibility and deters reliance on communal generosity as a substitute for individual effort. The stipulation that "neither let that person eat" is a communal directive to enforce this principle, ensuring that support is reserved for those genuinely in need rather than those who opt out of contributing to their upkeep.

Paul's reminder of this command provides a rationale for the community to cease support for the idle, reinforcing the value placed on work and self-sufficiency within the Christian community. This principle, deeply embedded in the ethical teachings Paul delivered to the Thessalonians, highlights the differentiation between lack of opportunity and willingness to work. By revisiting these instructions, Paul strengthens the community's resolve to uphold the standards of diligence and mutual support, framing idleness not as a mere personal choice but as a communal concern with spiritual and practical implications.

Paul's concerns came about by receiving reports that some members were engaging in idleness (3:11). Timothy's report probably brought this concern to his attention (1 Thess. 3:6-1; cf. 5:14), and whoever delivered the first letter, which caused Paul to write another. The phrase "for we hear" highlights that Paul had been made aware, possibly repeatedly given the present tense of "hear," that a segment of the community was not contributing to their support but instead was disrupting by meddling in the affairs of others. The destructive behaviour is highlighted in Paul's wordplay, "not busy at work, but busybodies," which stresses the contrast between being constructively busy and being destructively busy with matters that do not concern them.

In his instructions to the Thessalonian community, Paul employs a combination of commands and exhortations to address the issue of idleness directly. In 3:12, he explicitly targets those within the church who have been leading idle lives, using strong language to command and demand that they engage in productive work under the full authority and Lordship of Jesus Christ. This approach underscores the seriousness of the directive, suggesting that failure to comply is akin to rejecting the Lord himself, with potential exclusion from the community consequently. Paul's instruction is explicit: those who have been idle are to work "with quietness," a principle aimed at ensuring they contribute to their sustenance by earning their bread, thereby eliminating any dependency on others, particularly the community's wealthier members.

While addressing the immediate problem of idleness and its disruption, this directive also serves a broader purpose by promoting self-reliance and quiet industriousness as alternatives to meddling in others' affairs. Paul's emphasis on working quietly and self-sufficiency echoes his earlier teachings (1 Thess. 4:11), reinforcing the value of calm, orderly living free from the anxieties stirred by eschatological expectations.

In 2 Thessalonians 3:13, Paul shifts his focus back to the diligent members of the Thessalonian church (cf. 3:6, 7a), urging them not to become disheartened by the actions of those who shirk their

CONCLUSION: COMPELLING EVIDENCE FOR PRE-MILLENNIAL DISPENSATIONALISM

responsibilities. This verse, while appearing to introduce a new section, continues the discussion on community conduct, explicitly addressing the challenge of maintaining good deeds amidst discouragement. Despite the temptation to join the seemingly prosperous but irresponsible path some choose (1 Thess. 2:5-6), Paul emphasises the importance of perseverance in righteousness. He differentiates between the diligent, referred to as brothers (and sisters), and the idle, labelled merely as "such people" in verse 12, highlighting a self-imposed separation within the community based on behaviour. This distinction underscores a broader theme: the essential unity of the church is maintained not just by shared beliefs but by shared practices of responsibility and beneficence. Paul's exhortation to "do not grow weary of doing good" is not merely a general call to morality but a specific encouragement to continue acting charitably and justly, even when faced with indolence within the community. He implies that true adherence to God's directives is demonstrated through consistent good works, reinforcing the idea that actions reflecting God's teachings fortify the communal bond and individual integrity despite the negative examples set by others.

In 2 Thessalonians 3:14, Paul revisits the issue of disciplining uncooperative members within the community (cf. 3:6). He emphasises the importance of adhering to the instructions provided in his letter, framing disobedience not just as a personal failure but as a rejection of apostolic authority and, by extension, divine command. Paul's words ("if anyone does not obey what we say") underscore his authority as one in submission to the authority of Jesus Christ (cf. 3:6, 12).

Paul instructs the community to take decisive action against those who refuse to comply with these directives, advocating for a form of social ostracism. This approach, which includes avoiding association to the extent of not sharing meals, aims to prompt a sense of shame in the disobedient individual, encouraging repentance and reintegration into the community. This disciplinary measure is meant to rehabilitate the individual pro, protect the community from corrupt influences, and maintain its integrity in the eyes of both members and outsiders. By employing such measures, Paul hopes to foster a behaviour change, leveraging the power of social pressure and community standards to uphold a collective ethic rooted in productive engagement and mutual responsibility.

In closing, verse 15, Paul addresses the delicate balance required in disciplining community members who disregard his instructions about work, cautioning against treating the disciplined as enemies. Recognising the potential for such exclusion to be misconstrued as enmity, Paul clarifies that the intention is not to alienate but to correct, urging the community to view and treat the offender as a brother rather than an adversary. Instead, Paul advocates for a constructive approach, encouraging the Thessalonians to admonish the individual patiently and guide them back to the right path without severing all forms of contact. This nuanced stance aims to ensure that discipline remains a corrective measure rooted in brotherly love rather than punishment, emphasising restoration over retribution. Paul's guidance reflects a deep concern for maintaining both the integrity of the community and the possibility of reconciliation, indicating that such disciplinary measures should not be seen as final but as steps towards eventual reintegration, underscoring the Christian imperative to warn and correct in love rather than to denounce or ostracise.

In conclusion, Paul's epistle to the Thessalonian church deftly navigates the tension between eschatological anticipation and the exigencies of everyday life, offering a comprehensive directive against idleness. He advocates for a community characterised by industriousness and mutual

CONCLUSION: COMPELLING EVIDENCE FOR PRE-MILLENNIAL DISPENSATIONALISM

accountability, drawing on his example and apostolic authority to steer the believers towards a balanced Christian life. The emphasis on active engagement in work serves as ethical instruction and an essential element of faithfulness in the interim before Christ's return. Paul's counsel moves from general encouragement to specific admonitions to mitigate the detrimental effects of laziness on the individual and the community.

By recommending separation from the idle, Paul underscores a concern for the collective integrity and testimony of the church. He views discipline not as punitive but as corrective, aiming to safeguard the community's spiritual health and societal reputation. The nuanced recommendation in verse 15, advocating for a disciplinary approach imbued with love, showcases Paul's pastoral concern for unity and restoration. This part of his letter weaves theological and ethical threads, advocating a lived faith that harmonises belief with tangible action.

This passage from Paul's letter to the Thessalonians is a call to action, urging believers to integrate their eschatological hope with daily responsibilities. His admonition against idleness is framed as practical advice and a vital aspect of Christian discipleship. Paul's call for perseverance in good works amidst challenges is a testament to the enduring call for Christian service. His teachings provide timeless guidance for maintaining a purposeful and faithful witness, emphasising that true faith manifests in diligent work and loving correction within the community. Thus, Paul's message to the Thessalonians continues to resonate, offering enduring principles for living out the gospel in anticipation of Christ's return, where faith and action converge to reflect the gospel's transformative influence on life.

PURPOSE AND PEACE IN THE LAST DAYS

'Final Blessings as We Await His Coming'
(3:16-18)

In conclusion, the epistles of Paul to the Thessalonians stand as a profound testament to the apostle's deep pastoral concern, theological insight, and eschatological hope. In these letters, Paul navigates the complexities of Christian life and doctrine, weaving together themes of faith, love, hope, persecution, and the anticipation of Jesus Christ's return. The culmination of his correspondence, particularly highlighted in 2 Thessalonians 3:16-18, offers a poignant reflection on the necessity of divine peace and the apostle's earnest prayers for the well-being of the Thessalonian church.

Paul offers eleven prayers throughout the two letters, concluding with his prayer in 2 Thessalonians 3:16. The keywords and contextual themes of the prayers are as follows:

1. 1 Thessalonians 1:2–3: Keywords and theme: Gratitude, faith, love, hope. Paul expresses thanksgiving for the Thessalonians' work of faith, a labour of love, and steadfastness of hope in Jesus Christ.
2. 1 Thessalonians 2:13–16: Keywords and theme: Reception of God's word, suffering, persecution. Paul thanks God that the Thessalonians received his message not as the word of men, but

as what it truly is, the word of God, and notes their suffering from their own countrymen as the Judeans did from theirs.
3. 1 Thessalonians 3:9–13: Keywords and theme: Joy, love, strength. Paul expresses joy for the Thessalonians' faith, prays for an opportunity to visit them, and for their love to increase and strengthen so they may be blameless at Jesus' coming.
4. 1 Thessalonians 5:23–24: Keywords and theme: Sanctification, faithfulness. Paul prays for the Thessalonians' whole spirit, soul, and body to be kept blameless at Jesus' coming, emphasising God's faithfulness to do so.
5. 1 Thessalonians 5:28: Keywords and theme: Grace. A short prayer wishing the grace of our Lord Jesus Christ to be with the Thessalonians.
6. 2 Thessalonians 1:3: Keywords and theme: Growth in faith, love. Paul thanks God for the Thessalonians' growing faith and abounding love for one another.
7. 2 Thessalonians 1:11–12: Keywords and theme: Worthiness, power, glory. Paul prays for God to make the Thessalonians worthy of His calling, fulfilling every resolve for good and work of faith by His power, so that Jesus may be glorified in them.
8. 2 Thessalonians 2:13–14: Keywords and theme: Salvation, sanctification, glory. Paul gives thanks for the Thessalonians' salvation through sanctification by the Spirit and belief in the truth, to which God called them through the gospel.
9. 2 Thessalonians 2:16–17: Keywords and theme: Eternal comfort, good hope, strength. Paul prays for Jesus and God our Father to comfort the Thessalonians' hearts and establish them in every good work and word.

10. 2 Thessalonians 3:1–5: Keywords and theme: Spread of the word, protection, steadfastness, love. Paul requests prayer for the word of the Lord to speed ahead and be honoured, for deliverance from wicked men, and for the Thessalonians to be directed in God's love and Christ's steadfastness.
11. 2 Thessalonians 3:16: Keywords and theme: Peace. Paul prays for the Lord of Peace Himself to give the Thessalonians peace at all times in every way.

From the outset, Paul establishes a tone of gratitude and affirmation for the Thessalonians' faith, love, and hope (1 Thess. 1:2-3), acknowledging the gospel's transformative power in their lives amidst significant persecution (1 Thess. 2:13-16). His prayers, especially those uttered in the quiet of the night (1 Thess. 3:9-10), reveal an apostolic desire to see their faith strengthened, their love for one another deepened (1 Thess. 3:12-13), and their entire being—spirit, soul, and body—preserved blameless at the coming of Jesus Christ (1 Thess. 5:23-24).

This spiritual mentorship and care extend into the second epistle, where Paul continues to commend the Thessalonians for their steadfast faith and love in the face of ongoing persecution (2 Thess. 1:3-4) while also interceding on their behalf for worthiness and fulfilment of good purposes (2 Thess. 1:11-12) and divine encouragement and strength (2 Thess. 2:16-17).

Paul's invocation of the "Lord of peace" in 2 Thessalonians 3:16 serves as a pivotal moment in his correspondence, seeking not just the cessation of conflict thereafter but a profound sense of well-being for the community, rooted in Christ's presence, here and now. This prayer encompasses the church's internal challenges, including dealing with idleness (2 Thess. 3:6, 11-12), sexual sin (1 Thess. 4:3-8), and external pressures from persecution by their countrymen and Jews (1 Thess. 2:14-16), as well as the broader cosmic struggle against Satan's schemes (1 Thess. 3:5; 2 Thess. 2:9-10; 3:3). Paul also addresses the threat posed by false teachers (2 Thess. 2:2, 11-12), and those motivated by greed or seeking personal glory (1 Thess. 2:5-6), urging the community towards a life of humbleness and holiness.

Paul's appeal to the "Lord of peace" in 2 Thessalonians 3:16 underscores an essential aspect of Christian eschatology and daily living: the peace of Christ that transcends the mere absence of conflict, embedding itself into the fabric of the believer's life and the community at large. This concept of peace is not just a temporary respite from turmoil but a permanent state of well-being and harmony emanating from Jesus Christ's presence. It speaks to the immediate comfort and assurance believers can experience in their daily lives amidst personal and communal challenges and points towards a future eschatological peace that will be fully realised in the coming kingdom of God.

In the Old Testament, Isaiah 9:6 foretells the coming of Christ, calling Him the "Prince of Peace," indicating that His reign will bring about everlasting peace. Similarly, in the New Testament, Jesus Himself declares in John 14:27, "Peace I leave with you; my peace I give to you. Not as the world gives do I give to you. Let not your hearts be troubled, neither let them be afraid." This peace is part of the inheritance of the kingdom, a profound tranquillity that surpasses understanding, as mentioned in Philippians 4:7, guarding the hearts and minds of those in Christ Jesus.

The invocation of the "Lord of peace" is thus a prayer for both the present and the future: a request for God to manifest His peace in the here and now, helping believers navigate through life's tumultuous seas, and an anticipation of the ultimate fulfilment of God's promise of eternal peace in the new creation. It is a comprehensive peace, covering every aspect of life—spiritual, physical, emotional, and social. This peace is foundational to the Christian hope, assuring us that despite the chaos of the current world, God's ultimate plan is for a creation where peace reigns supreme, achieved through the redemptive work of Christ, and to be fully realised in His second coming.

Yet, this portrayal of the "Lord of peace" encompasses a paradoxical aspect of His divine nature, especially concerning the Second Coming and the judgment of the nations. While the Scripture heralds Jesus as the Prince of Peace, it also depicts a moment when He returns not as a gentle shepherd but as a righteous judge, wielding authority, and power to execute judgment upon the earth. This facet of Christ's return suggests that the peace He ultimately brings comes through the establishment of justice, which includes the confrontation and subjugation of all rebellion against God's sovereign rule.

For instance, 1 Thessalonians 1:6-9 speaks to this reality, highlighting how the Thessalonians turned to God from idols to serve the living and true God and to wait for His Son from heaven, whom He raised from the dead—Jesus, who rescues us from the coming wrath. This "coming wrath" alludes to a time when the Lord will exercise judgment against those who have rejected Him and oppressed His people. Similarly, 2 Thessalonians 1:7-9 foretells a time of retribution for those who do not know God or obey our Lord Jesus's gospel. They will suffer the punishment of eternal destruction, away from the presence of the Lord and the glory of His might when He comes to be glorified in His saints. These passages underscore a stark contrast between the fate of those in Christ and those who are not, delineating a period of judgment preceding the establishment of eternal peace.

CONCLUSION: COMPELLING EVIDENCE FOR PRE-MILLENNIAL DISPENSATIONALISM

Moreover, 2 Thessalonians 2:8 further illustrates this theme, describing how the Lord Jesus will overthrow the lawless one with the breath of His mouth and destroy him by the splendour of His coming. This imagery is far from peaceful in the conventional sense; instead, it depicts divine power and justice in action, affirming that true peace cannot coexist with evil and rebellion.

Thus, the biblical narrative holds in tension the dual aspects of Jesus' mission: to bring peace and to execute judgment. The peace Jesus offers is deeply intertwined with His justice, affirming that the new creation, where peace reigns supreme, is predicated on removing sin, evil, and death. In this light, the "Lord of peace" embodies the fullness of God's plan for redemption and restoration—a plan that encompasses both the merciful invitation to salvation and the righteous judgment of those who oppose His sovereign will. This understanding challenges believers to grasp the comprehensive nature of divine peace, which secures personal tranquillity and cosmic justice, culminating in the ultimate reconciliation of all things under Christ.

The personal touch of Paul's handwritten greeting in verses 17 and 18 of 2 Thessalonians underscores the authenticity of his message and his investment in the Thessalonian believers. This act of apostolic authority, coupled with his final benediction, calls for unity and peace in alignment with Christ's teachings, extending grace to all members of the community, irrespective of their circumstances.

Paul's reflections on the eschatological return of Jesus Christ, as conveyed in his letters to the Thessalonians, are deeply intertwined with themes of divine judgment and salvation. He offers an inspiring vision of hope, emphasising the believers' aspiration to be presented blameless before Christ and to partake in the joy of eternal communion with Him (1 Thess. 2:19). Paul reassures the Thessalonian believers of their deliverance from the impending wrath, a theme resonating with the promise of rescue for those faithful to Christ (1 Thess. 1:10; 4:15-17; 5:9). He vividly describes the gathering of the faithful at Christ's return, which contrasts sharply with the fate of those unprepared for the Day of the Lord (1 Thess. 4:13-17, 5:2-3, 2 Thess. 2:1, 7b). This narrative of hope and divine selection finds a profound echo in the apocryphal text of 2 Esdras, particularly in 7:1-19, where the discourse between Ezra and the Lord unveils the sobering reality that although many are created, few will be saved. This revelation underscores a recurring biblical theme: the path to salvation is narrow, and despite the Lord's deep desire for all to attain life, many will miss out due to their own choices and the hardness of their hearts. This reflection is further elaborated in 2 Esdras 8:4-63, highlighting the reward awaiting the humble—those who recognise their need for God's grace and have lived faithfully and with humility. Here, the text anticipates a moment of eschatological reversal, where the humble are exalted, receive their inheritance and fulfil God's promises.

In this light, the apostolic exhortations to the Thessalonians are not just calls to individual purity and communal holiness but are also deeply connected to the broader scriptural theme of God's justice and mercy. Paul's prayers for the Thessalonians' protection, spiritual stability, and sanctification reflect a pastoral concern for their readiness to meet the Lord, resonating with the message of 2 Esdras that highlights the critical importance of humility and faithfulness in securing one's place in the kingdom of God. Again, these texts underscore the dual themes of divine judgment and the gracious reward of the humble, offering a nuanced perspective on the Christian hope for the end times.

In a similar vein of eschatological exploration, 2 Esdras 7:1-25 delves into the mysteries of the end times and the judgment that awaits

CONCLUSION: COMPELLING EVIDENCE FOR PRE-MILLENNIAL DISPENSATIONALISM

humanity, offering insights that parallel and extend the themes Paul discusses in his letters to the Thessalonians. In this passage, Ezra engages in a dialogue with an angel who reveals to him the challenges of the path to salvation and the stark realities of divine judgment. The angel describes a future where the righteous face a narrow and perilous journey, likened to walking on a city's edge, to attain eternal life, emphasising the difficulty of achieving salvation and the ease with which one can fall into condemnation. This narrative starkly contrasts the fate of the wicked with that of the righteous, underscoring the importance of living a life in accordance with God's commandments to secure a place in the age to come. The angel's revelations to Ezra serve to reinforce the notion of the Day of the Lord as a time of decisive separation between those who have lived righteously and those who have not, mirroring Paul's emphasis on the necessity of being found blameless at Christ's return. Through Ezra's visionary experience, 2 Esdras further elucidates the intricate dynamics of divine justice and mercy, offering a complementary perspective to Paul's teachings on the resurrection, judgment, and the hope of eternal fellowship with God for those who endure in faith and obedience.

Building on the eschatological themes outlined in both the Pauline epistles and 2 Esdras, the concept of the rapture—a moment when God will remove those whom He is pleased with from the earth prior to unleashing a period of tribulation—finds resonance and support in specific verses from these texts. 2 Esdras 2:38-39; 6:23 and 26 speak to a time when those who are faithful will be separated from the prevailing corruption of the world, echoing the sudden and selective nature of deliverance. This is paralleled in the New Testament, where 1 Thessalonians 1:10 mentions Jesus delivering us from the coming wrath, and 1 Thessalonians 4:15-17 vividly describes the faithful being caught up together with the resurrected in the clouds to meet the Lord in the air, an event that epitomises the rapture. Further, 1 Thessalonians 5:9 underscores God's intention for believers to obtain salvation through Jesus Christ rather than facing wrath, aligning with the notion of a pre-tribulation rapture. Paul's discussion in 2 Thessalonians 2:1, 6-7, about the restraining force that must be taken out of the way before the end can come, can be interpreted as a reference to the removal of the church, thus preventing the righteous from enduring the tribulation. This collective scriptural narrative suggests a divine pattern of rescue for the faithful, reminiscent of Enoch's translation from the earth, as a merciful act by God to spare His people from the impending judgment and tribulation meant for those who have turned away from Him. Through these passages, the scripture provides a foundation for the belief in a rapture, a hopeful promise for those who live by God's will, eagerly awaiting the return of Christ.

Following from the discussion on the rapture and the insights provided by both Pauline epistles and 2 Esdras, it becomes evident that Paul's correspondence with the Thessalonians paints a holistic picture of the Christian experience. This narrative skilfully bridges the gap between believers' present adversities and the glorious future that awaits them. By integrating the immediate experiences of the Thessalonian church with broader, universal themes of faith, endurance, and hope, Paul transcends the specific challenges of Thessalonica. His approach fosters a community that navigates the complexities of its current trials with grace and looks forward with eager anticipation to the return of Jesus Christ.

Through his pastoral guidance, theological depth, and visionary outlook on the end times, Paul cultivates a sense of identity among the believers deeply rooted in a steadfast commitment to the gospel. This commitment is further highlighted by their dedication to leading holy

CONCLUSION: COMPELLING EVIDENCE FOR PRE-MILLENNIAL DISPENSATIONALISM

lives and maintaining a vibrant hope in the ultimate redemption and victory promised by Christ's second coming.

The early Christian community was given this message of instruction, encouragement, and blessing to guide them. It still resonates with believers today, providing a timeless message of divine peace, communal unity, and eternal hope.

In conclusion to this conclusion, the epistles of Paul to the Thessalonians, enriched with pastoral wisdom, theological depth, and a forward-looking eschatological vision, culminate in a powerful message that resonates through the ages, encapsulating the essence of the Christian journey towards the anticipated return of Jesus Christ. Paul's final blessings, especially as articulated in 2 Thessalonians 3:16-18, serve as a beacon of hope, emphasising the paramount importance of peace and persistent prayers for the well-being of the believers. This message, which commenced with expressions of gratitude and recognition of the Thessalonians' faith and perseverance, evolves into a comprehensive narrative that addresses the immediate concerns of a first-century church and casts a vision for the enduring spiritual journey of all Christians.

Paul's strategic interweaving of personal, communal, and cosmic concerns throughout these letters showcases his mastery in nurturing a faith community grounded in the present realities of Christian living and dynamically oriented towards the ultimate fulfilment of God's promises. His emphasis on peace, sanctification, and grace in the face of persecution, moral challenges, and theological confusion underscores the gospel's transformative power and the sustaining presence of the Holy Spirit amidst the church's trials and tribulations.

Moreover, Paul's discourse on eschatological themes, such as the rapture and the Day of the Lord, coupled with his reflections on divine justice and mercy as revealed in 2 Esdras, provides a solid framework for understanding the Christian hope in the context of God's overarching plan for redemption and restoration. The anticipation of Christ's return motivates ethical living and spiritual vigilance and offers comfort and assurance to those facing the complexities and uncertainties of life.

As believers today reflect on these letters, they are invited into a narrative transcending time and place, echoing the call to live in a manner worthy of God's calling. The final blessings pronounced by Paul, rooted in the promise of peace and the assurance of Christ's grace, affirm the continuous presence of God's love and the hope of eternal fellowship with Him. In this way, the messages to the Thessalonians stand as a testament to the enduring relevance of Scripture, guiding believers towards purposeful living and peace in the last days as they await the glorious coming of our Lord Jesus Christ with eager anticipation. This enduring message, encapsulating divine peace, communal unity, and eternal hope, fortified the early Christian community and continues to inspire and guide believers today in their spiritual journey towards the fulfilment of God's kingdom.